The Habits of Racism

Philosophy of Race

Series Editor: George Yancy, Emory University

Editorial Board: Sybol Anderson, Barbara Applebaum, Alison Bailey, Chike Jeffers, Janine Jones, David Kim, Emily S. Lee, Zeus Leonardo, Falguni A. Sheth, Grant Silva

The Philosophy of Race book series publishes interdisciplinary projects that center upon the concept of race, a concept that continues to have very profound contemporary implications. Philosophers and other scholars, more generally, are strongly encouraged to submit book projects that seriously address race and the process of racialization as a deeply embodied, existential, political, social, and historical phenomenon. The series is open to examine monographs, edited collections, and revised dissertations that critically engage the concept of race from multiple perspectives: sociopolitical, feminist, existential, phenomenological, theological, and historical.

White Self-Criticality beyond Anti-racism, edited by George Yancy
The Post-Racial Limits of Memorialization: Toward a Political Sense of Mourning,
    by Alfred Frankowski
Philosophy and the Mixed Race Experience, edited by Tina Fernandes Botts
The Habits of Racism: A Phenomenology of Racism and Racialized Embodiment,
    by Helen Ngo

The Habits of Racism

A Phenomenology of Racism and Racialized Embodiment

Helen Ngo

LEXINGTON BOOKS
Lanham • Boulder • New York • London

Phenomenology of Perception, Maurice Merleau-Ponty, trans. Donald A. Landes, Copyright © 2012 Routledge. Excerpts reproduced by permission of Taylor & Francis Books UK.

Black Bodies, White Gazes: The Continuing Significance of Race, George Yancy, 2008. Excerpts reproduced with permission of Rowman & Littlefield Publishing Group, permission conveyed through Copyright Clearance Center, Inc.

Published by Lexington Books
An imprint of The Rowman & Littlefield Publishing Group, Inc.
4501 Forbes Boulevard, Suite 200, Lanham, Maryland 20706
www.rowman.com

Unit A, Whitacre Mews, 26-34 Stannary Street, London SE11 4AB

Copyright © 2017 by Lexington Books

British Library Cataloguing in Publication Information Available

The hardback edition of this book was previously catalogued by the Library of Congress as follows:

Library of Congress Cataloging-in-Publication Data

Names: Ngo, Helen, 1981- author.
Title: The habits of racism : a phenomenology of racism and racialized
    embodiment / Helen Ngo.
Description: Lanham : Lexington, 2017. | Series: Philosophy of race |
    Includes bibliographical references and index.
Identifiers: LCCN 2017022513 (print) | LCCN 2017024838 (ebook) | ISBN
    9781498534659 (Electronic) | ISBN 9781498534666 (pbk. : alk. paper) | ISBN
    9781498534642 (cloth : alk. paper)
Subjects: LCSH: Racism--Psychological aspects. | Phenomenology.
Classification: LCC HT1521 (ebook) | LCC HT1521 .N396 2017 (print) | DDC
    305.8--dc23
LC record available at https://lccn.loc.gov/2017022513

∞™ The paper used in this publication meets the minimum requirements of American National Standard for Information Sciences—Permanence of Paper for Printed Library Materials, ANSI/NISO Z39.48-1992.

Printed in the United States of America

Contents

Acknowledgments

My first thanks go to series editor George Yancy, whose vision and infectious enthusiasm helped bring this book into fruition. I also owe a special debt of gratitude to my doctoral advisors, Anne O'Byrne and Ed Casey, for their valuable guidance and close reading in the formative stages of this project; and to Alia Al-Saji, Eduardo Mendieta, and George Yancy for their insightful feedback on subsequent drafts. I count myself lucky to have benefitted from the expertise and generous attention of such wonderful, inspiring thinkers.

For their sustained friendship and engagement with the ideas in this text, I wish to thank Brian Irwin and Amir Jaima; they have been excellent philosophical interlocutors. For their encouragement, motivation, camaraderie, or mentoring throughout the different stages of writing, I thank: Eunah Lee, Tim Johnston, Daniel Susser, Lori Gallegos de Castillo, Eva Kittay, Mary Rawlinson, Amma Asare, Ramesh Fernandez, Nathalie Batraville, Robert Ramos, Gustavo Gómez Perez, Hugues Dusausoit, Laura Roberts, Bryan Mukandi, Simone Gustafsson, Rebecca Hill, Catherine Mills, and Michelle Boulous Walker. I also thank the Stony Brook philosophy graduate student community for the supportive environment that nurtured the first seeds of this project, along with participants of the Collegium Phaenomenologicum (2013), PIKSI (2013), and audience members at conferences where I have presented early work from this book.

I extend a deep thanks to my parents, Thanh Chi and Thuc Trinh, whose resilience inspire and sustain me more than they know, and to Cathy and Steven, for being the most supportive (and fun!) siblings I could ask for.

Finally, I thank Patrick for seeing this project through with me from its inception to its completion, for living through its many highs and lows (rallying me through those lows), and for making the time and space for this book to come into being. And to Maia, whose recent appearance in the world has made the final period of writing a most happy one.

Introduction

When I was young—around eight or nine years old—I remember having a conversation with my older sister, whom I looked up to a great deal. We were talking about the jade bracelet around her wrist; a nice enough looking red Chinese jade bracelet, similar to the one my mother and her generation of friends wore. I neither particularly liked nor disliked these bracelets, but even back then they were to my mind associated with the cumbersome and often painful experience of removal; a simple, circular, hard-stone bangle designed to fit the narrowness of a wrist, its removal would usually involve wringing it over the width of your hand with the help of soapy water and a fair amount of force. For this reason one wore the bracelet either as a semi-permanent appendage or suffered the sore and reddened hand upon its removal. Given that, along with its weightiness, and obtrusive clunk when inadvertently struck against a hard surface, I wondered why my sister bothered with it. "I wear it to remind myself that I'm Asian," she, then aged 12 or 13, said. "When I look down at my wrist and see the jade bracelet, I remember that I'm not white." *How funny*, I remember thinking to myself. *Of course you're Asian, why would you need reminding of that?* And yet at the same time, there was something in her response that I understood immediately and intuitively. I, too, would sometimes "forget" I was Asian, even growing up as we did, in a migrant suburb among other Chinese-Vietnamese refugee families. *Sometimes*, I thought with a tiny pang of guilt, *it was nicer to "forget."* Reflecting on that conversation now, I am struck by the deep and poignant insight of two young girls navigating the complex world of race, alterity, embodiment. and identity. The quiet hegemony of whiteness, the tension in experiencing oneself from the "inside" as invisible but from the "outside" as visibly "raced," and the sense of "burden" that this duality brought with it (much like the clunkiness of the jade bracelet itself)—all these were, naturally, absent from our exchange, but each silently evoked.

This book is an effort to philosophically address some of the complex questions raised by the phenomenon and experience of racism, presented both in this vignette and in the testimonies of other "racialized bodies." I am, in particular, interested in the *lived and experiential* dimension of racism and racialization, and for this reason, draw on the philosophical tradition of phenomenology, and specifically, of phenomenological embodiment. My inquiry is guided by two main questions: First, how do phenomenological analyses help us to identify new registers or modes of racist praxis? Here I draw on the resources of French phenomenologist Maurice Merleau-Ponty, arguing that his conception of the habitual body opens up a way into some of the more subtle and basic workings of racism. Second, I ask: what is the bodily experience of racism and racialization, and what does it tell us about the nature of our embodied—and concomitantly socially situated—being? In other words, how does *racialized* embodiment problematize and extend existing accounts of embodied experience more generally? Here I draw on the analyses of critical race thinkers such as Frantz Fanon to call into question some of the dominant paradigms in philosophical and phenomenological conceptions of the self. In pursuing these two lines of inquiry, I hope to demonstrate how phenomenology and critical philosophy of race can come together in a mutually instructive way, each enriching while also challenging the limits of the other.

Chapter 1 begins in a constructive spirit. I take up Merleau-Ponty's conceptual reworking of habit and the habitual body in the *Phenomenology of Perception*, and argue that, following his account, we can begin to see how racism entails a set of practices that are embedded in bodily and habitual registers. Recast in terms of orientation and movement, Merleau-Ponty's concept of habit allows us to catch the insidious, gestural expressions of racism—for example, the clutching of one's handbag upon the approach of a Black man. Drawing on examples such as George Yancy's "Elevator Effect," I argue that bodily responses and gestures such as these can be considered habitual insofar as they articulate an underlying bodily *habituation* with respect to the racialized "other." This argument pertains also to racialized perception, which I explore through Linda Martín Alcoff's work on the visibility of race, and Alia Al-Saji's extension of this in relation to the perception of veiled Muslim women. Following these analyses, I examine how the framing of racism as habitual raises questions concerning responsibility, arguing that we can hold open this important ethical concern only insofar as we conceptualize habit anew. Here, my rereading of habit not only as sedimentation but also as active and ongoing—habits are *held*, not merely acquired—serves to insert a new space for the question of responsibility in racist habits.

In chapter 2, I turn from the bodily modes of racist praxis to the *bodily experience* of it. I ask: What is the lived experience of racism and racialization for those on its "receiving end"? Here I draw on the work of Fanon among others to explore the stress and "work" entailed in living and coping with racism, as well as the sense of body schema fragmentation that arises from the experience of being "in front" or "ahead" of oneself. Together, these analyses allow us to see the ways in which the racialized body is not experienced as fluid, coordinated, or transparent, in other words, how it does not square with the usual phenomenological descriptions of the lived body. This in turn prompts us to consider some of the limits of phenomenology (especially in its more existentialist mood), insofar as it tends to treat the body as synchronously experienced, and unthematized for itself; that is, insofar as it tends to take as its subject, a white (cis-male, able) body. Turning to the question of white embodiment, I draw on Shannon Sullivan's account of "ontological expansiveness" to highlight how the sense of spatial entitlement significantly contrasts with racialized embodiment.

Having provided a phenomenological reading of both the practices and experience of racism, the second part of this book then moves to a more thematic register. Chapter 3 picks up the notion of *inhabiting* heard in Merleau-Ponty's account of the habitual body, to explore the sense of dwelling and being-at-home in relation to racialized embodiment. Following the account of body schema fragmentation considered earlier, this chapter proceeds from the premise that the racialized body is experienced as *uncanny*. Here I turn to Martin Heidegger, who reminds us that the uncanny (*unheimlich*)—which usually means strange or alien—also bears a literal signification as un-homely (*un-heim-lich*). The racialized body, as strange or "other," is also the body displaced, or "not-at-home." To draw out the significance of this claim, I work through what it means to dwell or to find oneself "at-home." In contrast, María Lugones' account of "'world'-travelling" in the case of women of color highlights the way in which racialized embodiment entails a perennial displacement or "unhomeliness." And yet, taking her cue with regard to the celebratory aspects of "world"-travelling and the home-and-travel tension this betrays, I call for a reconceptualization of home in its porosity (and bodies in their intercorporeality) to usher in a more nuanced account of the uncanniness of racialized embodiment—specifically, one which gives voice to the enriching dimensions of displacement while holding onto the profound senses of suffering and disorientation.

Finally, in chapter 4 I turn to the question of the racializing gaze and its underlying subject–object ontology. In doing so, I address a persistent tension arising from phenomenology's lingering existentialism and its attempts to move toward a more relational ontology—a tension which, in my view, plays out clearly in the analyses of racialized uncanniness. Having drawn on critical race scholarship throughout the book, I note that this literature often invokes the concept of "objectification" in describing how the racialized "other" comes to be overdetermined from outside through the racist gaze. However, as I will argue, this discourse needs to allow for more complexity in its conceptualization of the subject–object relation; after all, the racialized body is seen, but also sees itself being seen. There is, in the experience of racialized embodiment, a concomitant being-subject-*and*-object. I begin therefore by examining the parameters of the subject–object relation through the figure of Jean-Paul Sartre, whose work on the gaze (*le regard*) in *Being and Nothingness* articulates some of the ontological presuppositions undergirding critical analyses of the racializing gaze. While in many respects useful, I nonetheless argue that he ultimately offers too reductive a paradigm in his account of being-for-itself and being-for-others. Consequently, I turn to the resources of Merleau-Ponty in *The Visible and the Invisible*, and in particular his efforts to dissolve the subject–object distinction through the concept of the chiasm or intertwining. I argue that this offers us a better framework through which to capture the complexity of racialized embodiment, so long as it holds open space for the necessary analyses of power and socio-historical situatedness advanced by critical race scholars. This, I argue in the closing moments of the chapter, offers us the occasion to cast anew, the ontological violence of racism; a violence not of one's subjectivity, but a more urgent and more profound violence of *inter*subjectivity.

SOME TERMS

Below are a few remarks concerning some terms recurring throughout the book.

Race. This central term is, of course, multilayered and complex. While much of the book ostensibly hangs on the definition or meaning of "race"—insofar as the terms "racism" and "racialization" are derivative of it—I refrain from staking out my definition of the term for the reason that my present inquiry is concerned with the bodily registers of *racism* and lived experience of *racialization*. The meaning of "race" itself therefore bears on my inquiry only to the extent that the phenomena of racism and racialization, as experienced and practiced, are activated through a notion (or *several notions*) of race and racial difference. That is to say, the machinations of racism and racialization unfold according to whatever conceptions of race gain traction in any given cultural-historico-political milieu, or whether they are biologically or socially defined. Moreover, there is no guarantee that these conceptions will be consistent or internally coherent—indeed they seldom are. Having said that, my own thoughts track those working with a hybrid definition of race, where race is seen neither as a pure biological fact (and determined by "nature") nor merely a social construct (and thus not "real"). Following thinkers such as Alcoff, I am of the view that our rejection of the naturalistic fallacy of "biological race" (and correlating acknowledgement of its socio-historic contingency) does not diminish the fact that race has and continues to structure our lives, relationships, projects, and possibilities. Indeed, this book is an effort in negotiating these positions by tracking some of the real, lived, and embodied dimensions of race.

Racism and Racialization. While I sometimes use these terms interchangeably, there is an important distinction to be made. Of the first, I appear to take a fairly standard definition: racism designates a belief system in which certain "races" (and their members) are considered inferior by virtue of characteristics or traits pertaining to that "race." This echoes, for example, the Oxford English Dictionary definition.[1] Where my version differs however is in carving out the scope of what it means to consider another race inferior. For example, while racism takes the most common form of discrimination and violence, it is also true that condescension and pity constitute racism insofar as they take a certain race to be inferior (and thus in need of pity). This is fairly uncontroversial. But in addition to this, I think racism's violence can also be an epistemic one, that is, an insistence on certain ways of knowing and perceiving, and the imposition of those ways onto others. This is where "racialization" becomes relevant. Given the ambiguity of the concept of "race" noted above, the term racialization (and racializing/racialized) becomes more useful. Throughout this book, "racialization" designates the process by which one is deemed to *have "race."* In the context of the West, this invariably means the process by which people of color are assigned a racial identity, whereas people of Caucasian description are not; racialization is about the production of a racialized "other" and a concurrent non-naming, normalizing, and centering of the white "I." Where this rejoins our definition of racism is that the process of racialization speaks to a superior–inferior complex; the imposition of a white epistemic perspective, and the corresponding exercise of power (of naming, of visibility) upon others is borne of the assumption that other ways of knowing and perceiving do not matter. *Racialization, then, is almost always a form of racism.* And yet because the term "racism" occupies a much more limited space in the public imaginary, and because racialization designates a very specific (and somewhat abstract) kind of racism, I am careful to distinguish the two. Moreover, I use separate terms also to draw attention to the way racialization—the process of assigning a racial identity to a person of color, with all its associated meaning and trappings—forms the basis of racism understood in its narrower sense. For example, the use of a racial slur on someone (an uncontroversial form of racism) is first predicated on the assignment to that person, a racial identity as a salient feature of their being; they are deemed to have—and be—this racial identity, and it is on that basis that they can be insulted for it. Given this definition of racialization, we can see how the concept will become especially important for the analysis of the racist gaze in chapter 4.

The Body. This book is firmly anchored in a phenomenological account of embodiment proffered by Merleau-Ponty (and his readers), and, as such, employs a usage for the term "body" that does not accord with its general meaning throughout most of the Western philosophical canon. In short, I use the term "body" or "lived body" throughout this book to broadly designate "person," "self," or other (disembodied) terms traditionally used to refer to the human being. My choice of "body" as the primary term for person reflects Merleau-Ponty's own efforts to reanimate the lived body as an important site of philosophical inquiry. Against the Cartesian dualism of mind and body, Merleau-Ponty insists on the philosophical significance of the body not only as the medium through which we engage with the world (ourselves, and others) but also the *condition* of our having a world. Being, traditionally located in the "mind," is as Merleau-Ponty shows thoroughly embodied, and as more recent scholars have argued[2], it is conversely true that the (human) body is thoroughly mindful. My references to the "racialized body" throughout this book speak metonymically to the "racialized person," but in line with the aims of this project, do so by drawing emphasis to the embodied dimension of such racialized being.

With these terminological remarks out of the way, we can now proceed to our analysis.

NOTES

1. The OED definition reads: "The belief that all members of each race possess characteristics, abilities, or qualities specific to that race, especially so as to distinguish it as inferior or superior to another race or races."

2. See, for example, Evan Thompson, "The Mindful Body: Embodiment and Cognitive Science," in Michael O'Donovan-Anderson (ed.), *The Incorporated Self: Interdisciplinary Perspectives on Embodiment* (Rowman & Littlefield, 1996), 127–144; Shaun Gallagher, *How the Body Shapes the Mind* (New York: Oxford University Press, 2005); Shaun Gallagher and Dan Zahavi, *The Phenomenological Mind: An Introduction to Philosophy of Mind and Cognitive Science* (New York: Routledge, 2008).

Chapter 1

Racist Habits*

Bodily Gesture, Perception, and Orientation

Why frame the problem of racism in terms of habit? As expressions of racist discrimination, hate, and violence persist under ever-changing guises, intensifying in recent times, does it make sense to frame the practice and phenomenon of racism through a concept that appears to blunt its political force? In this chapter, I argue that such framing is not only defensible, but also necessary. Racism in its many and varied expressions is undergirded by a habitual bodily orientation that often lies undetected and consequently under-examined. In this chapter, I embark on the analysis of racism as bodily habit in order to open up new domains for analyses, and in particular, to make possible an analysis of racism in its more subtle and insidious registers. Racism, I argue, is not simply a practice one engages in through conscious words or actions, and nor is it merely a set of attitudes held in thoughts; rather, it is more deeply embedded in our bodily habits of movement, gesture, perception, and orientation. However, to claim that racism is habitual is not therefore to say that it is unthinking, since I develop a reading of bodily habit grounded in Merleau-Ponty's account in the *Phenomenology of Perception*. In this phenomenological tradition, habit more closely resembles bodily orientation or habituation, which as I will argue, pushes us beyond its usual characterization as "sedimentation" or "calcification." This in turn opens up the possibility for locating both the active moment and question of responsibility in habitual racism, which I argue, affords us new ethical and political insights that may be productive for anti-racist efforts.

This chapter proceeds in four parts: first, I set up the conceptual apparatus by giving an account of habit and the habitual body as refigured by

* Based on an essay that originally appeared in *Philosophy & Social Criticism*; Volume 42, Issue 9; November 2016. Sage Publications.

Merleau-Ponty, flagging key aspects of his reconceptualization that will pave the way for this chapter's argument. This is followed in part 2 with a brief discussion of the question of the sociality of habits—via Bourdieu and Young—by way of preparation for the analysis of racism on the level of bodily habit. Part 3 takes up this task, with an extended analysis of how racism as practiced can be productively framed in terms of habit, both on the level of bodily gesture and perception. Here I draw on the work of critical race thinkers such as Yancy, Alcoff, and Al-Saji, to explore the rich and multifarious ways racism manifests in the habitual body. Finally, the chapter closes with a return to the concept of habit in part 4, where I offer a rereading of habit and sedimentation in order to locate its active moment, thereby opening up questions of responsibility for one's racist habits.

PART 1—HABIT AND THE HABITUAL BODY

Habit in the Body Schema

To embark on the task of recasting racism as a habitual practice, I begin by clarifying what I mean by the term "habit." While the concept enjoys a long and rich history in the Western philosophical tradition (from Aristotle, to Hume, James, Dewey, Husserl, and Ryle, to name but a few), in this chapter I draw primarily on the account presented in Merleau-Ponty's *Phenomenology of Perception*, where habit is wedded to the lived body. For him, habit describes our bodily manner of being in and moving through the world. Whereas we might in everyday language associate habit with repetition, absentmindedness, and lack of control or conscious intention—for example, the habits of biting one's nails or clicking a pen—Merleau-Ponty invokes habit in a different way. For him, habits are that which one cultivates or that to which one becomes accustomed. He writes, for example: "If I possess the habit of driving a car, then I enter into a lane and see that 'I can pass' without comparing the width of the lane to that of the fender, just as I go through a door without comparing the width of the door to that of my body."[1] Habit, then, describes a certain embodied way of being in the world. In particular, it describes a mode of moving in and responding to the world that is marked with ease, familiarity, and confidence. There is an ease with which I pass through the door in the sense that the movement is smooth, and not interrupted by a need to stop, wonder, or calculate. Oftentimes I pass through the door without even giving any thought to the fact of my doing so, much less whether I can do so. In this way, habit shares with the everyday examples of nail-biting and pen-clicking, a sense of absentmindedness—and yet Merleau-Ponty's account of habit is also more than this. For it is not just that case that we *have* habits and accumulate them in and through our bodies, for Merleau-Ponty habit represents a fundamental and primordial feature of embodied being; it forms an integral part of what it means to exist as a lived body in a world: "Moreover, my own body is the primordial habit, the one that conditions all others and by which they can be understood."[2]

But what does habit, in his rendering, entail? First, while it is true that habitual movements take place below the level of conscious activity, this is not to designate them to a level of automaticity or reflex. Habit occupies the hazy space between conscious and non-conscious being. In his example of the woman who moves about seamlessly in the world, without having to pay explicit attention to the objects that might damage the feather sticking out of her hat, the woman does not hold knowledge of the feather's precise position at all times, but rather has a "sense" of it. Her habitual movements amount to what Merleau-Ponty calls "a knowledge in [the] hands";[3] a knowledge that is not necessarily reflective or precise, but nonetheless practical and meaningful—indeed think of how we often employ our hands to convey indications of size, distance, direction, or shape in imprecise yet still meaningful ways. In Merleau-Ponty's analysis, habit works on the level of the body schema—an often contested and ambivalent term,[4] but which for Merleau-Ponty designates something like "the global awareness of my posture in the inter-sensory world."[5] The acquisition of new habits is described as the "reworking and renewal of the body schema"[6] such that it comes to move in certain ways and take on a certain stance or orientation to the world. Here we can start to reconnect Merleau-Ponty's version of habit to the earlier discussion of "becoming accustomed to something," insofar as we understand that becoming accustomed to something new involves adjusting and adapting our bodies to a new situation or behavior. Further, this understanding of habit, as an adapting or reworking of the body schema, is significant because of what it reveals about the future- and forward-orientation of habit in both the temporal and spatial registers.

The Temporal and Spatial Structure of Habit

One way habit is often described is through the motif of sedimentation; in other words, as movements or dispositions that have sedimented or "congealed" in our bodies. While the deployment of this metaphor is something I will critically examine later in the chapter, one reason for its pervasiveness lies in the way it captures the role of history in grounding or anchoring bodily movement. Like sediments, habits attest to the weightiness of the past in the present lived body. We acquire new habits by drawing on a repertoire of existing and readily available bodily movement; we take skills previously acquired and employ them as the medium through which we try to grasp at, translate, and fold in, new movements and habits. As Merleau-Ponty writes: "in learning the habit of a certain dance, do we not find the formula of movement through analysis and then recompose it, taking this ideal sketch as a guide and drawing upon already acquired movements (such as walking and running)?"[7] Habits such as dance—and we can generalize this to any number of activities—rely on the accumulation of bodily motility acquired in earlier life; they build upon existing movements gathered by the body, and motor capacities which in turn serve as a ground or a foundational base. If our bodies serve as the means through which we come to acquire new habits, then it is significant that bodies come with histories. And these histories can range from the complex and general histories of cultural practices, social organization, and power relations to the immediate and singular histories involved in moving one's arm.[8] In this sense, the sedimentation analogy is useful insofar as it allows us to tell a story of the past as it comes to ground and remain immanent in the present.

But at the same time, habit is forward looking, and embeds within it possibilities for future acting and modes of being. This is where I argue the metaphor of sedimentation reaches the limit of its utility, for while it helps us to visualize the "settling in" of bodily habit, the relative inertia or passivity entailed in sedimentation obscures the fact that habits are also future-looking: they launch us forward. Continuing with Merleau-Ponty's dance example, the bodily habits and motor capabilities that have thus far settled into my body schema do not just ground the habits of dance I have acquired, they also influence which new habits of dance I *can* acquire—and which for now, remain too ambitious. Further, they influence the *manner* in which they will get translated into my body schema. A trained ballet dancer, for example, will take to breakdancing differently than a street dancer, because they each have come to move to music and inhabit their own bodies in different ways. Habits, then, are also inherently futural. They are not just descriptive histories of the sedimentations that have accumulated in our bodies over time; they also look forward, at once serving as both a medium and gateway to that which we may incorporate into our body schemata, and how.

But first, to mark the point as it emerges: what we have in Merleau-Ponty's version of habit is an analysis that pulls us across the temporal horizon; habits look *at once* to the past and to the future, while being instantiated in the present. That is, habits function outside a linear scheme of time held together through a chain of past–present–future. Rather, their synchronic historical grounding *and* futural orientation means that both the past and the future are at each moment enveloped in the present; we might think of it as the past and future offering themselves up as the depths of a present. In an earlier passage of the *Phenomenology*, Merleau-Ponty writes:

Each present definitively establishes a point of time that solicits the recognition of all others. The present still holds in hand the immediate past, *but without positing it as an object*, and since this immediate past likewise retains the past that immediately preceded it, time gone by is entirely taken up and grasped in the present. The same goes for the imminent future that will itself have its own horizon of imminence. But along with my immediate past, I also have the horizon of the future that surrounded it; that is, I have my actual present seen as the future of that past. Along with the imminent future, I also have the horizon of the past that will surround it; that is, I have my actual present as a past of that future (my emphasis).[9]

The Husserlian movement of temporal protention and retention is helpful here. Habit reflects an accumulated past, but seen from another temporal horizon, each new (present) instantiation holds, at the same time, a projected future, whether the future of a past or the future of a present. Thus habit does more than provide "[a] past to a distended present" as Edward S. Casey writes in his essay, "Habitual Body and Memory in Merleau-Ponty."[10] Their enlivening of the past through the present also actively modulates that which is to come. As with a conception of time that harbors in each breath, the always-already here, the ready-to-come, and even the not-ready-to-come (the futures that do not materialize), bodily habits are at each moment laden with the histories that precede them, while at the same time, beholding *and* foreclosing possibilities of new ones to follow. Habits have a bearing on which futures will become readily available and those which will not.

A similar analysis to the temporal structure of habit can be advanced in the spatial register, by transposing the temporal analysis of habit into a spatial register; as with the "now," the "here" unites the expanse of the "from whence" and the "to where" (much like the German *woher* and *wohin*), holding them all in its grasp. But what is especially helpful about the framing of habit spatially is the way this illuminates the forward-facing possibility of action harbored in habit. Recall our opening distinction between the ordinary understanding of habit and Merleau-Ponty's use of the term, in which we noted the difference between habit as repetitive gesture (pen-clicking, nail-biting) and habit as a bodily activity to which I become accustomed (the habit of dance or driving). In both cases, we have a spatial posturing, a bodily arrangement in which the body is held—but, also *poised to act*—in a certain way. But whereas in the first case the body is spatially arranged for the ritual repetition of certain familiar gestures, gestures that more truly reflect a "sedimentation" in the body (which are of course open to change—one may, slowly, work to change one's habits), in the case of dance and driving we have a different kind of habit, one which entails bodily familiarity in equal measure, but which also entails a greater sense of bodily ability and possibility.

Habitual versus Habituating: Bodily Habit as Orientation and an Expression of Possibility

The move to frame habit in terms of orientation is perhaps better explained by a clearer parsing of the term. In his essay, Casey draws a helpful distinction between the *habitual* and *habituated*, splitting the difference thus:

> First of all, habit memory is repetitive: not just as steps on the way to learning something . . . but also as exactly re-enacting earlier performances of the same action. An example would be habitual action of staring [sic] my Honda Civic, an action which since first being learned has become routinized. On the other hand, "habituated" refers specifically to situations of being oriented in a general situation by having become familiar with its particular structure.[11]

In Merleau-Ponty's discussion of habit as the acquisition of new bodily signification, what he is concerned with is not only the habitual (the repeated, routinized gestures), but also the *habituated*. This is why he can speak of the habit of dance or the habit of driving—it is not that we engage in these activities with any particular frequency in our lives, but we have engaged in them enough to find ourselves habituated or accustomed to them. Of course the two are related: we become habituated to something only after a certain amount of practice, experience, or repetition—in other words, after a certain amount of habitual activity. But in bringing forth the sense of habituation in Merleau-Ponty's habit, what we can start to discern more clearly are the two important dimensions embedded within his account, that of orientation and possibility.

For example, in a key passage Merleau-Ponty considers the bodily habituation of an experienced organist, who after a relatively short period of acquaintance can proceed to play adroitly on a new and unfamiliar instrument on which the number of keyboards may be more or fewer, and on which the stops may be differently arranged. The explanation here cannot be an unusually quick aptitude for representing correspondences to organist's habitual instrument (there is no sign of, nor time for, translation and transposition), nor is it a case of reflex or muscle memory, given the new instrument's different topography. The clue, rather, lies in Merleau-Ponty's description: "He sits on the bench, engages with the pedals, and pulls out the stops, he seizes up the instrument with his body, he incorporates its direction and dimensions, *and he settles into the organ as one settles into a house*" (my emphasis).[12] The image of the house is surely deliberate, invoking the *inhabiting* of habit by our bodies, and their inhabiting of ours. Habit as habituation involves actively taking up residence in the spatiality of the organ, and to comport and orient oneself bodily such that one comes to relate to the organ as an open field of possibility. This kind of bodily orientation engenders not just a familiarity that is present in habitual (repetitive, routinized) activities, but trades also on the twin notions of power and possibility. Merleau-Ponty's organist relates to the instrument not as a series of static "heres" and "theres" which get reproduced or reconfigured in sitting down at a differently arranged organ, but rather he settles into the spatiality of the organ as a region of power (in the sense of *pouvoir* rather than *puissance*). This coheres with the account of bodily spatiality more generally, where he writes: "Consciousness is originarily not an 'I think that,' but rather an 'I can.'"[13] Habit thus, as a spatial organization and co-ordination of the body, opens oneself up to a range of motor and motile possibilities, and it is in this sense that Merleau-Ponty, in speaking of the example of a "blind man's cane," comes to describe it as "express[ing] the power we have of dilating our being in the world, or of altering our existence through incorporating new instruments."[14]

This reading of habit as habituation must always remain, however, in productive tension with the reading of habit as habitual. This is due not only to their entwinement noted above, but also because the routinized nature of the habitual allows us to draw emphasis to the temporality of habit, and in particular, its grounding in the temporal past. The organist settles into the spatiality of the organ and becomes habituated to it only after a period of habitual engagement (i.e., practice) with it. This is true of the engagement with any musical instrument or sport; a parkourist for example, whose sport exemplifies this kind of bodily habituation,[15] does not merely train for a series of repetitive movements, though her training will certainly *consist of* this. In parkour, as in art forms involving improvisation (jazz, acting, contact-dance), we encounter Merleau-Pontian habit at both ends: they are habitual in the first sense of repetition and familiarity (in their training), but also examples of how such training is *enabling*, in the cultivation of a bodily orientation that is future- and forward-facing, in the second sense of Merleau-Pontian habituating. This interplay between the habitual and the habituating captures the spirit of Merleau-Ponty's account, and shows us how habit, when understood in its fullness, can entail not just a "dilation" of one's spatial world as Merleau-Ponty puts it, but also a qualitatively changed relation to it.

Habit as *In*habiting

Already animated in this discussion of habit and spatiality then is a conceptual reworking of habit such that it enlivens an important etymological connection between habit and inhabiting, which is present both in French (*l'habitude* and *habiter*) and German (*die Gewohnheit* and *wohnen*). This is a connection that Merleau-Ponty himself exploits in his exploration of habit: "To habituate oneself to a hat, an automobile, or a cane is to *take up residence in them*, or inversely, to make them participate within the voluminosity of one's own body"[16] (my emphasis). That is, we accumulate habits and it is through these habits that we live in or inhabit the world, but at the same time, so too do these habits come to inhabit us. So in the example of the automobile above, we might say that the process of habituating ourselves to it is twofold: on the one hand we draw upon our existing motor skills (steering, pressing, releasing, turning) in order to learn the motions involved in operating the automobile, but we are not fully habituated to it until these new movements take up residence in us, among the repertoire of our existing movements. Insofar as habits reflect a spatial orientation and possibility of the body (when I sit down before a keyboard to type, "a motor space stretches beneath my hands where I will play out what I have read."[17]), so too does this spatial schema settle into the body ("The subject who learns to type literally incorporates the space of the keyboard into his bodily space"[18]). Furthermore, in becoming incorporated into bodily space, that space is changed; habits allow for a dynamic interchange between body and world, or we might say, it serves as an intermediary between the two. The same is true of the inverse, that is, in as much as habits come to dwell and feel "at home" in us, so too do we dwell *through them*, and make ourselves "at home" through the cultivation of habits: we come to inhabit new cities first by orienting ourselves and attending to basic needs (navigating public transport, bureaucracy, and so forth), but at the same time, we don't really feel "at home" in a city until we start to gather habits—visiting the same *boulangerie* every morning, figuring out one's route to the metro, or finding a local hangout spot to frequent. In this sense, habit entails more than a posturing in relation to the specific activity or movement at hand, the inhabiting through habit can also mean taking on a particular posture or stance towards one's *general* environment, in such a way that one starts to feel at ease, and at home. The significance of inhabiting in this sense and the related questions of home-making and home-space are questions that I will take up in greater detail in chapter 3.

We have, then, illuminated some important aspects of habit in this initial analysis. First, habit in Merleau-Ponty's account moves beyond its everyday association with repetitive, routinized gesture, designating instead something closer to bodily orientation. In this version habit has both a more general and a more fundamental connection with the body, describing the way we *inhabit* our bodies and the world. Conceptualized in this way, we also see how habit becomes aligned with the body's sense of possibility or "I can" in a way that will become relevant for our discussion of racialized embodiment in chapter 2. Finally, as we will reconsider toward the end of this chapter, the sense of spatio-temporal bidirectionality embedded within this conception of habit draws us into more complex questions of responsibility.

PART 2—CAN HABITS BE SOCIAL?

Before moving onto a direct consideration of habit with respect to racism, I want to first briefly address the question of whether this conception of bodily habit also works on a social level. That is, does it make sense to speak of habits that respond to socially meaningful interactions between people? Or put differently, Merleau-Ponty's examples of habitual action and movement throughout the *Phenomenology of Perception* tend to emphasize motoricity and motility in individual bodily movement; he speaks of walking through doorways, driving cars, playing organs, navigating with a "blind man's cane"—in short, activities which have become habituated and incorporated into a person's bodily schema as they move through space and engage with instruments or objects, but not with people. This is not to say that the examples of interaction with "things" are devoid of any social dimension—a Heideggerian analysis of the equiprimordiality of *Mitsein* even in our use of tools can swiftly dispel that—but what is distinct about these kinds of interactions is that they refer to habits operative within a *relatively* stable and closed circuit. A doorway affords entry and exit, solicits a certain spatial orientation or intentional action, and invites a certain aesthetic punctuation or focal point in our perception of buildings. And yet, even if we grant that doorways can be more than these—acknowledging the multistability of objects, which leaves open always the possibility of new significances to coalesce and emerge— the depth and variety of possibilities for interaction with a doorway remain relatively limited *in comparison* to interactions with other beings. The bodily habit of walking through doorways is thus a habit acquired within a relatively stable environment. There is a material difference when we begin to talk about bodily habits and dispositions in the context of intersubjective encounters, because their relative open-endedness and unpredictability require or engender a kind of bodily readiness and responsivity.[19] People talk back, but doorways do not—though this is not to discount the ways in which objects figure in our lived experience as things to *inter-act with*. And yet, there is an important added dimension in intersubjective interaction that bears remarking upon as we attempt to transpose Merleau-Ponty's analysis from the domain of individual bodies to that of inter-bodies, or the intersubjective and the social.

Pierre Bourdieu's *Habitus*

This attentiveness to the difference between Merleau-Ponty's typically motor-oriented and individual examples of bodily habit, and our concern with habit in the intersubjective and collective realm, opens up a further question: can we talk about habits that are socially acquired? Here I draw on French sociologist Pierre Bourdieu, whose work on *habitus*—a similar though not identical concept to habit—considers how social and cultural milieux profoundly shape our behavior, actions, and attitudes. Grounding his analysis is the proposition that habits are acquired and operative in a collective or group environment. For Bourdieu, our socialization entails acquiring and acting through a collectively intelligible *habitus*, and in fact, that we do so is the *condition* upon which social life is possible at all. *Habitus* serves as an ever-present structure—or a structuring structure—through which behaviors and interactions are formed, so thoroughly shaping them that one cannot step outside its influence. The idea of "pure" interactions then, or interactions that are not already informed by the *habitus*, become unthinkable. In *Outline of a Theory of Practice* he writes:

> Thus, when we speak of class habitus, we are insisting, against all forms of the occasionalist illusion which consists in directly relating practices to properties inscribed in the situation, that 'interpersonal' relations are never, except in appearance, *individual-to-individual* relationships and that the truth of the interaction is never entirely contained in the interaction. . . . In fact it is their present and past positions in the social structure that biological individuals carry with them, at all times and in all places, in the form of dispositions.[20]

In other moments Bourdieu insists more strongly that *habitus* not only influences ways of being and acting, but actually produces them.[21] For him, insofar as *habitus* propels us forward, it does so primarily through the reproductive force intrinsic to it. Thus in his field investigations on marriage practices in Kabylia, Algeria which inform much of this book, Bourdieu identifies the many ways in which rituals, negotiations, understandings of self-interests, and so forth are predetermined by the *habitus*, which are then in turn reproduced by it.[22] This is not to say that there exists no room for divergence from or evolution in the practices or behaviors engendered in any given *habitus*— that Bourdieu emphasizes the *tendency* toward (and not *certainty of*) reproduction clearly indicates to us that he does not foreclose this possibility. And while this sense of predetermination is a criticism most commonly leveraged against Bourdieu, as sociologist Nick Crossley argues, such critiques are misguided insofar as Bourdieu is more appropriately read as illuminating the organizing structures and practices that supply the milieux of our interactions. Nonetheless, Crossley readily admits that Bourdieu underplays this aspect of creative possibility to his own detriment: "It is because Bourdieu ignores this generative role of agency, in my view, that he leaves himself vulnerable to the charge of determinism."[23]

Despite the importance of Bourdieu's work in introducing an explicitly social dimension to our consideration of habit, there are important reasons for remaining within Merleau-Ponty's phenomenological framework in our present investigation, over that of Bourdieu's sociology (and the tradition he carries through from Durkheim to Mauss[24]). While Bourdieu's account helps us to broaden our working concept of habit by lending it a distinctly social and historical dimension, the diminution of the role of the lived body[25] and its relation to this *habitus* fails to sufficiently capture not only the way habits are alive and changing, but also how habits are *in*habited—that is to say, taken up, activated, and *held*. Bourdieu's habitus thus succumbs to a more or less passive construction of habit as sedimentation (which we will consider further toward the end of the chapter), and as already noted, is therefore frequently criticized for presenting too determinist a picture.[26] And despite his efforts to rescue Bourdieu from these criticisms (which interestingly, he does by way of tracing some continuity between Merleau-Ponty and Bourdieu), Crossley concedes in his article, "Habit and Habitus," that it is the question of the body which stands as a key distinguishing feature separating their respective versions:

> in contrast to Mauss and Bourdieu, Merleau-Ponty offers a dynamic account of the process in which habits are formed, reformed and, in some cases, extinguished across time. . . . Habits, for Merleau-Ponty, are structures of behaviour, attaching the embodied actor to their world, which take shape and are reshaped (and sometimes extinguished) in the dynamic and always ongoing process of interaction between actor and world.[27]

Because of this, the phenomenological framework inaugurated by Merleau-Ponty, with its distinctive emphasis on the *embodied* dimensions of habit, proves most pertinent for our investigation as it will allow us to consider racism on the level of bodily gesture, posture, and disposition—that is, the socially and historically situated practice of racism as it gets taken up by the body. Moreover, situating our inquiry in the phenomenological tradition also allows an articulation of the *experiential* dimension of racism and racialization, with its broader implication for the experience of and relation to one's self—something which is not readily available to us in the sociological *habitus*. What Bourdieu's habitus does offer us however, despite its methodological limitations, is a way to transition from a strictly individualistic bodily register of habit and experience characteristic of phenomenology (and of Merleau-Ponty's account), to broader considerations of social, historical, and power relations, in the accumulation of habit or *habitus*.)

Iris Marion Young on Female Bodily Comportment

Indeed we find an example of such an effort in Iris Marion Young's iconic essay, "Throwing Like a Girl: A Phenomenology of Feminine Body

Comportment, Motility, and Spatiality." In that piece, Young takes up the Merleau-Pontian concerns of bodily movement, motility, and comportment in the explicitly historical and social context of gender. She argues that the relatively impoverished motor capacities observed in young girls in various studies are attributable not to female biology, physiology, or mysterious "feminine essence" as early phenomenologist and psychologist Erwin Straus concludes, but rather to the way women and girls are socialized in patriarchal societies. Whereas boys exhibit more open postures and wider walking strides, girls are more likely to walk with disproportionately smaller strides, with arms held closer to bodies, and without the loose swinging motion observed in boys.[28] Even in the act of throwing a ball, girls are less likely to engage their lower leg and back muscles, or to make good use of space by taking up wide supporting stances. According to Young, these features of feminine motility and movement speak to a lived contradiction, whereby the "I can" of the phenomenal body is countered with an "I cannot," supplied by the girl's social situation.[29] As a result of this lived contradiction as subject *and* object, feminine bodily movement is characterized by three modalities, which she identifies as: ambiguous transcendence, inhibited intentionality, and discontinuous unity.[30] She explains the relation thus:

> At the root of these modalities . . . is the fact that the woman lives her body as *object* as well as subject. The source of this is that patriarchal society defines woman as object . . . and that in sexist society women are in fact frequently regarded by others as objects and mere bodies. An essential part of the situation of being a woman is that of living the ever-present possibility that one will be gazed upon as a mere body, as shape and flesh that presents itself as the potential object of another subject's intentions and manipulations, rather than as a living manifestation of an action and intention.[31]

While not framed explicitly in terms of habit or habitual expressions of sexism, Young's analysis of female bodily movement is indeed an analysis of how female bodies habitually move (in throwing a ball, in walking, etc.), and how they come to *in*habit their own bodies in the context of patriarchal society. As such it offers us a clear example of the application of Merleau-Ponty's account of the lived body in a socially and historically situated context, and in doing so opens up a way for us to proceed in our phenomenological inquiry into racism, despite Merleau-Ponty's own silence on such questions. Interestingly, in a different essay intervening on the "sex versus gender" debate concerning ways to understand the category of "woman," Young too offers a brief comparison between Bourdieu and Merleau-Ponty, concluding:

> Pierre Bourdieu's concept of the *habitus* offers one interpretation of how generalized social structures are produced and reproduced in the movement and

interaction of bodies. Especially in his understanding of gender structures, however, Bourdieu's understanding of the relation of social structures to actors and experience conceptualizes these structures too rigidly. It may be more fruitful to draw on a theory of the lived body like that of Maurice Merleau-Ponty but connect it more explicitly than he does to how the body lives out its position in social structures[32]

In other words, while Young recognizes the contribution of Bourdieu's work insofar as it extends to habit an explicitly social and historical dimension, she too notes the limitations of any analysis of habit that is not grounded in the lived body. Given that a phenomenological inquiry into habitual racism will in many ways track the trajectory of phenomenological analyses of gender and sexism, I find Young's turn to Merleau-Ponty, while retaining the social dimension introduced by Bourdieu, instructive.

PART 3—RACISM IN HABITUAL BODILY GESTURE AND PERCEPTION

To turn now directly to the problem of racism, how does the account of phenomenological habit as developed so far open up new insight or critical analyses? How does this account of habit provide us with a useful way to think about the phenomenon of racism, with a particular view to its embodied and experiential dimensions? I want to propose two such ways. First, there is a growing body of literature which analyzes the way in which racist praxis does indeed operate on a habitual level. This is the idea that racism finds expression not only in public discourse, overt acts of racial violence, hatred, or discrimination, but also and perhaps more potently in the subtle bodily gestures, reactions, and behaviors—not always explicitly intended—that are routinely enacted in response to an encounter with the racialized "other." Second, and relatedly, I want to argue that this "habitual racism"[33] is not only limited to expressions of the body through gesture and movement, but also through habitual perception—that is, that the perception of "racialized others" is already operative on a bodily and habitual level.

Bodily Racism: (Micro-) Gestures and Bodily Responses

In thinking about racism on the level of bodily gesture, it is first important to delineate between different categories of gestures. One could, for example, trace a long history of racist gestures which unambiguously degrade, mock, and threaten their racialized targets. This would include performing the Nazi salute to reference the genocide of Jewish people in the Holocaust, pulling back the sides of one's face to make "slanty eyes" in mock of Asian people, or performing ape-like gestures to link African, Caribbean, or Australian Aboriginal peoples with primates. Such examples are relatively uncontroversial in their racist content, and constitute gestures in which the meaning is immediately clear to those who see themselves referenced in them.[34] In part they are so because they have crossed a threshold in public discourse; they are highly visible and recognizable gestures that carry clearly intended and precisely executed racist messages. But in addition, these also pass the threshold of recognition because they are *performative* gestures: lifting one's hand to perform the Nazi salute means to momentarily inhabit the character of an SS soldier (or in the case of the salute with the other hand making a moustache, Hitler himself), and to invoke or recreate the racist world and worldview of the Third Reich in which Jews were an "inferior race." Or in the case "slanty eyes," the gesture entails inhabiting not the perpetrator but the Asian persona directly, to embody it and project the caricature of an ugly, foolish, or conniving figure. It performs to the Asian person how they are seen, and how they are being mocked. As performances, these kinds of gestures are highly visible; they are enacted *in order to be seen* by their intended audiences, but also to the world at large. They constitute a type of speech that carry an intended message, and in doing so they employ rhetorical and theatrical devices such as humor, mockery, metaphor, and hyperbole. We can liken these gestural forms of racism to other broader performance-based practices, such as donning "blackface" in minstrel shows, imitating speech (particularly where it is broken or heavily accented), and so forth. These kinds of racist gestures sit within a broader spectrum of racist speech, insofar as they seek to communicate racist messages to the people they degrade, or to solicit agreement from onlookers. As explicit performances, these gestures are intended to be seen, and so they have in-built, a certain measure of intelligibility.

This kind of embodied gestural racism, however, is not what I am most interested in here. While it is of course important to attend to the different ways this kind of performative racism persists in daily life and public discourse, and indeed takes on new forms—the debate around white rappers as a new incarnation of "blackface" is a good example of this[35]—in this section I am interested in the kinds of bodily gestures and movements which, at first glance, might not appear to constitute performance or speech, as ordinarily construed. However given our earlier reconceptualization of habit as bodily orientation, what Merleau-Ponty's work opens up is a way to bring such unassuming bodily responses and movements—glances, flinches, and the like—into the purview of our discussion around racism and racist gesture. This is important because while there exists a reasonably developed discourse around forms of racism in this explicit register of performance and speech, analyses of bodily gesture and responses as racist are much harder to ground.

Thus it is blackface, for example, that will solicit collective outrage and condemnation, while the clutching of a handbag in response to the approaching figure of a Black man will solicit anything from defenses, denials, to accusations of "over-sensitivity"—despite the way they both structure the lived experience of Black people and in particular Black men. In what follows then, I take up the question of embodied gestures that at first glance do not so much seek to "perform" racist messages, but rather those gestures that "express" them, although noting the tenuous distinction between them insofar as they *both* constitute forms of bodily speech.

"The Elevator Effect"

In his book *Black Bodies, White Gazes*, George Yancy traces precisely this bodily and gestural mode of racism. Following in the footsteps of Frantz Fanon's seminal text, *Black Skin, White Masks* (Yancy's title contains a direct allusion to this earlier work), Yancy draws from his own lived experience as a Black man in the United States, with particular attention to the ways racism can be performed through (micro-) gestures and expressions of the body. Take, for example, a phenomenon which Yancy calls "The Elevator Effect":

> Well-dressed, I enter an elevator where a white woman waits to reach her floor. She "sees" my Black body, though not the same one I have seen reflected back to me from the mirror on any number of occasions. Buying into the myth that one's dress says something about the person, one might think that the markers of my dress (suit and tie) should ease her tension.[36]

And later:

> I walk into the elevator and she feels apprehension. Her body shifts nervously and her heart beats more quickly as she clutches her purse more closely to her. She feels anxiety in the pit of her stomach. Her perception of time in the elevator may feel like an eternity. The space within the elevator is surrounded from all sides with my Black presence. It is as if I have become omnipresent within that space, ready to attack from all sides. Like choking black smoke, my Blackness permeates the enclosed space of the elevator. Her palms become clammy. She feels herself on the precipice of taking flight, the desperation to flee. There is panic, there is difficulty swallowing, and there is a slight trembling of her white torso, dry mouth, nausea.[37]

The example is a controversial one, and for reasons we will explore later, perhaps necessarily so. Yancy himself notes that it is one which frequently draws critical questions (or defensive re-interpretations) as to its validity as a reading of the situation. I leave these aside for the moment, as they raise very real and complex questions of epistemology and hermeneutics in phenomenological method, to which we will need to return. Further, while the example offers only one specific expression of racism—and some might argue, not an especially devastating one considered against the spectrum of racial violence—I argue that as a seemingly unmediated and beneath-surface instance of racism, the example focuses our attention to the bodily orientation that undergirds and unites other forms of racism, from the highly publicized recent spate of racist killings in the United States to racial discrimination and violence in its more structural forms. There is, in other words, much at stake in this bodily mode of racism.

Taking up to the scenario outlined by Yancy, then, in what sense can this woman's bodily response be analyzed as habitually racist? In order to arrive at this question, we need first to work through two others, namely: What is the significance of the bodily register in this woman's response? and, Can her response be called racist? After working through these questions, I will then turn to the chapter's primary question: Can this kind of bodily response be understood in terms of habit, and if so, what does this framing contribute to our broader analyses of racism?

Racism in a Bodily Register

Beginning with the first, one could argue that the response of the white woman—the tensing, the constricted breathing, the uneasy shifting of the body—these are all enacted responses to the confrontation with Yancy's Black male body, or more precisely, with that which is inscribed or projected onto his body, for it is not Yancy's body in its particularity that solicits the response. Rather, what she responds to is a generalized racist projection of Blackness, instantiated in the singularity of his Black male body. In a world where racism exists, racialized bodies come predetermined or "*over-*determined" to borrow Jean-Paul Sartre's term (who in turn borrowed from Freud)[38], with coded meanings. As Yancy writes earlier:

> My darkness is a signifier of negative values grounded within a racist social and historical matrix that predates my existential emergence. The meaning of my Blackness is not intrinsic to my natural pigment, but has *become* a value-laden "given," an object presumed untouched and unmediated by various contingent discursive practices, history, time, and context. My Blackness functions as a stipulatory axiom from which conclusions can be drawn: "Blackness is evil, not to be trusted, and guilty as such."[39]

Insofar as these constructions form the horizon of the woman's bodily responses, we can argue that such gestures constitute racism in a bodily register, drawing upon and responding to racist representations of the Black male body, and taken up in the white woman's own bodily comportment.

One might be tempted to argue that nonetheless this is not enough to render the gestures themselves racist, that instead what we are confronted with are gestures that merely express racist modes of thinking. In other words, it is the *idea*, and not its bodily manifestation, that is properly racist. The problem with this argument, however, is that it insists on a distinction between the idea and its expression, which, as Merleau-Ponty points out, enforces a misleading separation. In a section entitled "The Body as Speech and Expression," Merleau-Ponty writes, "speech does not translate a ready-made thought; rather, speech accomplishes thought."[40] Insofar as gesture is a kind of bodily speech, it becomes difficult to separate a gesture from the content of its expression; as embodied speech, gesture *accomplishes* the body's thoughts. As Merleau-Ponty notes, "The gesture does not *make me think* of anger, it is the anger itself."[41] One could argue, then, that the racist tropes around Blackness are not only invoked at the woman's tensing of the body, but rather are *accomplished* by them. And given that we are presently concerned with racism in the form of *responsive* gesture, that is to say, as distinct from other explicitly intended forms of gestural racism mentioned above ("slanty-eyes" or the Nazi salute), the distinction between idea and expression such that racism is located exclusively in the former, becomes tenuous. While the woman's response in Yancy's example undoubtedly draws on a racist discourse in which Black male bodies are constructed as dangerous, rapacious, uncontrolled, and so forth, it is also the case that her response *participates* in this discourse and breathes life into it, giving a lived reality to the projections and thereby reinscribing them onto the body.

Such re-inscriptions happen not by way of further discursive contribution, but rather through direct bodily movement and gesture. Yancy himself remarks: "Notice that she need not speak a word (speech-acts are not necessary) to render my Black body 'captive.' She need not scream 'Rape!' She need not call me 'Nigger!' to my face. . . . Her nonverbal movements construct me, creating their own socio-ontological effects on my body."[42] Put differently, it is not just that discursive representations tell women (and in particular white women) that Black men ought to be feared; bodily responses such as these enact the fear, and the Black man *is* feared. Of course this is not to say that the fear is thereby rendered disingenuous—as if sincerity excludes the possibility of racism, or indeed, racism the possibility of sincerity. The point is, rather, that discursive representations come into being through their enactment and embodiment. Indeed the "idea versus enactment" problem itself underscores the very importance of looking to the body and not only to discourse or ideas when dealing with racism, since one may, as Yancy points out, take a critical stance to dominant racist practices and discourses, and yet still find a disjuncture at the level of bodily response and gesture.

As such, the woman on the elevator does not really "see" me . . . To begin to
see me from a perspective that effectively challenges her racism, however,
would involve more than a *cognitive* shift in her perspective. It would involve a
continuous effort at performing her body's racialized interactions with the world
differently. This additional shift resides at the somatic level as well. After all,
she may come to judge her perception of the Black body as epistemologically
false, but her racism may still have a hold on her lived body.[43]

By pointing out the cognitive-embodied dissonance, this analysis opens up a
way for us to think more seriously about the role of bodily habit in racism.

"But is it Racist?": On Social Epistemology and Hermeneutics

"But is it racist?" one may object. And in fact, this is the question most commonly and eagerly put to Yancy when presenting his work, and indeed a
question often posed any time more "controversial" assertions of racism are
raised (especially when raised by people of color, which itself is instructive).
Our second question, then, speaks directly to this concern. Is the ascription
of "racism" to the woman's gesture valid? Given Yancy cannot speak for this
woman's habitual bodily movement and body schema, can he have misread
the situation? Or even if it may fall within her body schema to respond in
such a way in encounters with the Black man, does that necessarily make *this*
particular instance an irrefutable expression of racism? Isn't it possible that
Yancy is wrong? The answer of course has to be "yes"—but this is only as
meaningful as saying that there is always room for misreading in hermeneutic
events such as these. Meaning is necessarily slippery and inexhaustible in
non-verbal communication (indeed even in verbal communication), and as
such resists definition. Still, the objection would run, perhaps Yancy *has* misread the woman's bodily movements, perhaps this is "all inside his head." Or,
perhaps he is simply being "oversensitive" and projecting all these responses
onto her. Given the challenge they pose to the credibility of Yancy's phenomenological reading, and given what the objections themselves reveal about the
nature of racism, these questions require some methodical working-through.

Epistemic Privilege

Yancy proceeds first by writing:

One important objection that might be raised at this juncture is that I have simply misread the white woman's intentions. I have read racism into a situation
where it simply does not exist. This objection raises the issue of how it is that
Blacks learn to read white gestures, gazes, and other forms of apparently racially
benign behaviors. I want to avoid the claim that the white woman's response
to me is simply a case of 'direct' observation, as if any other person (even any

other Black or white person) need only 'observe' her behavior and will ipso facto come to justifiably believe what I do about her comportment. That is, it is not as if *any* knower can "see" this and claim, "Yes, her gesture was racist."[44]

By positing that the woman's response is not manifestly evident for everyone and anyone to observe, Yancy is claiming that there are specific epistemological conditions under which some things can be perceived. This is compatible with basic phenomenological analyses of the way in which our lived bodily concerns shape how and what we perceive. But if this is the case, then it follows that some groups are better placed—or epistemically privileged—in reading situations such as these. This is because what becomes relevant in such hermeneutic bodily encounters includes personal history and experience, shared histories and shared experiences, direct experience and cognizance of the fundamental role of racism in structuring society, and Yancy will add, *the extent to which the woman's gesture coheres with these.* In his discussion of the "Elevator Effect," it is in this spirit that Yancy identifies African Americans as forming a kind of "epistemological community," whereby they stand in privileged—though this is not to say exclusive[45]—position to its interpretation. He writes for example:

So, what is the evidence for my claim that the white woman's behavior in the elevator is racist? Her gestures cohere both with my knowledge of white racism and with past experiences I have had with whites performing racist gestures, and my experience is consistent with the shared experiences of other Blacks, who have a long history of having become adept at recognizing these gestures for purposes of resistance and survival.[46]

And further:

Not only I but others in my epistemological community have seen white women pull their purses close to them when in our presence. I, and others in my epistemological community, later came to learn that many of those tugs turned out to be based upon racist prejudices. What's more, the hypothesis that "pulling one's purse under such-and-such circumstances is an expression of racist prejudice" coheres with a number of other facts, for example, the racist portrayals of African Americans in the media[47]

To take stock for a moment, we should note that there are different threads of coherences here, pulling across different directions. On the one hand we have the coherence of the same experience shared across a community of Black men. That there exist other anecdotes, articles, videos, and popular culture references to the elevator phenomenon partly testifies to this. When I said earlier that Yancy's example was a "controversial" one, I should have actually said that it is a controversial example *to some* (primarily whites)—as it is not particularly controversial for Black men, for whom the experience is common place, and what Yancy calls, "a form of commonsense knowledge."[48] I will call this a coherence of *breadth*; the same phenomenon is experienced across a range of people in independent circumstances. Second, the interpretation coheres with a range of *other experiences* which reflect similar habitually racist responses to the encounter with the Black man, including the locking of car doors, crossing the street, being followed by security guards in malls (a phenomenon known as "shopping while Black"[49]), or even at the more extreme end, the immediate perception of threat by Black bodies as played out in the cases of Rodney King and Trayvon Martin. This is a coherence of *kind*; Yancy's reading of the "Elevator Effect" coheres with other personal experiences that fall into the same *kind* of phenomenon. Note that coherence of breadth is also at play here—it is well documented that other Black men routinely experience these different bodily responses. Third, as Yancy indicates above, the reading of the "Elevator Effect" coheres with the history of racist practices and representations of Black people, and in particular Black men, embedded in public life, discourse, and imagination. I will call this final one a coherence of *depth*; where responses such as the bodily tensing and handbag-grabbing cohere with the weight of historical practices and systematization of racism. As Yancy notes in the article, "Elevators, Social Spaces, and Racism," "The history of racism in the USA underwrites and supports my knowledge regarding the white woman's gestures."[50]

Still, even while Yancy may have justifiable grounds for his reading, based in part on his shared epistemic privilege, is it not still possible that he is wrong, either because he is "oversensitive" to the possibility of racism or because he has interpreted *this* woman's bodily responses incorrectly? Maybe she is of nervous constitution, maybe she has a history with sexual violence, maybe she is just having a bad day? To these again, the answer is yes—however, not without qualification. In the first instance, it may well be the case that by virtue of one's epistemic privilege as a Black man, or as a person of color more generally, that one is inclined to read racism into situations where they don't "exist." This is a frequent accusation leveraged against people of color when they call racism where it is not perceived by others; we are "oversensitive," and "*everything* is about race." However we can once again point to concordance with phenomenological and gestalt accounts of perception (which we consider further below), whereby one's experiences, framework, and embodied concerns play an active role in shaping one's perceptions. Thus insofar as this supports the charge of oversensitivity, at the same time it *also* supports the claim of epistemic privilege. This in turn prompts us to question whether the charge of oversensitivity in fact belies an epistemological ignorance on the part of the skeptic.[51] Further, as Yancy points out, the matter is complicated by a question of political exigency:

> Whiteness theorist Christine Sleeter notes that "what white students often find . . . more difficult to understand is that generally people of color know that they may over-interpret race, but can't afford not to because most of the time the interpretation is correct." I would add that it could also prove fatal for people of color to respond to each situation as if it were sui generis.[52]

That is, there exists a political exigency to the perceptual disposition of being "on guard" against racism, for those who bear the weight of it of most acutely, for those who are most at risk of being disadvantaged, discriminated, harmed, or endangered by it. The weight of this threat cannot be overstated. As Yancy writes, with reference to Rodney King, "On any given late evening, I *know* that white police officers might kill me as I reach for identifying information."[53] Note that in contrast, because of their comparatively protected positions, the consequences of white people under-interpreting racism are not as grave; at most they are proved wrong, which may occasion self-reflection. This disparity does not itself mean that all judgments of racism will always be correctly identified by people of color, but it does dispel the notion that there is an "epistemological level playing field" in which the stakes are evenly distributed among those who do and don't bear the brunt of racism. Given this reality of racism, insofar as we can speak of a "heightened sensitivity" in the perception of racism, it is a sensitivity which is epistemologically meaningful, but also, politically intelligible and defensible. Or to put the point differently, the processes of hermeneutic interpretation are not only *informed by* social, historical, and political horizons, but they also *participate in* actively constituted social and political fields, and thus can themselves serve as tools or coping strategies within these fields. For our present purposes then, given we can never be so intimately acquainted with each person's habitual body and orientation to evidentially justify the claim of habitual racism (even if such a thing were possible), it is enough to note the epistemic privilege and political exigencies of those racialized bodies at the coalface of such encounters.

Finally, granting (even despite all of this) that Yancy is wrong about the claim of racism in the woman's gesture—and this remains a distinct possibility—the case of being wrong in a particular instance does not in itself invalidate the epistemological frameworks in place supporting the judgment. As Yancy writes, "Being incorrect or highlighting exceptions to acts of racism does not unseat claims regarding racist patterns and proclivities, since being incorrect or having exceptions are compatible with such racist patterns and proclivities."[54] For example, the question of gender is an important one to consider, although I address it only summarily here. Following Young's analysis considered earlier, we can speak of a habitual bodily comportment specific to women in patriarchal societies, which *do* cohere with some though not all of Yancy's descriptions of the white woman in the elevator. Young, for example, notes that women and girls tend to hold themselves closer to their bodies, in an inward direction. Moreover, it remains a real possibility that past experiences with sexual violence, or even what Susan Brison in *Aftermath* calls "prememories (of one's own future rape)"[55], can provide some explanation of the woman's comportment. These ought to be taken seriously, if we also take seriously the claim that social situation bears itself out on the level of bodily posture and comportment. However taking them seriously does not, on the other hand, discount Yancy's interpretive framework, but rather complicates it:

> Critical pedagogy theorist Audrey Thompson points out that if the white male student's objective in the counter-reading is to use complexity to make the problem of racism disappear, then this is an invalid use of complexity. She also notes, and I agree, that what is interesting is that whites may worry about whether someone is being obnoxious, having a bad day, and so on, but they don't worry about racism when it comes to how they are addressed.[56]

Two important points are addressed here: first, that questions of gender don't render ineffective Yancy's interpretation but rather demand more nuance. A woman with an experience (or "prememory") of sexual violence may respond *both* to the bodily presence of *a* man, *and* to the racialized presence of *this Black* man; one does not discount the other, but may even potentiate the other. That is, both gender *and* race are already at play insofar as the woman's response in the elevator is a response *qua* white *woman* (and not just any white) to the presentation of a Black *man* (and not just any Black), with both race and gender embedding certain features into their social identities. Further, Thompson's second point, which is corroborated in Yancy's own anecdotal evidence concerning the reception of his work at lectures, questions the motivations and haste to explain away the possibility of racism when a more reasonable starting position, in a climate of systematic racism, would be to first assume it. The danger, then, is that when questions of gender are raised in relation to this reading of racism, they may be offered up disingenuously to diffuse the diagnosis of racism, and in doing so, further obviating the possibility for critical analysis and intervention.

Habitual Racism

Having now engaged with some of the salient points arising from the "Elevator Effect"—namely the significance of its bodily register, the defensibility

of its ascription as racist, and the differential epistemic positions in inter-
preting such gestures—we are in a position to extend the analysis in order to
argue that what we are facing here is not just racism in an embodied register,
but also in a habitual[57] one. We can return here to our primary question: can
the woman's response in the elevator be considered properly habitual, in a
Merleau-Pontian sense explicated above? Proceeding on the basis of not
knowing the woman's particular bodily habits, history, and mode of being
in the world—indeed not knowing anyone's, except perhaps one's own[58]—
but, knowing the history of racism in its depth, character, and scope, it is
possible to speak at a level of generality, about the broad class of gestures
associated with those described in Yancy's "Elevator Effect." Of this class
of gestures (which also include: locking car doors, suspicious surveilling in
shops, holding onto one's handbag, pointedly crossing the street), can we
justifiably consider them habitual? Recall that in the discussion of habit in
part 1 of this chapter, we made an important distinction between habit as
repetitive or *habitual* gesture that has "sedimented" (in its narrower sense)
in the body, and habit as a more general bodily orientation, or that to which
we are *habituated*. It is this latter conception of habit which I suggest can
be useful here. The flinches, the tensing, the moving away, the calling
toward, the panic—these are examples of habits insofar as they represent
a kind of response that is unthinking and nearby; they are responses that
reside within the body schema, such that they become called upon readily
and effortlessly in navigating encounters with the racialized "other." They
represent a certain bodily *habituation*. The white woman's body is oriented
such that responses of fear, suspicion, self-concern, and self-preservation
have settled into her bodily repertoire, and are made immediately available to her upon the unanticipated interaction with a Black man; her bodily
habits are racist.

While this claim might appear to dovetail the discourse on unconscious
or implicit bias, I suggest that they differ in some important ways. Many
studies have shown the way in which we may "unconsciously" hold certain
biases or ascribe certain stereotypes to differently racialized "others" in situations of work, education, public life, and so forth.[59] However, while this
discourse is effective in illuminating the depth of racist attitudes and perceptions in our psychical being, as well as their near-imperceptibility (often
the results of these studies surprise participants themselves), its framing in
terms of the unconscious makes it difficult to give an account of the *uptake*
involved in such racist orientations. That is, there is little room for asking
how racist stereotypes and attitudes come to be embedded, and the role or
participation of the bias-holder in this process; unconscious or implicit bias
confirms that these biases *exist*, but says little about the way they come to be
actively embedded in our ways of being. The potential for habit to address

such questions, through its analysis as habituation and through a rereading of sedimentation, is something I will explore toward the end of this chapter.

Moreover, nor do the terms "casual racism" or "microaggression" sufficiently adequate what I am seeking to capture here. The term "casual racism," which has gained some traction in public discourse in Australia, for example, refers to the small "everyday" acts of racism, much like the kinds we have been considering in this chapter. For example, in 2014 a far-reaching public television campaign portrayed similar scenarios in relation to Indigenous Australians—people shuffling away in public seats, suspicious surveilling in shops, heightened skepticism at job interviews, the subtle rejection of an open bus seat, and the casual racist joking among white friends at a pub.[60] However, I argue that what there gets called "casual racism" is in fact a misnomer; for while such forms of racism are casual in the sense of being relaxed or unreflective on the part of racist whites, they are not casual in the sense of being irregular, unexpected, or intermittent. Rather they are held together by a certain underlying and overarching bodily orientation toward racialized "others." Casting it as "casual," then, misses the systematicity and cohesion of the separate acts with related expressions of racism in that same person, and in the broader cultural milieu. A similar argument pertains to the discourse of "microaggression," a term coined by psychiatrist Chester Pierce in the 1970s, and subsequently expanded in the psychological literature (and now widely levied in public discourse). This concept, defined by Pierce and others as the "subtle, stunning, often automatic, and non-verbal exchanges which are 'put downs' of blacks by offenders,"[61] identifies two important things: first, the micro-level coding of anti-Black racist messages into the fabric of popular culture (Pierce and his team of researchers were interested in TV commercials), and second, its psychical impact on Blacks. In addition to effectively naming racism's beneath-surface register and infusion into all aspects of public life, the concept also points to the affective toll accumulated and experienced by those on the "receiving" end (a toll which thinkers such as Fanon have also sought to articulate). This is undoubtedly critical work, but it draws a slightly different emphasis from my present concern by focusing on the perspective of the racialized person. While I take up such questions in chapter 2, what I am after in this present analysis is a way to consider racism from the vantage point of its "doing" or its "doer," that is, to find ways to think about racism as it is enacted or performed, and to open up questions about the complicity and responsibility of those who perform it.

In view of these concerns, I suggest that these kinds of gestural and responsive modes of racism—such as the kind elucidated by Yancy—are better framed as habits, both in the narrower sense of repetition and in the broader sense of habituation. Recall that Merleau-Ponty earlier speaks of habit in terms of "the power of responding with a certain type of solution to a certain form of situation."[62] The ease with which such gestures are enacted in response to the racialized "other"—that is to say, the extent to which they are not anomalous or exceptional in the history of one's body schema, but rather coherent and consistent with it—supports the ascription of habit. These kinds of responses are habits insofar as they reflect a comportment or mode of responding that has "sedimented" in and been taken up by the body, supported by deeply embedded discourses and histories of racist praxis. Further, following our earlier analysis, we can say that such racist responses are neither conscious in the sense of fully deliberate and considered (indeed, they are most often denied and defended precisely on the grounds of being "unintentional"), nor non-conscious in the sense of unmediated bodily reflex,[63] but rather sit in the grey region of acquired orientation—and in this case, they reflect an orientation that is shaped by and enacts racist stereotypes and projections. Racism, on this account, is not only or always consciously enacted, but operates equally—indeed more insidiously—beneath the level of consciousness. But this is not to say that questions of culpability and responsibility therefore fail to get off the ground, since as I will argue in part 4 of this chapter, our reworking of the concept of habit is *precisely* what will open up such questions for consideration. More forcefully than the discourse of implicit bias, I will claim, framing racism in terms of phenomenological habit shows that there exist certain modes of being in the world that are not simply nor naïvely acquired, but rather involve some complicity or complacency on the part of the subject. Before moving on to this argument, however, I wish first to round out the present analysis of habitual racism by taking up the question of racism in the register of habitual perception.

Habitual Perception of the "Racialized Other"

Having considered at some length, the way in which racist gestures and responses can become inscribed on the level of the body schema through habits and habituated bodily orientation, along with the difficulties entailed in such a claim, I propose now to consider embodied racism in the form of habitual perception. The question here becomes: how does racist practice manifest in the basic level of bodily (and primarily visual) perception? This question is, of course, intimately bound up with the preceding analysis of bodily response and gesture, and indeed in some sense it seems logically prior: surely it is in *response* to a racialized perception that certain bodily movements or gestures are invoked? However, as we will see from the Merleau-Pontian accounts developed by Linda Martín Alcoff and Alia Al-Saji, the rigid insistence of a perception-then-expression logic obscures the way in which our processes of perception are *themselves* developed through embodied and lived experiences. In view of this, I present the following analysis of racialized perception

alongside the earlier analysis of racist gesture and orientation, as a complementary and supplementary contribution to the broader investigation into the
different aspects of embodied racism.

The (Hermeneutic) Visibility of Race

Drawing on the phenomenological tradition, Linda Martín Alcoff in *Visible
Identities* argues that the perception of race is informed by our perceptual
frameworks, themselves learnt and acquired through bodily habit. She writes:
"Because race works through the domain of the visible, the experience of race
is predicated first and foremost on the perception of race, a perception whose
specific mode is *a learned ability*" (my emphasis).[64] One of her claims, then,
is that contrary to what we might ordinarily assume, race "is the [perceptual]
field, rather than that which stands out."[65] That is to say, whereas we usually
take race to be the *characteristic* we perceive, Alcoff instead argues that
race is in fact operative at the level of our perceptual framework or horizon,
and is that *through and against which* we perceive. In earlier passages of the
Phenomenology, Merleau-Ponty offers a corrective classical psychology's
version of gestalt perception, arguing that "one's own body is the always
implied third term of the figure-background structure, and each figure appears
perspectivally against the double horizon of external space and bodily
space."[66] The statement resonates with Alcoff's claim in that whereas we
might usually consider race as the "figure" perceived against the ground of
morphological variation in general, given the significance of racial difference
in lived experience, it in fact serves as an organizing "structure of contemporary perception,"[67] constituting the ground against which we come to perceive
particular races (and not others). In other words, the lived body, situated as it
is in a racially differentiated world with meanings and signification flowing
from this differentiation, supplies race as one of the horizons against which
particular races emerge in our perception of others. The lived experience of
race as meaningful is what renders it intelligible and perceptible to us in our
perceptual schemata. If this appears to invite a certain circular kind of logic—
Alcoff seems to be claiming race as both ground *and* figure—this is because
she is reminding us here that the interplay between ground and figure that
constitutes perception is itself embedded in, and emerges from, a meaningful
context. For her, extrapolating from Merleau-Ponty, the perception of race, in
a certain sense, presupposes itself.[68]

What Alcoff rallies against with this argument is a naturalistic account
which uncritically accepts the "self-evidence" of race and racial difference,
and to which phenomenology may itself fall susceptible.[69] That is, in attending to the experience of racialization, one risks mistaking experience for
explanation, the result being that perceptible racial differences get chalked

down to naturalistic bodily coping mechanisms in response to living among racial diversity. Alcoff writes:

> Against this, I will argue that although racial classification does operate on the basis of perceptual difference, it is also the case that, as Merleau-Ponty argues, perception represents sedimented contextual knowledges. So the process by which human bodies are differentiated and categorized by type is a process *preceded* by group oppression, rather than one that causes and thus "explains" racism.[70]

Alcoff's phenomenological approach, then, is explicitly attentive to the historical and discursive practices that structure our perceptual and expressive horizons. Thus, despite the reservation, it becomes evident why Alcoff does choose to engage with phenomenology, albeit critically. In arguing that racialized perception is itself already structured by our bodily and lived concerns, and in drawing on Merleau-Ponty's account of embodied perception in this process, Alcoff is able to draw attention to an aspect of racist practice we might otherwise miss, since "perceptual practices involved in racializations are . . . tacit, almost hidden from view, and thus almost immune from critical reflection."[71] In the case of racism, this can mean that a "fear of African Americans or a condescension toward Latinos is seen as simple perception of the real, justified by the nature of things in themselves without the need of an interpretive intermediary of historico-cultural schemas of meaning."[72]

Further, according to Alcoff, the pertinence of phenomenological investigation to racism in particular is underscored by the specific way in which race is especially designated through the visual register more than other sensory registers, and more so than other forms of oppression (sexism, ableism, etc.). Regarding the first claim, while commentators such as Eduardo Mendieta have contributed important phenomenological explorations of racist hatred through other bodily (or what he calls somatological) registers[73], I think Alcoff is right when she argues that there is a distinctly privileged relationship between racism and the visual. (Although this of course is not to say that race functions *exclusively* in the visual register; I take up this theme in relation to the phenomenon of "racial passing" in chapter 4.) Alcoff argues, for example, that although "race" has always been conceptually fluid, with shifting definitions and metrics throughout its history—a claim supported by the genealogical investigations of Ladelle McWhorter[74]—these varied organizing schemata have always found their translation through visual bodily markers: "The criteria thought to determine racial identity have ranged from ancestry, experience, self-understanding, to habits and practices, yet these sources are coded through visible inscriptions on the body."[75] That race is taken to be expressed most saliently through the visual was attested to in the controversial and bewildering case of Rachel Dolezal in 2015, whose highly contentious and fraught claims to Black identity were significantly performed through the transformation of her visual presentation.[76]

The visual inscription of race onto the body, according to Alcoff, is by no means accidental: "Locating race in the visible thus produces the experience that racial identity is immutable."[77] It also refers us back to the privileged realm of the visible—what she calls an *ocularcentrism*—long-established in the Western philosophical and cultural tradition.[78] Given this, phenomenology's attentiveness to the dynamics of visual experience provide some welcome philosophical tools for thinking about the way racism works through the visual register. Alcoff's deployment of Merleau-Ponty's insight into the structure of perception, filtered through an engagement with questions of the social and political, is here put to work in opening up a space for political critique and intervention. One such example of this is Alia Al-Saji's analysis of perception in the case of veiled Muslim women.

Racialized Perception of the Muslim Veil

In her article "The Racialization of Muslim Veils," Al-Saji examines the French public debate in 2009 around proposals to ban the wearing of Muslim veils in government service and spaces, a debate which has seen many iterations in the post 9/11 world, in countries such as France, Canada, Australia, and the United Kingdom. (In the French case, the matter reached peak absurdity in 2016 when local bans were instituted against the "burkini," resulting in the fining or mandatory de-robing of covered Muslim women on beaches along the French Riviera.) Itself a renewal of an earlier debate and legislative prohibition of all "conspicuous" religious signs in 2004, Al-Saji argues that in both cases, the prevailing discourses were grounded in various habitual modes of racialized perception. For example, she argues that one of the bases (although importantly, not the *only* basis) upon which the 2004 law was justified was through the French legal doctrine of *laïcité*, or state secularism. Justified on this ground alone, one could argue that the law applied equally and indiscriminately to signs of *all* religions, indicated by its reluctance to call out the veil in its specificity, but instead referencing any signs that were "*ostensiblement*" religious. However, as Al-Saji argues, in both its application and even colloquial naming as "*la loi sur le foulard*" (the headscarf law),[79] this was manifestly untrue. This is in part due to the nature of the historico-cultural schema, to borrow Alcoff's term, operative in the political and legal context of this debate. Al-Saji writes:

> The assumption in most French discourse on *laïcité* is that all religious signs are equally foregrounded, and hence made visible, against a neutral, secular

background from which religion is absent (in public schools, administration, government). This is understood to apply as much to crosses as veils. But French secularism was built on a history of Christianity; that it has had to accommodate and coexist with Catholicism has meant, as some commentators argue, that secular public space is not a generalized but a structured absence.[80]

In other words, while *laïcité* was invoked to underscore the neutrality of the law, French cultural, political, and religious history was such that the traces of Christianity and particularly Catholicism[81] remained present though not necessarily "visible," in the structuring of that so-called secular space. Invoking a gestalt-like analysis, Al-Saji therefore argues that the seemingly neutral criterion of *"ostensiblement"* in the law was in fact coded against this historical context:

> This invisible structure of secular space (and time) means that cultural-religious practices are rendered differentially visible when put into coexistence with it. Some attract attention more than others: we may imagine that some signs and practices appear compatible with this space (and hence "discreet") . . . and further signs are in conflict and hence "conspicuous."[82]

This, however, was not the full extent of the story insofar as public discourse leading up to 2004, and the renewed debates in 2009 became centered not around conspicuous religious signs, generally, but on the female Muslim veil specifically. Al-Saji thus posits that there was something *in particular* about the veil—as distinct from any or all non-Christian signs—that rendered it especially suspect to French lawmakers. The key move which allowed this transition, she contends, was the "inscription of gender oppression as an essential feature of the representation of the Muslim veil," accompanied by a complementary and concurrent assertion of "presumed gender equality of French society (conceived as continuous with and even an outcome of secularism)."[83] It is the intertwining of these two discourses which, according to Al-Saji, render the Muslim veil *immediately* conspicuous and suspect against the secular and egalitarian self-image of French society. Thus as Al-Saji writes: "Against this complex ground, veiling was doubly adumbrated and came to appear as an over-determined figure—not merely visible in belonging to a different religion but hypervisible as the symbol of gender oppression of that religion."[84]

In this argument, Al-Saji moves beyond the gestalt analysis that reveals the "ground" or perceptual framework according to which we see, to argue that there is also a predetermined seeing of the "figure" that takes place when the veiled Muslim woman is seen *as* a woman oppressed by the faith and practices of Islam. Said differently, it is not only that there is discursively informed perceptual horizon determining how and what we see, but this mode of perception has already marked or predetermined the veiled Muslim woman as the oppressed woman, such that she is *each time* seen in this way. She writes:

> the relative intransigence of colonial and contemporary western representations of Muslim women—their surprising immunity to empirical cases and counter-examples—reveals something of the mechanism at play. These representations put Muslim women in positions scripted in advance, where veiling is constituted as the equivalent of *de-subjectification*—a lack of subjectivity, a victimhood or voicelessness, that these images in turn work to enforce.[85]

Our perceptual habits can thus work on these two levels, of ground *and* figure. Following Alcoff's analysis of race as supplying the perceptual horizon or "ground" of visual perception, in Al-Saji's analysis we have a complementary claim of racialized bodies appearing as "figure." As Al-Saji argues, veiled Muslim women are within this schema, seen as oppressed regardless of their diverse situations, self-perceptions, practices, or self-understandings. That this is the case is both confirmed by many Muslim women in their first person testimonies as well as by Muslim women's movements criticizing radical feminist organizations such as Femen for seeking to "liberate" them.[86]

Further, the perception of veiled Muslim women as oppressed, according to Al-Saji, reveals at once both a "more" *and* "less" in habitual perception. First, the racialized seeing in the case of veiled Muslim women is "more" in the sense that her body is laden with attributes, or "overdetermined," to recall Sartre and Fanon's term. Indeed, there is an affinity here between Al-Saji's descriptions of the habitual perception of Muslim women, and what Fanon describes as the "absolute density"[87] of black consciousness, a density which is given in the moment of perception, rather than at the moment of recognition.[88] In both cases of the Black man and veiled Muslim woman, their racialized bodies come already loaded with meaning and determination in the moment of visual perception.[89] And this, of course, extends to differently racialized bodies, whether Black women who are perceived as sexually available, Latino men as uneducated laborers, Asian women as exotic, and so forth.[90] Such wealth of personages, coded onto the bodies of differently racialized people, leads us to an important point: in the process of racialized perception analyzed by Al-Saji (following Alcoff and Fanon), what is also revealed is a point of convergence between representation and phenomenon. That is to say, if phenomenology purports to return us "to the things themselves" (per Husserl), then what the analysis of racialized perception shows us is that these "things" are not simply "themselves" but are already shaped by, and participate in, discursive practices. In other words, the appearance of a thing and its perception do not occur in some phenomenologically "pure" way, but rather they are already informed by, and indeed can be put in service of, discursive representations. Thus when Fanon writes that he is "a slave not of the 'idea' that others have or me but of my own appearance" in order to draw a contrast between the Black man and the Jew (a distinction we will consider more carefully in chapter 4), he is right to draw attention to the visual givenness of the Black body and the seemingly immutable inscription of race onto its epidermal layer. However as I would argue, it is also the case that the appearance of his Black body solicits such determination precisely *because* it is already supported by a long history of construction as inferior, savage, and so forth—in other words, the *idea* of the Black. I contend therefore that the distinction between the "idea" (or representation) and "appearance" which Fanon seeks to draw is somewhat overstated, insofar as his appearance is one that is *already* discursive (and representationally) constituted.

But as Al-Saji also argues, racialized perception is at the same time marked by seeing "less," evident in this case, in the way veiled Muslim women were effectively excluded from the French public debate, and from the possibility of being taken seriously as rational interlocutors or actors.

> Racializing vision is *less* in that the responsivity and affectivity of vision are circumscribed—the openness of vision to other ways of being, which may destabilize or shatter its perceptual schemata, delimited. The dynamic ability of vision to change is partially closed down. Racialized bodies are not only seen as naturally inferior, they *cannot be seen as otherwise*. The veiled body is not merely seen as oppressed, but cannot be seen as a subject who takes up and constitutes itself through that oppression.[91]

The description echoes some of Yancy's own remarks on the simultaneous hypervisibility *and* invisibility of the Black body, where this invisibility stands in for the inability to see the person as they are to themselves or to others.[92] However, couched in terms of an impoverished seeing, with the "dynamic ability of vision" of the seer being "closed down," I think that Al-Saji more suggestively points us to the contours of an *ethical* question on perception. (Indeed, she offers a rich account of the possibility of a "critical-ethical vision" in an earlier essay.[93]) Here, the several references to the disenfranchisement of veiled Muslim women and their effective "de-subjectification" in the French debate draw our attention to the way in which modes of perception—especially where the power structure is such that this perception frames the terms of public discourse—carry important political consequences and ethical import. It is not just that veiled Muslim women in this case are "not seen" or invisible, it is that this refusal or impoverished seeing *divests them of a self-originating voice* in public debate and participation in political life more generally, thus denying them political and ethical agency. And as thinkers such as Levinas and Waldenfels have shown, our openness, receptivity, and responsivity to others as they are (and not as they are *for us*) offer a more meaningful basis upon which an ethical relation with the other can unfold.[94]

Such connections in turn raise questions about ethics and normativity in relation to phenomenology more generally—something not explicitly considered by Merleau-Ponty in his account of the body, nor thematized by the phenomenological tradition more generally. If, as we see here, habits of perception can on a generous reading carry harmful unintended consequences in the realm of politics, or less generously, be strategically deployed to maintain oppressive power relations, can we speak of an ethics of perception and bodily disposition? This question, which I argue is especially well illuminated when we consider the way racist practices are inscribed in a bodily register, was in fact already implicitly raised in our earlier consideration of racist habits and habitual dispositions. Given Merleau-Ponty allows that we are intersubjectively constituted in our interactions with the world and with each other, if these modes of interaction (whether through bodily expression or perception) are such that they generate or contribute to a thoroughgoing denial of self, or breakdown of body image and body schema, this opens us to the question of whether there are normatively ideal (or normatively harmful) ways of comporting one's bodily self. This question, which I raise here only in a cursory way, appears to invite a repositioning of Merleau-Ponty's account of embodiment in the milieu of Aristotlean ethics, although as we will see in the discussion on responsibility toward the end of the chapter, as well as in our consideration of the racist gaze in chapter 4, with some subtle differences in play.

Returning to our present analysis, it is also worth noting the ways in which the account of racialized perception folds back into our earlier analysis of habit. For example, the "seeing less" which Al-Saji describes in the case of the public positioning of veiled Muslim women (such that they are each time seen in a predetermined way) also returns us to the concept of habit in two ways. First, it returns us to the narrower sense of habit as habitual, whereby the perception of veiled Muslim women as oppressed is routinized through repetition, without meaningful room for variation. This is habitual racialized perception in its usual understanding of the term. But, in addition, we can also identify here habit in its broader sense of habituation. That is, such racist seeing speaks to an underlying perceptual orientation; *one inhabits this mode of racialized perception.* As Al-Saji writes in the essay, "A Phenomenology of Critical-Ethical Vision: Merleau-Ponty, Bergson, and the Question of Seeing Differently":

> The perceived world mirrors the practical possibilities . . . of my body and changes in conjunction with my changing habits. Seeing is therefore not an

indifferent and neutral recording of the visible. Seeing configures the visible according to the ways my eyes have of wandering in it, according not only to my habitual eye movements but the habitual and nascent motor anticipations of my body.[95]

And as we noted in our earlier explication of Merleau-Ponty, it is the hallmark of habits that they are seamlessly integrated into our body schemata so as to render themselves invisible to us, absent their explicit thematization. Or as Al-Saji writes, "Through sedimentation and habituation, the constitutive operations of vision remain tacit or pre-reflective. . . . We see through our habits; we do not see them, Alcoff notes."[96] This explains why, for example, human-resources managers can be "stunned" when experiments show them to significantly favor "White sounding names" (Emily, Greg) over "African-American sounding names" (Lakisha, Jamal) in assessing identical fictitious résumés, despite their stated commitment to diversity in the workplace.[97] Likewise, the habitual perception of veiled Muslim women works in this way, quietly structuring the tenor and content of public discourse while obscuring its own perceptual framework. We may inhabit such modes of racialized perception, but we do not always do so knowingly.

Gender in Racialized Perception

Finally, it is also important to note the central role that gender plays in the habitual perception of veiled Muslim women. Al-Saji's argument here is not just that veiled Muslim women are racialized as "other" or "conspicuous" against the purportedly neutral ground of French *laïcité*, it is additionally that veiled Muslim women are racialized specifically as oppressed and agent-less because a gendered (and heteronormative) account is mobilized in this racialized seeing. In laying out this argument, Al-Saji draws on Fanon's account of the French colonial project to "unveil" Algerian women in the 1930s. In his essay, Fanon contrasts the striking difference between the hypervisibility of veiled women to the colonial male gaze, with her non-visibility to the Algerian man, since "their gaze is trained 'not to perceive the feminine profile'."[98] That veiled women are assumed oppressed by virtue of their covering up, exposes certain gendered and heteronormative expectations around how much, in what way, *and to whom* one ought to be visible. As Al-Saji argues, "Representations of veiled women—as sites of sexual repression and gender oppression—are generated by . . . a gaze that desires possession of women's bodies and 'wants to see.'"[99] In other words, Western patriarchal perceptual schemata which posit women as visual objects for the male gaze are also operative in the perception of veiled women as oppressed. Considered from a different vantage point, insofar as the seer (or gaze-holder) is usually understood to occupy a position of relative power in the relation of seer—seen (to be explored in chapter 4), this would suggest that veiled women—and in particular women more fully veiled, such as those in *niqāb*—actually *occupy* positions of power insofar as they becomes seers but not themselves seen, and insofar as their veiling is what creates and gives meaning and texture to differential social relations. That this is not a prevalent or even a *possible* narrative in the usual discourse, where veiled women are seen as almost exclusively oppressed, suggests that the operative perceptual framework is one which is imbued with patriarchal norms around the visibility of women's body to a certain, male gaze.[100] Al-Saji thus writes: "Women who continue to veil seem to place themselves beyond (colonial male) recognition. They have no place within this heterosocial and scopic economy. *Not even objects, their ability to return the gaze, to see and to actively make meaning, cannot be imagined within this field*" (my emphasis).[101]

We should take note that the analysis offered here is not *quite* one of intersectionality, which occupies lively debate in race and gender studies. As Al-Saji has elsewhere argued, intersectionality can be problematic insofar as it can operate on the assumption that there already exists relatively stable axes of race and gender (or any other social identities) which converge or "intersect" when a person falls concurrently within both categories.[102] The problem here is that unless and until this intersection occurs, these axes are otherwise undisturbed by the presence of the other—and the face of the racialized body usually becomes the *male* racialized body, as the face of the woman becomes the *white* woman. Needless to say, such a conceptual framework risks reinscribing its own hierarchies and further oppressive practices. Perhaps unsurprisingly—given it is women of color who are the ones traditionally caught out in this model of intersectionality or the failure to consider it—Al-Saji's account, which centers around Muslim women, instead advances the idea that gendered schemata are *already* intrinsic to racialized perception. That is, they are not the intersection of two distinct problems, but rather, "continuous":

> Though I argue in the rest of this article (beyond Fanon) that the process by which the veiled Muslim woman is "othered" in western and colonial perception is double—her racialization being inseparably intertwined with gender—I also maintain that this othering is a form of racism continuous with the racialization that Fanon has described.[103]

The habitual and gendered perception of veiled Muslim women as oppressed serves to support the general racialized perception of Muslim men and Muslim culture (interpellated primarily through the actions of men) *as oppressive*, and thus is in this way continuous with racism.

With this in mind, if we return to Yancy's example of the dangerous Black man, also recounted by Fanon among others, we see that so too is there already a gendered dimension to these racist perceptions. The narrative there is not simply (or only) that Black *people* are dangerous, but that Black *men* are particularly (though not exclusively) dangerous, and this is an image both constituted and sustained through a complementary construction of the "purity" of the white woman alluded to by Yancy[104], and with its own pitfalls and oppressive practices for white women. Consider for example, the "King Kong" narrative which has long animated popular imagination and periodically re-enlivened in popular culture. Can this be connected to the fact that Black men seldom speak of the purse-clutching practices from Asian, Latina, or Black women, instead calling out almost exclusively of their experiences in relation to white women in this practice? The Black man is constructed as dangerous or "rapacious" specifically in relation to the gendered *and* racialized constructions of the white woman (as opposed to the Black, Asian, or Latina woman). In a similar vein, I would extend Al-Saji's account to argue that it is not just the *same* desiring patriarchal gaze that is imposed in habitual modes of perception toward Muslim women, but rather a specific, racialized gaze which fetishizes the "exoticism" of women from the Orient,[105] and which is interrupted by veiling practices. In our analyses of the habitual perceptions of racialized bodies then, there exists always and already an interlaced gendered dimension which, if sometimes under-emphasized, ought not to be forgotten, to say nothing of the heteronormative framework that organizes these gendered and racialized relations.

PART 4—HABITUAL RACISM AND RESPONSIBILITY

Habitual Perception and Response: Two Cases of Embodied Racism

As I have tried to emphasize throughout the discussion of the different aspects of embodied racism (habitual perception and bodily gesture or orientation), these two threads are not brought together by a relationship of causality, but as intertwining and mutually reinforcing aspects of bodily racism. And while it might be argued that the examples I have discussed so far have involved relatively "benign" or "harmless" forms of racism, a position I would not accede to (they are harmful precisely because they are insidious and seemingly benign), I also argue that the structural operations at work in these analyses can have far more extreme expressions. Here I turn briefly to the cases of Jonathan Ferrell and Renisha McBride, which bring together the two sides of habitual perception and bodily response or orientation, while bearing out the gravity of these racialized modes of bodily habituation.

In the early hours of September 14, 2013, a young Black man by the name of Jonathan Ferrell, aged twenty-four, was gunned down by police in a residential North Carolina street.[106] Around 2 a.m. that morning, Ferrell was driving home before getting into a serious car crash on a quiet country road; so badly damaged was his car that he had to kick through the rear window in order to escape. Having done that, he then—most likely in a considerable amount of shock, pain, disorientation, and fear—climbed through a thicket of bushes and trees in the dead of the night, to reach a residential street where he sought help at the first house he saw. Sarah McCartney, a young white woman, and mother of a young child sleeping upstairs, answered the door expecting it to be her husband. Upon seeing Ferrell, however, she immediately mistook him for an intruder. McCartney called 911 in a state of distress, reporting that a man was banging on her door, trying to break in. Three white police officers arrived, and when Ferrell—unarmed and, it bears repeating, *injured and in need of help*—started moving toward them, one police officer shot him with a taser. Since that did not stop him, another police officer proceeded to fire twelve shots, ten of which hit Ferrell, shooting him dead. As exceptional an event as this would appear to be, a chillingly similar scene unfolded only six weeks later on November 2 in Detroit, involving a young Black woman named Renisha McBride, aged nineteen. Like Ferrell, McBride got into a car accident early one morning. In a disoriented state (in her case partly due to intoxication, but also due to shock and possible brain injury), McBride was described by a first witness as having held her head in her bloodied hands, repeatedly stating that she wanted to go home.[107] After wandering off she eventually found her way to the front porch of another house, where in seeking assistance, she was mistaken for an intruder, and shot in the face at close range by a white middle-aged man, Theodore Wafer.[108]

While both cases call for more careful analysis, I raise them briefly here to offer examples of how habitual racialized perceptions—the acquired, sedimented, and *maintained* perceptions—of Blackness as dangerous, threatening, or "thuggish," accompanied by habitual responses of fear, defensiveness, or even dis-empathy, operate across a wide spectrum of racist response and action. That a Black person seeking help or refuge is instantly—though by no means randomly—perceived as violent or threatening, and responded to without hesitation[109] in violence, indicates that the problem of habitual racism is not merely some disinterested academic question, but one of profound and urgent import, even if that urgency that can at times become obfuscated or derailed by the slowness and precision of academic inquiry.[110] Further, while both cases resonate strongly with the more recent and heavily criticized fatal police shooting of Mike Brown in Ferguson, Missouri, and police choking of Eric Garner in Staten Island, New York, the cases of Ferrell and McBride show us that the problem of habitual and embodied racism lies not only with the police and authorities[111]—although institutional violence against Blacks in the United States is desperately real and chronic—but also with regular citizens in the course of their daily lives. While the Brown and Garner cases generated much heated public debate and scrutiny of practices in the policing of Black bodies (entirely justified, given public power and responsibility vested in police), what Ferrell and McBride's deaths remind us is that there is a broader narrative uniting all of these tragic cases, that of the habitual perception of Blacks and bodily responses to them as dangerous, violent, and less worthy.

While not framed in terms of habit, Judith Butler's reading of the Rodney King beating some twenty years ago, which of course is silently recalled in these contemporary cases, shows how pervasive and deeply embedded this hermeneutic and embodied racism is. In her chapter "Endangered/Endangering," Butler argues that such predeterminations of Blackness are operative not only in the moment of racist violence, but are powerful enough to secure "not guilty" verdicts and editorial vindication long after the "heat" of that moment has faded. She writes:

> What struck me on the morning after the verdict was delivered were reports which reiterated the phantasmic production of "intention," the intention inscribed in and read off Rodney King's frozen body on the street, his intention to do harm, to endanger. The video was used as "evidence" to support the claim that the frozen black male body on the ground receiving blows was himself producing those blows, about to produce them, was himself the imminent threat of a blow and, therefore, was himself responsible for the blows he received. That body thus received those blows in return for the ones it was about to deliver, the blows which were that body in its essential gestures, even as the one gesture that body can be seen to make is to raise its palm outward to stave off the blows against it. According to this racist episteme, he is hit in exchange for the blows he never delivered, but which he is, by virtue of his blackness, always about to deliver.[112]

Resonating with Al-Saji's analysis of the "too late," Butler here describes the way the King's Black male body appeared on the scene already fixed in its meaning, already guilty of the blows he did not deliver. The potency of racialized perception is such that it needs neither time to deliberate nor facts to corroborate. This mode of seeing is, as we noted earlier, "sedimented" in our perceptual habits. And yet as I have flagged throughout our discussion of habit, I think there are some limits to the characterization of habit purely in these terms. Where for example, do we locate the ethical moment of responsibility (not to mention the possibility for change) in these acquired habits?

In closing out this chapter, I propose revisiting the question of sedimentation in order to see how we might think habit anew.

Rethinking Sedimentation: The *Holding* of Habits

It is of course true that Merleau-Ponty invokes the motif of sedimentation on several occasions, not only in his reference to the "double moment of sedimentation and spontaneity,"[113] but also in his consideration of the practices or behaviors that become in his word (following Bergson) "deposited"[114] in our cultural world. Commentators are therefore right to run with the analogy; habits are sedimentations insofar as they express the past's grounding or anchoring effect on our present and anticipatory bodies. Further, the cases above seem to confirm this; Black bodies are perceived as violent and responded to unreflectively in defense because of the long and fraught histories of racism collected or "sedimented" in the body schema. And yet as I have suggested, the problem in invoking sedimentation is that it tends to point to the passive and inert—both of which obscure the innovative moment in Merleau-Ponty's presentation of habit, and which I argue further obscure questions of responsibility in the cultivation and persistence of one's bodily habits. This claim, however, presumes a meaning for the term which we have not yet sufficiently interrogated.

The term sedimentation is commonly employed in scientific fields such as Geology, where it designates the process in which minerals get deposited on surfaces and which in time turn into rock. Significantly, this usage already betrays the sense of passivity and inertia we normally attribute to it: materials get *deposited* on a surface (passivity), and once sedimented the materials solidify and remain fixed in their layers and order (inertia).[115] We see similar connections if we look to other domains: the word "sedentary" in our everyday language refers to inactivity, slowness, even stillness. Think, for example, of the contemporary occupational health discourse around the problem of our increasingly *sedentary* work and life-styles. In Zoology, the term refers to species that are non-migratory and inhabit the same place (sessile animals). If the weight of sedimentation is heavy and unmoving, how then does this square with our earlier descriptions of habit as bodily habituation and *orientation* and the sense of "I can" embedded within Merleau-Ponty's habitual body? Further, how can we begin to articulate a notion of responsibility for one's habits if their acquisition is mostly passive and inert?

But we should press further. For example, in geological sedimentation, the depositing of materials is passive insofar as surfaces do not solicit them—but they do *receive* them. This entails a measure of material and compositional compatibility such that the new material does not simply "run off" the existing surface. In the way that catching a ball involves receptivity—we open our hands to make the shape of the ball—something similar can be said here: the surface contains a receptivity to the material, with its own edges and formations codetermining which new materials get deposited, and how. If we transpose this to realm of bodily habit, then we could say that the acquisition of new habits depends not only on one's cultural and social milieu, but also on one's own bodily receptivity and compatibility. Sedimentation on this reading is not *wholly* passive; habits do not just get "deposited" in our bodies. In the habitual response of clutching of one's handbag upon the approach of the Black man for example, does the acquisition of this habit cohere with existing bodily habituations, or does it in fact jar with one's bodily orientation? The question of receptivity thus figures importantly in our consideration of sedimentation and habit.

In addition to this receptivity (as opposed to pure passivity), I want to suggest that habit also entails an *ongoing* activity (as opposed to pure inertia). Note that in Merleau-Ponty's account, the acquisition and possession of habit is never fully accomplished, but rather undergoes continual reworking and instantiation. The movement is similar to his account of time and thought, in which he writes: "Likewise, my acquired thoughts are not an absolute acquisition; they feed off my present thought at each moment; they offer me a sense, but this is a sense that I reflect back to them. In fact, the acquisition that is available to us expresses, at each moment, the energy of our present consciousness."[116] Habit is constantly in play, shaping our movements and responses. The organist sitting down to the different organ does not just "apply" or put to use her habit of organ playing to the new instrument, in settling into its spatiality the habit of organ playing is at once exercised and expanded. As Casey adds: "The process of sedimentation is ever at work: intentional threads go back and forth between body and its ever-changing phases, which are continually reanimated by current experience. If sedimentation is to be conceived as a precipitation of the past into the present, it is an active precipitation actively maintained."[117]

If sedimentation is to be reanimated in a more active voice as suggested by Casey, then we would do well to turn to the term's etymology, which provides us with important cues. Sedimentation's Latin root *sedēre* refers not only "settling" (as invoked by chemical sedimentation), but also to "sitting." This term, heard distinct from "laying" (or layering, as in geological sedimentation), allows a new and more active sense to emerge. Sitting entails an active moment; it involves a *holding* of the body. (And we should note in turn that the Latin root for habit, *habēre*, can also mean "to hold.") To sit is to remain in one place perhaps, but it is nonetheless to hold or collect one's body in such a way so as to *maintain or keep* this position. This holding is what prevents our bodies from collapsing onto the floor in a way that gives us over wholly to the downward plunge of gravity. Moreover, this sense of holding in sitting is closely related to that of posture; the German noun for posture, for example, *die Haltung*, carries this sense of "holding" (*halten*) the body. One could go further to say that such maintaining or keeping is not just active, but also intentional. The Chinese martial arts *Wushu* is helpful here: when one *holds* a stance, such as the horse stance, this is an active endeavor (that the leg muscles begin to shake in resistance after a few short moments is testament to this). This is akin to the active voice in sedimentation. But while a horse stance can be held for the sake of training, it is also more: in the context of a form or routine, the stance serves as a foundation for transition, preparing and positioning the body for the next movement or strike. It is significant that in Chinese the word for stance, 步, can also be translated into English as "step." Holding is not only active, it also enables and prepares us for action and movement.

Habitual movements and orientations, insofar as they continue to participate in the body schema, are *held* in the body in a continuous and ongoing way. This reconceptualization of habit as being *held*—requiring ongoing maintenance and servicing—is made even clearer when we note that for Merleau-Ponty, habit has a distinctively "lived" dimension: the acquisition of a new habit never fully crosses over the threshold into the acquired, but involves a constant holding or "inhabiting." Speaking here of the body's familiar and habitual motility around the home-space, he writes:

> But this word "sedimentation" must not trick us: this contracted knowledge is not an inert mass at the foundation of our consciousness. For me, my apartment is not a series of strongly connected images. It only remains around me as my familiar domain if it still *hold* "in my hands" or "in my legs" its principal distances and directions, and only if a multitude of intentional threads run out toward it from my body.[118] (my emphasis)

This reference to holding takes up the sense of sitting in sedimentation discussed here. For Merleau-Ponty, habits are *held* rather than possessed; they are both active and continually *activated*. This reading, which renders passivity not only in a more receptive but also more active register, finds resonance with Merleau-Ponty's account of the past and our relation to it, as sketched out in his later *Collège de France* lectures on institution and passivity. He writes for example: "Human institution is not only the utilization of the past or the utilization of an experience as a substitute. . . . Human institution is still the integration of this past into a new signification. . . . Already in the animal there is prospection; there is never pure prospection in the human."[119] This integration of the past is continual and undetermined, such that it is as wrong to say "my past explains me entirely" as it is to say "I create the sense of my past ex nihilo."[120] According to Merleau-Ponty, we relate to the past not as an object, but as that which "creates a question, puts it in reserve, makes a situation that is indefinitely open."[121] As expressions of the anchoring past, habits therefore are never truly congealed or calcified, but are held over in our bodily horizons.

Responsibility and Change

If this is right then what we have is an opening *within* the concept of habit, for a consideration of questions of responsibility and change. For example, we do not have to locate the possibility of change in that which is external, as Alcoff does when she writes:

> are we not led to pessimism about the possibility of altering the perceptual habits of racializations? Here I would think that the multiple schemas operating in many if not most social spaces today would mitigate against an absolute determinism and thus pessimism. Perceptual practices are dynamic even when congealed into habit, and that dynamism can be activated by the existence of multiple forms of gaze in various cultural productions and by the challenge of contradictory perceptions.[122]

While it is surely true that social change is powerfully effected through intervening practices, the "loosening" of sedimentation's stranglehold in my reading of habit also offers a way to think through the possibility of change without sole recourse to disrupting schemata. Habits too can be receptive to change. More importantly, however, locating the active moment within habit also allows us to articulate more clearly a notion of responsibility in relation to one's own racist habits. The question that now becomes available to us is: to what extent can one be held responsible for one's habituated bodily orientations or modes of perception, when these habits are not merely passively "sedimented" in the body, but also *held* and *activated*? In the context of racist habits that bear negatively on the lived experience of racialized bodies—or as we have seen, can even prove fatal for some—what is the responsibility to continually interrogate, challenge, and rework such habits?

Returning to the cases of Jonathan Ferrell and Renisha McBride, what this analysis opens up is a way to talk about responsibility in relation to the racist habits that buttressed the immediate perception of and response to their bodies as dangerous and violent. To the extent that the first responses of Theodore Wafer and Sarah McCartney (to say nothing of the police) were to cast the bodies of McBride and Ferrell as criminal, according to the racist orientations of their bodily horizons, they can be held responsible for the racist habits which were acquired, maintained, and activated in those critical moments. Now of course we can—and *should*—be nuanced in our understanding of responsibility, allowing for important gradations across the range of actors involved (e.g., the police in Ferrell's case, who bear the greatest responsibility as people entrusted with state power), as well as the cultural and historical milieux that give rise, shape, and meaning to these particular habits of racist perception and response. In other words, my argument ought not distract us from these important conversations about the role of structures and institutions in racism, but instead broaden our purview so as to allow us to ask *how* such macro-level workings of racism can find expression in our bodily being, and what role we each play in the uptake, maintenance, and perpetuation of such racist schemata.[123] Further, this analysis of racism in terms of habit throws up another important consequence: in public discourse we too often see the diffusion of racist controversies with the unsatisfactory defense, "I did not *mean* to offend." This misplaces the meaning and significance of racism to its actor, sidelining the *experiential effect* on the offended person or community, which is endured independently of the actor's intentions, though *not* independently of the world already experienced racially. But in addition to the argument that meanings of gestures are located outside the exclusive control of their actors, habit renders blunt the notion of intention in a second way: by highlighting a register of movement and action that sits below cognitive intention, which nonetheless involves some *acquired* and *maintained* bodily orientation toward racial "others." In other words, my reading of habit in its more active voice assigns *some* responsibility to those whose racist habits and bodily orientations remain uninterrogated and unchallenged.

This is different from, though not unrelated, to the kind of responsibility Emily Lee discusses in her essay, "Body Movement and Responsibility for a Situation." Although she is concerned with the questions of the habitual body, her argument in relation to responsibility plays out primarily in the political context of the "race treason" movement, which entailed disavowing whiteness as an anti-racist strategy. Lee is rightly critical of such strategies insofar as they allow whites to avoid responsibility for the historical benefits that continue to accrue to them, regardless of their own intentions.[124] My claim, however, is that in addition to responsibility for one's *situation*, one can and ought to also be responsible for one's *bodily habits*, especially insofar as we *hold* habits in the active sense, and to the extent that such habits racially objectify, harm, and oppress others.[125] Racism is not a matter of wilful "intention" as noted, but is deeply embedded in our habitual bodies. And as I have argued, this level of inscription does not diminish the imperative or responsibility to work on our habits. George Yancy has argued elsewhere that "the threshold for perpetuating White racism is very low; all that is necessary is for White people to do nothing at all."[126] In part, this echoes Lee's point above; in a system of longstanding, entrenched, and continuing racism, whites who "do nothing" continue to benefit from the accrued advantages of white racism, which can range from economic benefits,[127] cultural and political benefits of representation and participation, to the existential benefits of facing a more open and not-yet-determined project of being and becoming, in contrast to the overdetermination of racialized bodies. In other words, "doing nothing" can still mean one benefits from one's *situation* within the racist schema. Following the analysis of habit, however, I argue that white racism can also take the form of "doing nothing" insofar as one's racist habits of perception and bodily orientation remain uninterrogated and unworked upon. As Yancy writes:

> By the time White students have arrived to our classrooms, they have already been shaped by White ways of being-in-the-world, White ways of avoiding the issue of White privilege, White ways of constructing nonwhite bodies as "different," White ways of seeing themselves as "innocent" of White racism, and White ways of taking up space and moving through that space in the capacity of ownership and possession.[128]

What I have tried to uncover through this chapter's analysis of racism as habit, then, are new sites of racism and racialization to which anti-racist efforts must attend.

NOTES

1. Maurice Merleau-Ponty, *Phenomenology of Perception*, trans. Donald A. Landes (New York: Routledge, 2012), 144.

2. Ibid., 93.

3. Ibid., 145.

4. There is a fair amount of ambiguity around the use of these two terms in philosophy. Shaun Gallagher and Jonathan Cole in their essay, "Body Image and Body Schema," present a helpful way to distinguish the two: "In contrast to the reflective intentionality of the body image, a *body schema* involves a system of motor capacities, abilities, and habits that enable movement and the maintenance of posture. The body schema is not a perception, a belief, or an attitude. Rather, it is a system of motor and postural functions that operate below the level of self-referential intentionality, although such functions can enter into and support intentional activity." (132). So, intentionality and consciousness, for them, seem to be the key distinguishing markers, although they also do admit that "the conceptual distinction should not imply that on the behavioral level the image and schema are unconnected or that they do not sometimes affect one another." Shaun Gallagher and Jonathan Cole, "Body Image and Body Schema in a Deafferented Subject" in Donn Welton (ed.), *Body and Flesh: A Philosophical Reader* (Oxford: Blackwell Publishers, 1998), 131.

5. Ibid., 102.

6. Ibid., 143.

7. Ibid., 144.

8. To the latter, Merleau-Ponty writes: "At each moment in a movement, the preceding instant is not forgotten but rather is somehow fit into the present, and in short the present perception consists in taking up the series of previous positions that envelop each other by relying upon the current position." Ibid., 141.

9. Ibid., 71.

10. Edward S. Casey, "Habitual Body and Memory in Merleau-Ponty" in Tom Sparrow and Adam Hutchinson (eds.), *A History of Habit: From Aristotle to Bourdieu* (Lanham: Lexington Books, 2013), 213.

11. Casey, "Habitual Body and Memory in Merleau-Ponty," 212–213.

12. Merleau-Ponty, *Phenomenology of Perception* (New York: Routledge, 2012), 146.

13. Ibid., 139.

14. Ibid., 145. For a critical reading of Merleau-Ponty's example of the "blind man's cane" and its ableist assumptions, see Joel Michael Reynolds, "Merleau-Ponty's Aveugle and the Phenomenology of Non-Normate Embodiment," Chiasmi International 18 (2017).

15. Parkour is an interesting example because it exhibits many of the qualities of a Merleau-Pontian account of habit. With its origins in military obstacle-course training, parkour today is practiced in the open field of urban landscapes. It consists of "free running" through streets, rebounding and responding to whatever objects or structures insert themselves into one's path. A typical run might therefore consist of bounding off walls some meters high, leaping up stairs, sliding down ramps, jumping from the tops of buildings, and so forth. It is a dynamic sport demanding a thrilling display of agility and responsivity. As an urban activity, people also constitute an essential element of the cityscape, and thus parkour also involves dodging bodies as they appear unannounced and unanticipated in the immediate horizon. More so than the organist, the parkourist trains to cultivate a certain bodily orientation or responsivity, such that in the course of a run they are well positioned to respond swiftly, creatively, and *spontaneously*, to what reveals itself upon the turn of a street corner.

16. Ibid., 145.

17. Ibid.

18. Ibid., 146.

19. This point partially draws from Hubert Dreyfus' argument concerning artificial intelligence (AI), and the closed-circuit nature of the simulated environments in which such machines are developed. The argument is that AI will fail (insofar as it seeks to emulate human intelligence) because human interaction is infinitely open; situations and significances are unpredictable, and our responsivity calls for more than rule-based learning. Hubert Dreyfus, *What Computers (Still) Can't Do: A Critique of Artificial Reason* (Cambridge: MIT Press, 1993).

20. Ibid., 81–82.

21. Bourdieu writes for example, "In short, the habitus, the product of history, produces the individual and collective practices, and hence history, in accordance with the schemes engendered by history." Ibid., 82.

22. "It follows that every marriage tends to reproduce the conditions which have made it possible. Matrimonial strategies . . . belong to the system of reproduction

strategies, defined as the sum total of the strategies through which individuals or groups objectively tend to reproduce the relations of production associated with a determinate mode of production by striving to reproduce or improve their position in the social structure." Ibid., 70.

23. Nick Crossley, "The Phenomenological Habitus and its Construction," *Theory and Society*, 30 (2001): 96.

24. Crossley traces Bourdieu's sociological genealogy in "Habit and Habitus," *Body & Society*, 19 (2013): 140.

25. This claim needs to be qualified. Bourdieu does speak of embodiment, but when doing so he invokes the term *hexis*, the Ancient Greek term which gets translated as habit. So Bourdieu seems to make a telling distinction, relegating *hexis* to the body and *habitus* to practices more generally: "Body *hexis* speaks directly to the motor function, in the form of patterns of postures that is both individual and systematic, because linked to a whole system of techniques involving the body and tools, and charged with a host of social meaning and values: in all societies, children are particularly attentive to the gestures and postures which, in their eyes, express everything that goes to make an accomplished adult—a way of walking, a tilt of the head, facial expressions, ways of sitting and of using implements, always associated with a tone of voice, a style of speech, and (how could it be otherwise?) a certain subjective experience." see Bourdieu, *Outline of a Theory of Practice*, 87.

26. For some examples of this criticism, see Nick Crossley, "The Phenomenological Habitus and its Construction," where he identifies sociologists such as Jeffrey Alexander and Richard Jenkins who present various criticisms against the deterministic nature of Bourdieu's theory of *habitus*.

27. Crossley, "Habit and Habitus," 147.

28. Iris Marion Young, "Throwing Like a Girl: A Phenomenology of Feminine Body Comportment, Motility, and Spatiality" in *On Female Body Experience: 'Throwing Like a Girl' and Other Essays* (New York: Oxford University Press, 2005), 32.

29. Ibid., 36.

30. Ibid., 38.

31. Ibid., 44.

32. Iris Marion Young, "Lived Body vs. Gender: Reflections on Social Structure and Subjectivity" in *On Female Body Experience*, 26.

33. Given the earlier distinction between "habitual" and "habituated," I note that my reference to "habitual" in the term "habitual racism" is adjectival, that is, I do not limit "habitual racism" the cases of unthinking repetition, but include in it the broader sense of habituation and orientation.

34. While I claim that these are "uncontroversial" examples of racist gestures, it is still the case that popular culture and discourse will often entertain questions of whether such gestures are "really racist." Some examples of this include: the public "debates" around Australian Football League (AFL) club president's public invocation of *King Kong* when talking about Aboriginal football player Adam Goodes on the radio in 2013, pop-star Miley Cyrus' slanty-eye photo poses in 2009, and Prince Harry's Nazi "fancy dress" costume in 2005.

35. There is, for example, a lively debate around white rappers such as Eminem, and more recently, Iggy Azalea, not only on questions of cultural appropriation and exploitation, but also on what has been variously termed "vocal blackface" or "verbal blackface." See, for example, "Jean Grae Talks New '#5' EP And Disdain For Iggy Azalea's 'Verbal Blackface'" (http://revolt.tv/news/jean-grae-talks-new-5-ep-and-disdain-for-iggy-azaleas-verbal-blackface/9029F87F-CA4B-4122-84AA-6A03E4611752 accessed March 01, 2015) and "Azealia Banks, Iggy Azalea and hip-hop's appropriation problem," *The Guardian,* December 27, 2014.

36. George Yancy, *Black Bodies, White Gazes: The Continuing Significance of Race* (Lanham: Rowman & Littlefield, 2008), 4.

37. Ibid., 5.

38. Jean-Paul Sartre, *Anti-Semite and Jew: An Exploration of the Etiology of Hate,* trans. George J. Becker (New York: Schocken Books, 1948), 79.

39. Yancy, *Black Bodies, White Gazes,* 3.

40. Merleau-Ponty, *Phenomenology of Perception,* 183. Note, however, that Merleau-Ponty does (in his footnotes) allow for distinction between "authentic or originary" speech and "secondary" speech, the former being that which he refers to in this claim.

41. Ibid., 190.

42. Yancy, *Black Bodies, White Gazes,* 16.

43. Ibid., 5.

44. Yancy, *Black Bodies, White Gazes,* 6.

45. In an important passage, Yancy explains that this epistemological community is not exclusively constituted *only* or *exclusively* by those in the Black community: "It is important to note that Black communities' perceptions are not in principle inaccessible to those not from them. In short, we can communicated the shared experiences, conceptual frameworks, and background assumptions to others if they are open to instruction and willing to take the time to listen. So even if all knowers are not intersubstitutable, it does not mean that non-Black knowers, once suitably instructed, cannot come to learn to cognize in ways that enable them to identify racist behavior readily. . . . Of course, this line of reasoning also allows for the possibility that even Blacks can disagree about what constitutes a racist form of behavior." Ibid., 9.

46. Ibid., 7.

47. Ibid., 7–8.

48. Yancy, *Black Bodies, White Gazes,* 7.

49. Ibid., 67 and "Barneys and Macy's Racial Discrimination Cases Stir Talk of 'Shopping While Black'," *Huffington Post,* October 31, 2013.

50. George Yancy, "Elevators, Social Spaces and Racism: A Philosophical Analysis," *Philosophy & Social Criticism,* 34(8) (2008): 843–876, 849.

51. The question of epistemological ignorance and racism is richly explored in the collection: eds. Shannon Sullivan and Nancy Tuana, *Race and Epistemologies of Ignorance* (Albany: SUNY Press, 2007).

52. Yancy, *Black Bodies, White Gazes,* 11.

53. Ibid., 25.

54. Ibid., 11.

55. This is the idea that women and girls in societies rife with gendered violence are "primed" to anticipate our own rape: "Postmemories (of other women's rapes) are

transmuted into prememories (of one's own future rape) through early and ongoing socialization of girls and women, and both inflect the actual experiences and moments of rape survivors." Susan J.H. Brison, *Aftermath: Violence and the Remaking of a Self* (Princeton: Princeton University Press, 2002), 87.

56. Yancy, *Black Bodies, White Gazes*, 11.

57. Following my parsing of habit into habitual and habituated, my adjectival use of the term "habitual" from here on refers to this dual and enlarged sense of habit. Where I revert to the use of "habitual" in the narrower sense of repetition and routine, I will indicate this in the text.

58. Although even then we may not really know our own habits since they are often more opaque to ourselves than they are to others.

59. The literature here is vast. A sample of relevant studies include: Marianne Bertrand and Sendhil Mullainathan, "Are Emily and Greg More Employable Than Lakisha and Jamal? A Field Experiment on Labor Market Discrimination," *American Economic Review*, 94(4) (2004): 991–1013; Katherine L. Milkman, Modupe Akinola, and Dolly Chugh, "What Happens Before? A Field Experiment Exploring How Pay and Representation Differentially Shape Bias on the Pathway Into Organizations," *Journal of Applied Psychology*, 100(6) (2015): 1678–1712; Kevin A. Schulman, Jesse A. Berlin, et al., "The Effect of Race and Sex on Physicians' Recommendations for Cardiac Catheterization," *New England Journal of Medicine*, 340(8) (1999): 618–626.

60. The campaign was produced and launched by Beyond Blue, a leading mental health organization in Australia, and accordingly was couched in terms of stress and depression, and the impact of such subtle forms of racism on the mental health of Indigenous Australians. While this is an undoubtedly an important message—and a sophisticated one, given the recent climate of racist denial in Australia—the emphasis is subtly different from what I am emphasizing with my present analysis, which is the collection of these bodily gestures under the banner of "habit" for the person performing such racist gestures.

61. Chester Pierce, Jean Carew, Diane Pierce-Gonzalez, and Deborah Wills, "An Experiment in Racism: TV Commercials," *Education and Urban Society*, 10(1) (1977): 61–87 (65).

62. Merleau-Ponty, *Phenomenology of Perception*, 143.

63. That gestures such as grabbing one's bag are not properly "reflexes" becomes clear when we compare them to neuro-physiological reflexes such as the knee-jerk, which is not cultivated, maintained, or structuring of ancillary behaviors (in the way that racist habits structure other behaviors and actions, such as whom we might sit next to on a subway, or whom we would take seriously as a job candidate).

64. Linda Martín Alcoff, *Visible Identities: Race, Gender, and the Self* (New York: Oxford University Press, 2006), 187.

65. Ibid., 188.

66. Merleau-Ponty, *Phenomenology of Perception*, 103.

67. Alcoff, *Visible Identities*, 188.

68. Alcoff cites the following passage from the preface of *Phenomenology*: "Perception is not a science of the world, nor even an act or a deliberate taking of a stand; it is the background against which all acts stand out and *is thus presupposed by them*" (my emphasis). Merleau-Ponty, *Phenomenology of Perception*, lxxiv (cited by Alcoff, *Visible Identities*, 187).

69. Indeed, Alcoff cites this as one reason critical race scholars may be reluctant to engage with phenomenology.

70. Alcoff, *Visible Identities*, 184.

71. Ibid., 188.

72. Ibid.

73. Eduardo Mendieta, "The Sound of Race: The Prosody of Affect," *Radical Philosophy Review* 17(1) (2014): 109–131.

74. Ladelle McWhorter, *Racism and Sexual Oppression in Anglo-America: A Genealogy* (Bloomington: Indiana University Press, 2009).

75. Alcoff, *Visible Identities*, 191.

76. Dolezal's case garnered widespread anger and cynicism not only because of her appropriation of Black identity and exploitation of its cultural capital to the benefit of her professional and social life, but also because of the dis-ingenuity entailed in her visual presentation as a Black woman, relying on the visual cues of augmented skin tone and hair to articulate an identity she claimed to feel personally, but which to the external world served as markers of a particular ancestry, lived experience, and so forth. In other words, there was a sense in which Dolezal managed to bypass the highly complex and contentious conversation around the bases of racial identity (a conversation which *ought* to have involved the community to which she was claiming membership) via her coded visual presentation, a fact that was underscored by the way news reporting of her case frequently counterposed her image with photos of her as a young white girl, complete with straight long blond hair, for striking visual effect.

77. Ibid., 192.

78. Alcoff herself is critical of this ocularcentrism: "A further danger of an ocularcentric epistemology follows from the fact that vision itself is all too often thought to operate as a *solitary* means to knowledge. Against claims from another, one demands to 'see for oneself,' as if sight is an individual operation that passes judgment on the claims that others make without also always relying on them. By contrast, knowledge based on the auditory sense, some have argued, is inherently dialogic, and encourages us to listen to what the other says, rather than merely confirming their claims or judging how they appear." Ibid., 198. Casey discusses a similar point in a chapter on "The Hegemony of the Gaze" in Edward S. Casey, *The World at a Glance* (Bloomington: Indiana University Press, 2007).

79. Note that even these choice of terms are instructive, as Al-Saji has argued. In contrast to "hijab" or even the common French word *voile* (veil), *foulard* is indicative insofar as it is a generic term referring to a scarf or covering worn around the head or shoulders that one may take off at whim. This characterization reveals a fundamental misunderstanding of the role of veil in religious or spiritual practice as something which is ancillary, and which has no role to play in the formation of self-identity, community, or kinship relations. Alia Al-Saji, "The Racialization of Muslim Veils: A Philosophical Analysis," *Philosophy and Social Criticism*, 36(8) (2010): 878.

80. Ibid., 881.

81. As Al-Saji notes, some of these "traces" have been removed (though not contradicted), while others (such as shortened school days on Wednesdays, limited Sunday trading) continue to exist despite the banner of *laïcité*.

82. Al-Saji, "The Racialization of Muslim Veils," 881–882.

83. Ibid., 882.

84. Ibid.

85. Ibid., 877.

86. See, for example, articles such as: "Muslim Women Against FEMEN," *Huffington Post*, April 5, 2013; and "Put Your Shirts Back On: Why Femen Is Wrong," *The Atlantic*, May 6, 2013.

87. Frantz Fanon, *Black Skin, White Masks*, trans. Charles L. Markmann (New York: Grove Press, 1967), 134.

88. What I mean by the "moment of recognition" is Fanon's distinction between the situation of the Black man and the situation of the Jew, which he argues differ insofar as the Black man is overdetermined in the moment of visual perception—a claim which has been contested by commentators such as Gail Weiss. I consider Fanon's distinction more carefully in chapter 4. Ibid., 115–116.

89. However, there is a tricky question here: how are anti-Muslim sentiments to be understood in relation to racist sentiments more generally? Al-Saji argues, for example, that they fall under the umbrella of what she calls "cultural racism," the qualification referring to the fact that Muslims do not of course come from one "race" (difficult though it may be to pinpoint what we might mean by "race"), but rather span across racial, spiritual, cultural, familial, and so forth communities. But it remains a type of, or continuous with, racism insofar as Islam is most strikingly identified with Arabic peoples, defined mostly in racial terms. (That is, white converts are not the image of the Muslim man or woman in the popular imagination.) The question thus bears a complex relation to Fanon's quote: does the experience of the veiled Muslim woman, who might present any range of ethnic, racial, and morphological features, more closely resemble the Jew—herself religiously rather than racially constituted— or the Black, given the iconic visual status of the Muslim veil (whether *hijab, burqa,* or *niqāb*) in post–9/11 society?

90. Indeed, in looking at racism at any level (structural, corporeal) I argue that it is important to move beyond Black/white binaries which have to a large extent (and not without good reason) dominated the way we think about racism. This is important in two reasons: (1) to give voice to the varied and equally important experiences of racism beyond the Black experience; and (2) to ask after other modes of racism that are not necessarily tied up with responses of *fear*, and thus harder still to "catch." Both speak to the fluidity of racism, in its target and in its forms, and these in themselves reflect back to us the highly complex and contextualized nature of racism. Further, I argue that we ought not to assume that any and all expressions of move from white to "other", which a white-Black model of racism tends to inscribe. It is of course the case that racism exists *between* differently racialized peoples, although this itself is further complicated by how whiteness remains an organizing schema in interracial relations (e.g., how the relation between Asians and Blacks are in part framed by hegemonic white conceptions of both, i.e., Asians as quiet/submissive, Blacks as dangerous, etc.).

91. Al-Saji, "The Racialization of Muslim Veils," 885.

92. "Trayvon Martin, like so many black boys and men, was under surveillance (etymologically, 'to keep watch'). Little did he know that on Feb. 26, 2012, that he would enter a space of social control and bodily policing, a kind of Benthamian

panoptic nightmare that would truncate his being as suspicious; *a space where he was, paradoxically, both invisible and yet hypervisible*" (my emphasis). George Yancy, "Walking While Black in the 'White Gaze,'" *The New York Times*, September 1, 2013.

93. Although Al-Saji's article traces a different ethical trajectory from the one I describe in this paragraph, in that essay she is concerned not so much with the ethico-political implications of our habits of seeing, but rather with how vision can be refigured such that we move beyond its "objectifying" mode, to arrive at a kind of seeing that is attuned to the conditions, "thickness," and "affective dimensions" of its own seeing. In the context of habitual racism, Al-Saji writes: "An anti-racist vision can learn to see the conditions, material, historical, social and discursive, of racializing perception." Alia Al-Saji, "A Phenomenology of Critical-Ethical Vision: Merleau-Ponty, Bergson, and the Question of Seeing Differently," *Chiasmi International*, 11 (2009): 375–398, 376.

94. See, for example, Waldenfels, Bernhard, *The Question of the Other* (Albany: SUNY Press, 2007).

95. Alia Al-Saji, "A Phenomenology of Critical-Ethical Vision," 377.

96. Al-Saji, "The Racialization of Muslim Veils," 885.

97. For example, those with "White sounding names" received 50% greater callbacks as compared with those CVs bearing "African-American sounding names." Marianne Bertrand and Sendhil Mullainathan, "Are Emily and Greg More Employable Than Lakisha and Jamal? A Field Experiment on Labor Market Discrimination." The responses of HR managers upon learning the results of the experiment here: Sendhil Mullainathan, "Racial Bias, Even When We Have Good Intentions," *The New York Times*, January 3, 2015.

98. Al-Saji, "The Racialization of Muslim Veils," 886.

99. Ibid.

100. The argument might at first seem frivolous, but consider how in popular culture and imagination, figures such as the ninja or Australian bushranger with their *niqāb*-like attire (revealing only the eyes) are in contrast held out as dynamic, creative, safe, and if not powerful then at least occupying some position of power by virtue their being able to see but not be seen. That both characters are most commonly imagined as male is, I would argue, no coincidence. In my view this supports Al-Saji's argument about the colonial male gaze, which demands visual access to women's bodies, but not to men's. As indeed does the Catholic nun's veiling, the habit which is again non-contentious (even pious) given she is acceptably placed outside the male desiring gaze. This is not to say, however, that the circumstances around some Muslim veiling practices—notably, where women are pressured, required or coerced into wearing the veil, such as in Saudi Arabian society, or other communities—are an irrelevant consideration. These are surely relevant. However the point is that this model of repression—true for some women in some circumstances, but not true for others—is taken to be the case for *all* veiled women, and habitualized patriarchal and colonial modes of perception corroborate this. Thus veiled women's very diverse circumstances and reasons for veiling are not taken seriously. I would argue in addition to this that if the question of force or pressure were truly at the core of the concern around veiled women, then the differential levels of veiling—from

hijab to *niqāb*—would have no material difference *unless* this were accompanied by a normalizing male gaze, since to be partially or fully covered should make little difference if the question is primarily one of "choice" and autonomous decision-making. However given the *niqāb* solicits far more visceral responses than the *hijab* as *the* sign of oppression, this seems to confirm that a patriarchal gaze, and its desire to possess the woman's body as object, is imported into this colonial and/or racialized seeing.

101. Al-Saji, "The Racialization of Muslim Veils," 886–887.

102. Al-Saji writes for example: "Indeed, intersectional theories, in their assumption of preexistent and separate axes of identity that then cumulatively interact, perpetuate the picture of identity that McWhorter criticizes (see p. 15). What I mean to point to here is, rather, an architecture in which dimensions are inseparable because each is articulated and deployed through others (implicitly and by means of historically contingent junctures). It is in this way that I see McWhorter to be cutting across the dilemma of one or many oppressions: one oppression is already many." Alia Al-Saji, "White Normality, or Racism against the Abnormal: Comments on Ladelle McWhorter's Racism and Sexual Oppression in Anglo-America," *Symposia on Gender, Race and Philosophy*, 6 (2010): 2.

103. Al-Saji, "The Racialization of Muslim Veils," 883–884.

104. "Rarely do I face the anonymous white woman within the elevator in isolation from an informed history of the mythical purity of white female bodies and the myth of the Black male rapist." Yancy, *Black Bodies, White Gazes*, 8.

105. Edward Said, *Orientalism* (New York: Pantheon Books, 1978).

106. This occurred on September 14, 2013. Example articles discussing the event include: Tressie McMillan Cottom, "Jonathan Ferrell Is Dead. Whistling Vivaldi Wouldn't Have Saved Him," *Slate Magazine*, September 20, 2013.

107. This occurred on November 2, 2013. Example articles discussing the event include: "The Killing of Renisha McBride," *The New Yorker*, November 16, 2013.

108. "Theodore Wafer Sentenced to 17 Years in Michigan Shooting of Renisha McBride." *The New York Times*, September 3, 2014.

109. Indeed, this serves as a case in point for Al-Saji's argument elsewhere on hesitation as a productive interruption of racializing habits. In the chapter Al-Saji is concerned primarily with the habits of racializing vision, but the argument also works for habits of bodily movement and response. Alia Al-Saji, "A Phenomenology of Hesitation: Interrupting Racializing Habits of Seeing" in Emily S. Lee (ed.), *Living Alterities: Phenomenology, Embodiment, and Race* (Albany: SUNY Press, 2014), 133–172.

110. Yancy makes a similar point in relation to philosophical/academic activity more generally, when pitted up against the urgency of racism as a political problem, with real-world and real-time consequences: "Although there are many white antiracists who do fight and will continue to fight against the operations of white power, and while it is true that the regulatory power of whiteness will invariably attempt to undermine such efforts, it is important that white antiracists realize how much is at stake. While antiracist whites take time to get their shit together, a luxury that is a species of privilege, Black bodies and bodies of color continue to suffer, their bodies cry out for the political and existential urgency for the *immediate* undoing of the

oppressive operations of whiteness. Here, the very notion of the temporal gets racial-ized. My point here is that even as whites take the time to theorize the complexity of whiteness, revealing its various modes of resistance to radical transformation, Black bodies continue to endure tremendous pain and suffering. Doing theory in the service of undoing whiteness comes with its own snares and seductions, its own comfort zones, and reinscription of distances. Whites who deploy theory in the service of fighting against white racism must caution against the seduction of white narcissism, the recentering of whiteness, even if it is the object of critical reflection, and, hence, the process of sequestration from real world weeping, suffering, and traumatized Black bodies impacted by the operations of white power. As antiracist whites continue to make mistakes and continue to falter in the face of institutional interpellation and habituated racist reflexes, tomorrow, a Black body will be murdered as it innocently reaches for its wallet. The sheer weight of this reality mocks the patience of theory." Yancy, *Black Bodies, White Gazes*, 229.

111. Though not "police," we can invoke here also Trayvon Martin's shooting by private security guard, George Zimmerman.

112. Judith Butler, "Endangered/Endangering: Schematic Racism and White Paranoia" in Robert Gooding-Williams (ed.), *Reading Rodney King/Reading Urban Uprising* (New York: Routledge, 1993), 18–19.

113. Merleau-Ponty, *Phenomenology of Perception*, 132.

114. Ibid., 363. Henri Bergson also uses the term in *Matter and Memory*, trans. Nancy Margaret Paul and W. Scott Palmer (London: Allen and Unwin, 1911).

115. Of course, the rock itself might fracture and the form itself might change, but the particular ordering of the sediment remains always in place.

116. Merleau-Ponty, *Phenomenology of Perception*, 132.

117. Casey, "Habitual Body and Memory in Merleau-Ponty," 214.

118. Merleau-Ponty, *Phenomenology of Perception*, 131–132.

119. Maurice Merleau-Ponty, *Institution and Passivity: Course Notes from the Collège de France (1954–1955)*, trans. Lawlor and Massey (Evanston: Northwestern University Press, 2010), 19.

120. Ibid., 119.

121. Ibid., 22.

122. Alcoff, *Visible Identities*, 184.

123. For example, prominent race commentator Ta-Nehisi Coates notes in an article on the Ferrell shooting that McCartney cannot be attributed any blame; I dis-agree. While it is of course true that the police bear the ultimate responsibility for this as armed public officers (with institutional support), it is also true that the woman's bodily response ought to also be critically questioned. T. Coates, "The Killing of Jonathan Ferrell," *The Atlantic*, September 23, 2013.

124. Emily S. Lee, "Body Movement and Responsibility for a Situation" in Emily Lee (ed.), *Living Alterities*, 245.

125. This appears to echo aspects of Aristotle's ethical position on the cultivation of good habit, but differs in the sense that I am not arguing here for responsibility for one's habits insofar as we are ethically obligated to cultivate virtuous characters, but rather, responsibility insofar as our habits can harm others.

126. George Yancy, "White Crisis and the Value of *Losing One's Way*" in George Yancy and Maria del Guadalupe Davidson (eds.), *Exploring Race in Predominantly White Classrooms: Scholars of Color Reflect* (New York: Routledge, 2014), 10–11.

127. On this point George Lipsitz's work on racism and intergenerational wealth is particularly illuminating: George Lipsitz, *How Racism Takes Place* (Philadelphia: Temple University Press, 2011).

128. Yancy, "White Crisis and the Value of *Losing One's Way*," 11.

Chapter 2

The Lived Experience of Racism and Racialized Embodiment

PART 1—THE BODILY EXPERIENCE OF RACISM AND RACIALIZATION

Faire les marchés, or "doing the markets," is usually one of the weekly delights of Parisian life. Colorful fruit and vegetable stands line the morning boulevards, bursting with the season's freshest, while vendors compete animatedly to passing shoppers. *Madame! Les clémentines! Très doux, très doux, très doux . . . Aaaaallez-y, madame, allez-y! Pas cher, pas cher, pas cher . . .*

Heavy bags in hand and eyes searching ahead for the stand with Moroccan clementines (they are the sweetest of them all), when suddenly a loud, booming voice cuts across from the right. *NI HAO! (HELLO!)* My gut sinks. *Ni Hao!* I pretend not to notice, but a lump grows in my throat, my mouth goes dry. *Madame! Ni Hao! NiHaoNiHaoNiHaoNiHaoNiHaoNiHaoooo.* He's turned it into some screeching "Oriental"-sounding song. This is humiliating. The voice stops—or gives up—eventually, and I continue along, visibly unaffected to the vendor (*Maybe she didn't hear? Maybe she's not Chinese?*), but my eyes become fixed ahead on nothing in particular, my lips pursed, and my cheeks betray slight signs of the internal fluster. The color of the market returns to the scene, but this time at a distance. An internal monologue inserts itself between myself and the street. *Dammit. I should have said something. But what? Arghhh.* The frustration is directed toward myself as much as it is to the vendor. After all, this has become a semi-regular occurrence. *I should have been prepared! I should have said something back.* I work *on racism for god's sake!*

I continue along. The market noise washes over. I walk, but my gait feels hollow, mechanical. *I* feel hollow. *Fuck this. Fuck it all! This guy today, those kids in Belleville, the men on the park bench at night.* The singularity of this event recalls all the past ones. *The woman who tried to pay me for her Zen Buddhism book at the métro bookstand. The other woman who asked me for the price. The man calling out from the bodega in Brooklyn. The one who muttered it under his breath in East Village. All those times while travelling.* The list grows longer, I grow more agitated, angry, and distracted, until I blink myself back into the present moment and place. *Enough. This will just put me in a worse mood.* I give a little shake of the head in a feeble effort to expel the nasty feeling. The rage that appeared so quickly more or less quietens down, but I am left with a residual feeling of disappointment. *This again.* I turn around, and head home.

In chapter 1 we focused primarily on the question of the *expression* of bodily racism—its manifestation, through habitual bodily gesture and perception. While this was important for revealing the hidden sites and forms of racist praxis, it constitutes only one side of our phenomenological inquiry into racism. In what follows, I turn to a consideration of the *experience* of racism, with a particular emphasis on how those on the "receiving end" of racism come to experience the phenomenon, and their own bodies. In this chapter, I continue with a phenomenological analysis of the lived experience of racism, deferring for later chapters a more thematic consideration of racialized embodiment through the conceptual prisms of uncanniness and objectification. And while I am primarily concerned with the lived experience of the racialized body in this chapter, I follow this analysis with a brief consideration of the lived experience of whiteness, both to contrast and to round out the phenomenological account of racialized embodiment. But first: What is it like to experience oneself as a racialized body? How do those subjected to racism anticipate and respond to it? What kind of body schemata are at play?

"Whistling Vivaldi": Bodily Adjustments and the "Work" of Managing Habitual Racism

In the opening pages of social psychologist Claude Steele's book, *Whistling Vivaldi (and Other Clues to How Stereotypes Affect Us)*, Steele recounts the anecdote that gives rise to the book's novel title. The story comes from *New York Times* writer Brent Staples, speaking of his experience walking through the streets of Chicago's Hyde Park neighborhood as a young Black man:

> I became an expert in the language of fear. Couples locked arms or reached for each other's hand when they saw me. Some crossed to the other side of the street. People who were carrying on conversations went mute and stared straight ahead, as though avoiding my eyes would save them . . .
> I'd been a fool. I'd been walking the streets grinning good evening at people who were frightened to death of me. I did violence to them by just being. How had I missed this . . .
> I tried to be innocuous, but didn't know how. . . . Out of nervousness I began to whistle and discovered I was good at it. My whistle was pure and sweet—and

also in tune. On the street at night I whistled popular tunes from the Beatles and Vivaldi's *Four Seasons*. The tension drained from people's bodies when they heard me. A few even smiled as they passed me in the dark.[1]

The story tracks a common narrative: the way that racialized people manage the experience of bodily racism, or even its anticipation, through the adoption of various gestural, postural, and behavioral strategies. As Steele goes on to write in relation to Staples: "In a single stroke, he made the stereotype about violence-prone African American males less applicable to him personally. He displayed knowledge of white culture, even 'high white culture.'"[2] Columnist Tressie McMillan Cottom, who in reporting on Jonathan Ferrell's shooting references Steele's work, herself testifies to the prevalence of such "whistling Vivaldi" strategies:

> I do not know many black people who do not have some kind of similar coping mechanism. I have been known to wear university-branded clothing when I am shopping for real estate, hopefully drawing on the cultural value of colleges and students to counter any assumptions of me as buyer. A friend straightens her hair when she is job-seeking. Another friend, a Hispanic male, told me that he shaves all his facial hair when entertaining white clients to signal that he is respectable.[3]

Other examples abound: A Bangladeshi Australian friend speaks of his conscious efforts to smile more and speak in a higher, brighter tone of voice in his dealings with white women in bureaucracy. A Zimbabwean Australian friend speaks of the ritualized gestures he performs when preparing to disembark a bus late at night, when the only remaining commuter is a white woman: he stands up immediately upon passing the penultimate stop, presses the button straight away, puts his backpack on, and makes his way toward the exit door—all as if to signal, "I'm not following you. This is my stop, too." In the aftermath of the Michael Brown shooting and non-indictment of police officer Darren Wilson, comedian Kamau Bell wrote of his predicament as a "B.B.M.," a "big black male":

> Being a B.B.M. is why I smile quickly. It's why I don't usually stand to my full height. I slouch and bend. When acquaintances haven't seen me for awhile, I often hear, "I forgot how tall you are!" I know you did. It's because I'm trying to make you forget. This is what being black in America has done to me, to others like me, and in some sense, even to you.[4]

To some extent, we might say that such strategies reflect the broadly adaptable nature of bodily comportment to social situations, and that we all engage in them from time to time; in order to inspire a certain impression of ourselves, we dress more formally at conferences and job interviews, speak more politely in the course of business or bureaucratic transactions, and so forth. In other words, some of this may be attributed to the unavoidable work of self-presentation in a social economy that trades on image and appearance,[5] although this is not to say that there are no racialized dimensions even here. However, the examples above point to a different level of bodily adjustment, which extend far beyond what ordinary (read: white) people must attend to when they engage in such activities by virtue of the currency that whiteness brings (respectability, reliability, and so forth). They differ from the general "work" of self-presentation in the way that they respond to and work against existing, invariably negatively valenced determinations of the racialized person, in order to avoid or interrupt habitual, racialized perceptions. This "work" (as I am naming it) is entirely negatively constituted, but in addition, it is also entirely mundane. Whereas we all might comport ourselves differently for a job or bank interview—in other words, for *events* or *occasions*—in the case of racialized bodies, this kind of work is operative even during the *non-events* of strolling through a park, walking the streets, or doing the weekly shopping. Here there are two points to be considered: first, there exists a certain amount of work that pervades the movement and comportment of racialized bodies in such environments, which ought to be given some further thought. Second, this work can be called upon at almost any time and place, during *non-events*, piercing through the seemingly innocuous moments of daily living and challenging, as I will argue, the Merleau-Pontian version of the habitual body schema.

Turning first to the question of work: think of how a body loaded as it is with the work of anticipation and adjustment ceases to resemble a body at ease with itself, or a body focused and fluid in the execution of its projects, however banal or mundane. Instead, such a body is laden with the work of managing others' racialized anxieties and expectations, a burden that is both one-sided and counterproductive.[6] This work is in a sense reminiscent of Simone de Beauvoir's assessment of how women's bodies are tied down and kept busy through societal norms of appearance:

> The woman, on the other hand, knows that when people look at her, they do not distinguish her from her appearance: she is judged, respected, or desired in relation to how she looks. Her clothes were originally meant to doom her to impotence, and they still remain fragile: stockings run; heels wear down; light-colored blouses and dresses get dirty, pleats unpleat. . . . Whether she is a secretary or a student, when she goes home at night, there is always a stocking to mend, a blouse to wash, a skirt to iron.[7]

But whereas the work described by Beauvoir in this passage refers mostly to the ornamentation of the female body,[8] in the examples cited above, we can see how for racialized bodies, this work can operate at a more immediate and intimate level of gesture, timbre and tonality of voice, posture, gait—in other words, on the materiality of the body itself. It is the thickness of the body's medium, with all its expressivity, which gets worked upon directly; smiles get softened, hair is tamed, postures are opened up or closed down. And while these might seem relatively benign points of bodily adjustment, Beauvoir's point is precisely that activities as banal as ironing skirts and mending stockings count in our tallying up of the invisible labor undertaken by women in their adherence to, or "performance" of (Butler's word), societal gender roles. While the performance in relation to racism is less an *adherence* to societal expectations (as is the case with women) and more a *managing* of racist perception and bodily responses, the basic point remains the same; this requires labor. Moreover, a powerful picture emerges when we situate this level of bodily adjustment and work among the broader, more explicit, levels of work involved when encountering (and countering) racism in daily life: the work of calling it out (and when doing so, having to "prove" it), defending oneself and others from it, taking care of oneself and others in the face of it, and combatting it more generally. Once we add to these, the micro-level bodily adjustments I have been considering, we begin to make sense of why terms such as "fatigue," "exhaustion," and "stress" are so frequently invoked by people of color in describing their experience of anti-racist work and daily living. Indeed, this language of fatigue and exhaustion is instructive insofar as it leads us into another consideration. After all, it is not just the mere facticity of this work which we ought to register—in addition to the overloading of one's system in purely functional terms, we should consider also the *affective* dimension of this labor and stress.

Bodily and Existential Stress in the Experience of Racialization

More than the bodily "work" gets taken on in the anticipation and management of habitual racism directed to oneself, there is also a correlating experience of stress that often colors such encounters. It is a stress that cuts across several registers, and indeed is not even limited to phenomenological or existential registers. In recent years, researchers in sociology and public health have conducted studies confirming the increased levels of physiological stress among people of color experiencing or anticipating racism. Such results have been tracked across cardiovascular indicators (high blood pressure, heart rates) as well as expressions of emotional and psychological stress.[9] For example, in a 2012 study, researchers conducted an experiment in which they paired young Latina college students with young white female students. While preparing short speeches to be delivered to their white counterparts outlining why they personally would make good study partners, half the

Latina subjects were given indication that their white listeners held prejudicial views against Latino/as specifically, or racial minorities more generally. Researchers found that:

> Latinas led to believe that their partner was prejudiced against ethnic minorities showed greater blood pressure increases and sympathetic nervous system activation during speech anticipation, and reported more threat-related cognitions and emotions before and after the interaction than did those led to believe their partner was not prejudiced. These findings support the role of vigilance as a stressor in that situational cues can lead to a stress response characterized by heightened physiological arousal and greater self-reported concern.[10]

In other words, not just the management of racial prejudice, but even its anticipation is enough to trigger physiological stress responses in the racialized body, in ways that complement the first-person phenomenological accounts of such experiences.

> *"Man, I almost blew you away!"*
> Those were the terrifying words of a white police officer—one of those who policed black bodies in low income areas in North Philadelphia in the late 1970s—who caught sight of me carrying the new telescope my mother had just purchased for me.
> "I thought you had a weapon," he said.
> The words made me tremble and pause; I felt the sort of bodily stress and deep existential anguish that no teenager should have to endure.[11]

> *. . . tiens, un nègre, il fait froid, le nègre tremble, le nègre tremble parce qu'il a froid, le petit garçon tremble parce qu'il a peur du nègre, le nègre tremble de froid, ce froid qui vous tord les os, le beau petit garçon tremble parce qu'il croit que le nègre tremble de rage, le petit garçon blanc se jette dans les bras de sa mère: maman, le nègre va me manger.*[12]
> . . . look, a negro, it's cold, the negro trembles, the negro trembles because it is cold, the little boy trembles because he is afraid of the negro, the negro trembles from the cold, a cold that twists down into your bones, the handsome young boy trembles because he thinks the negro trembles from rage, the little white boy throws himself into his mother's arms: mummy, the negro is going to eat me! (my translation[13])

Yancy's anecdote, the first of the two appearing above, speaks to a kind of stress pertinent to the experience of anti-Black racism: the anguish and terrifying shock of having barely escaped being shot for "walking while Black." So too does Fanon give an account of anxiety and stress upon being publicly singled out for his blackness. The references to "trembling" in both accounts (recurring frequently in Fanon's[14]) are significant in the way they invoke the profound kind of existential anguish that flood the emotional and psychical (or better: bodily) senses, in the course of such pedestrian encounters. It is not only the externally observable and quantifiable signs of physiological stress that we can identify, then, but also their emotional and existential expressions that we ought to consider. The language of "tremble" is apt insofar as it lends imagery to the shakenness (and shakiness) of the self, or what one had taken to be the self. The racialized body here is not the habitual one—at ease or at rest in its holding of itself—but the one disturbed, desta-bilized, unsettled. One is shaken, figuratively and literally; fingers tremble, hearts beat louder, the body breaks out in sweat. These correspond to the feel-ings of rage and frustration that such encounters provoke. Even in relatively benign and harmless encounters such as the one relayed in the opening of this chapter (harmless in the sense of bearing no personal or immediate danger, as compared with that recounted by Yancy), there remains a distinctly affec-tive dimension to the experience of racialization. Racism and racialization take an emotional toll on those who routinely experience them, and this is distinct from (though not unrelated to) Beauvoir's description of the burden of material "work" in the case of women. There exists in addition, to adopt this terminology, an affective toll and emotional work in the situations of racialized bodies.

But why *existential* stress? Why does the experience or anticipation of racism inspire an anxiety so deep that it touches one's existential sense of being an intact self? The threat of imminent danger, as in Yancy's anecdote, may be one reason, but not itself a sufficient one. After all, had he narrowly avoided being hit by a car, he would have felt stressed to be sure—but not in this existential way. This is where phenomenological accounts do the crucial work of filling out the picture of bodily stress mapped out across physiological markers. The kind of bodily stress and anguish in question here is one connected to a profound loss of self, or sense of self—hence its exis-tential nature. It signals a moment in the experience of oneself reduced to an object for-other, and the denial of one's experience and identity as a subject for-oneself. There is a profound undoing of the self that gets called out in moments such as these. Of course to say this is perhaps to already assume too much in terms of a self or subject, and, and there are problems with this philosophical framework which will be treated in some length in chapter 4. Nonetheless, working for the moment with the language of stress and anguish as deployed by Yancy and Fanon, we gain some insight into how and where the bodily experience of racialization begins to run up against some of the limits in Merleau-Ponty's own existential-oriented phenomenology in this early period of his thought.

Being One's Body versus Being in Front of (or Before) One's Body

In his examination of the synthesis of the lived body, Merleau-Ponty declares in rebuke to Descartes' mind–body dualism: "I am not in front of my body, I am in my body, or rather *I am my body*"[15] (my emphasis). While the statement is clearly aimed at the Cartesian dualism that has animated much of our Western philosophical tradition, it also represents a positive statement of Merleau-Ponty's own phenomenological account of the body—at least in this early period of his thought, which is marked by a more pronounced existentialist inclination. For Merleau-Ponty, there is a certain fluidity entailed in the habitual body and its body schema, a fluidity that is explained by the fundamental relation of *being* one's body. In earlier passages of the *Phenomenology*, Merleau-Ponty establishes the fundamentally anchoring role of the body in phenomenological experience. Not only does the body supply the perceptual horizon which forms basis of our engagement with the world as we saw in chapter 1—the body "impose[s] on me a perspective on the world"[16]—but more profoundly and more simply: the body is *permanently present* for us. This, Merleau-Ponty insists, is no mere factical claim but a metaphysical one, since it is the body's permanent presence that allows other objects—and indeed the world—to appear for us; the body is thus the *condition* of one's phenomenological experience. What distinguishes the lived body from an object then is this permanent presence. Whereas the object "is only an object if it can be moved away and ultimately disappear from my visual field,"[17] the phenomenal body cannot move away from itself, it cannot be severed from itself in such a way as to be taken away, or *put in front of* itself. As Merleau-Ponty writes, "To say that my body is always near to me or always there for me is to say that it is never truly in front of me, *that I cannot spread it under my gaze,* that it remains on the margins of all of my perceptions, and that it is *with* me"[18] (my emphasis). In this account, it makes sense that the phenomenal body—which as we have seen tracks the habitual body—is marked with a fluidity and ease, since the body is co-extensive and co-present with itself, never wholly absent nor fully visible before itself.

However, while Merleau-Ponty's account appears to secure the centrality of embodied experience for phenomenological and philosophical inquiry more broadly, it also seems to sit jarringly with our many descriptions of racialized embodiment (and I note that this analysis may well apply to others, for example, trans* persons, people with visible disabilities, and so forth). In my opening account of grocery shopping at the weekly markets in Paris, the experience of being racially called out in such a spontaneous and public manner serves precisely to put my body in front of itself, to spread it under my gaze and place it on display along with the other produce for sale. Heads look up from sorting through potatoes or carrots and follow the vendor's voice until their eyes settle on my Asian body. My body is not, in that moment, on the "margins of my perception" as Merleau-Ponty writes above, but visually foregrounded, both for myself and for others. This experience is corroborated by the various other accounts we have considered throughout this book. Yancy's experience excerpted above is sometimes colloquially called "walking while Black," a phrase which strikes a deliberate discord, since who, least of all a young boy caught up in the excitement of carrying a new telescope, would think of themselves while walking down a street, as "raced"?[19] But in the moment of confrontation, the young Yancy comes to realize that that is precisely what he has been all along, to the police officer's normalizing white gaze. His "walking while Black" incorporates this third-person perspective into his own bodily experience of walking. In the moment of having escaped being "blown away" because his Blackness ascribed to him the default position of "dangerous," Yancy's body *is* spread under his own gaze, and he is not simply *his* body (prompting us to hear alternate emphases of Merleau-Ponty's statement, "I am my body"/"I *am* my body"/"I am *my* body"). Merleau-Ponty's analyses start from the experience of *le corps propre* or "one's *own* body," always supposing that the body experienced is the one *proper* to the self.

A more traumatic account still of this "not being one's body" comes in the form of a vicious rape case perpetrated in the western suburbs of Melbourne, Australia, in May 2013. There, two white middle-aged male friends, Matthew Brooke and Andrew Morris, smashed their way into a house at 2:45 a.m., having decided that it "would be fun" to rape someone. The two Asian women victims—a mother and daughter, who were targeted because Brooke "hated Asians"—were forcibly bound, drugged, and then repeatedly raped by over the course of two hours.[20] In their victim impact statements to the court, the daughter (who was so traumatized that it took her five days to complete her initial police statement) recounted:

> I was happy in my own skin, in my own body. After what happened all that has changed. . . . I am no longer confident in my own body.
> When I look at myself in the mirror, I see what the men see. It is a disgusting feeling. It makes me feel dirty.[21]

In a meaningful sense she is no longer *in* her body and no longer *is* her body, because of the way it was so violently and viciously stripped away from her. This sense of bodily dispossession is a narrative common to the experience of survivors of rape, as Susan Brison shows in *Aftermath*, and speaks to the way trauma (whether in the form of racist and sexual violence, or otherwise) can throw out this phenomenological synchronicity of the body Merleau-Ponty describes. In her statement the daughter, whose own upbringing in

Australia would have armed her with the coping mechanisms to fend off more pedestrian forms of racism, articulates how the attack had shaken her inner being, her deeper sense of self: "during the attack on my mum and myself it had impacted on me on a more personal level . . . it was not just my race and culture, but my self worth as a woman and as a person was affected."[22] The sexual violence, perpetrated against her not only as an Asian but as an Asian *woman*, struck at the core of her felt personhood. While on the extreme end of the spectrum of racial and sexual violence, these women's experiences show how such violence can profoundly disturb and shake up the seamless experience of one's own body.

We might then, in light of these varied but powerful reflections, start to question how Merleau-Ponty's account of the habitual body, while offering a useful framework from which to analyze how racist *practices* can become inscribed in bodies, at the same time fails to account for how one's body is *experienced* in the case of those who are at the receiving end of such practices. For example, in our earlier consideration of how certain racialized perceptions can become habituated in the body, there is an important counter narrative tracking what this experience entails for those who find themselves at the receiving end of such perceptual practices. In Al-Saji's and Yancy's accounts of the hypervisibility entailed in racialization, the racialized body is that which is seen, and, moreover, seen-*as* a series of pre-scripted or pre-determined possibilities. These echo Fanon's reflections on his own hyper-visibility in the midst of everyday living: "I cannot go a film without seeing myself. I wait for me. The people in the theater are watching me, examining me, waiting for me. A Negro groom is going to appear."[23] But this visibility or hypervisibility also holds a phenomenological significance: a body which goes from seeing to seen, from invisible (to itself) to hypervisible (to others), edges toward the threshold of what an early Merleau-Ponty wants to reserve exclusively for objects. The racialized body, on these various accounts, seems to cross over from subject to object.

This subject–object distinction, which is still pronounced in Merleau-Ponty's early work, in part hinges on the question of perspective. For example, unlike the body, an object is "in front of us because it is observable, which is to say, situated at our fingertips or at the end of our gaze."[24] Read against this, his claim that we are not in front of our bodies therefore serves to ground the fundamental position that we, as living bodies [*corps vivants*], are not objects, but rather subjects. But of course this is what Fanon directly challenges, when he comes to describe his experience of himself as an object. His Black body, always seen and *seen-as*, starts to drown out his own experience as a breathing, seeing, and living body. Further, it is not just that his body comes pre-loaded with meaning, it is that this perspective is also imposed upon him: at the cinema *he waits for himself*, his "distorted and recolored" body is given back to *him*.[25] Fanon is not just seen; he experiences himself being seen, anticipates himself being seen, and finally, *sees* himself being seen. This is what he sometimes calls, borrowing from Sartre in *Anti-Semite and Jew* (and echoing also W.E.B. Du Bois), double consciousness.[26] What then when we find our own bodies at the end of a gaze—not only the gaze of the other (although this alone is significant), but owing to its hegemonic force, a gaze which gets incorporated into our own seeing, displacing the seeing, perceiving, and moving of the habitual self? Do we become a kind of object? Fanon thinks so: "I came into the world imbued with the will to find a meaning in things, my spirit filled with the desire to attain to the source of the world, and then I found that I was an object in the midst of other objects."[27] The language of "object" becomes problematic for the later Merleau-Ponty, and so this is something I give only cursory consideration here, deferring a more thorough and nuanced treatment for chapter 4. The point at present, however, is that the account of the habitual body which undergirds Merleau-Ponty's thinking does not satisfactorily account for experiences such as those recounted by Fanon or Yancy. Racialized bodies frequently *do* find themselves in front of their bodies, through the specific function of visibility in racism.

Being in front of one's body has a distinct spatial sense, whether it is through the imposed distance of a subject–object relation, or through the distance imposed by a hypervisible experience of the self (captured nicely in the locutions, "to be spread *under* one's gaze" and "at the *end* of the gaze"). This spatial distance with oneself can translate to a kind of inhibited or self-conscious being and moving in the body, as explored by Young in relation to feminine bodily motility as discussed in chapter 1. There, the (visual) objectification of women's bodies at the general level of culture and society meant that girls and women lived the contradiction of being at once subject *and* object. As Young argued, girls consequently experienced their bodily motility in terms of an intentional "I can" *and* "I cannot," which for her explained the impoverished bodily movements observed in young girls and the reluctant integration of extended space into their own bodily space and vice versa (e.g., when preparing to throw a ball). Of course, there is a specificity to the case of female bodily comportment and the movement through space that does not necessarily carry over to the case of racialized embodiment.[28] Nonetheless, the central point remains: the visibility of racialized bodies, marked in advance by the mechanisms of racist seeing, through the specific markers of skin color, phenotypes, cultural or religious dress (e.g., hijab), and so forth, means that one's own body is always experienced with a special kind of distance.

This is a distance that inserts itself not only in the relation of body image and body schema, but in the coming together of the body schema itself. The body schema, as we saw in chapter 1, functions in Merleau-Ponty's account in the manner of a "unique law" of the body, coordinating and constituting bodily experience.[29] It is the layer that collects together bodily habits, dispositions, and motor capacities to support bodily movement. There is then, a sense of fluidity and coordinated effort in the body schema, a "spatial and temporal unity,"[30] that becomes fragmented in the experience of racialization. Insofar as the body schema is that which coordinates and supports intentional (or conscious) bodily activity, the experience of racism and racialization intrudes into this coordination, straining the fluidity of the experience of the body. Yancy, for example, writes in relation to anti-Black racism: "With white gazes everywhere waiting to put you in your place, you begin to move in this world slowly, as if dragging the weight of an unsought burden. It is a form of motility that takes effort. . . . Within an anti-black world, effortless grace is precluded."[31] Notably, this sense of "heaviness" echoes Fanon's earlier reflections when he writes: "I move slowly in the world, accustomed now to seek no longer for upheaval. I progress by crawling."[32]

In part this is because the subject–object distinction starts to break down: unlike Merleau-Ponty's account of the lived body, racialization entails the experience of oneself from "this side" *and* "that side." While for some (including Fanon at times) this has been translated into the language of "objectification," I argue that the situation is more complex. The sense of being "in front" of oneself does not quite amount to a *dis*-placement of the self in its fullest sense, but rather a spatial fragmentation, in which one is both here *and* there, and with a perspective so constituted. It is not that one is simply taken away or separated from a "real" or "genuine" self (even if we are taken away from the self that we recognize), but rather as a racialized body, one stands in *multiple relations to and perspectives upon* the self, in a way that disrupts the spatial cohesion of the body schema. In the specific case of Black male bodies, where the hypervisibility is usually bound with associations of danger and violence, their bodily sense of spatiality can come to reflect such fragmentation. Of the elevator example, Yancy writes:

> My movements become and remain stilted. I dare not move suddenly. The apparent racial neutrality of the space within the elevator (when I am standing alone) has become an axiological plenum, one filled with white normativity. As Shannon Sullivan would say, I no longer inhabit the space of the elevator "as a corporeal entitlement to spatiality." I feel trapped. I no longer feel bodily expansiveness within the elevator, but corporeally constrained, limited. I now begin to calculate, paying almost neurotic attention to my body movements, making sure that this "Black object," what now feels like an appendage, a weight, is not too close, not too tall, not too threatening. [33]

But there exists, in addition to this spatial register, an important temporal dimension to the experience of racialization. For as much as we can speak of being "in front" (*devant*) of our bodies, we can also speak of being "before" (*avant*) our bodies. What might this mean? In Al-Saji's account of veiled Muslim women's being determined in advanced as "oppressed" women, what she describes is the way in which these women are presumed to be known *before* they actually are. Not only are they "over-determined," but they are also *pre*-determined; determined *ahead* of themselves, ahead of what any genuine encounter with them may reveal, and ahead of how they may wish to present themselves. We saw a version of this played out in the case of a ten-year-old Muslim boy in Lancashire, UK, in early 2016, whose primary school reported him to police for questioning when he wrote in his home-work that he lived in a "terrorist house," misspelling "terraced house"[34]—an episode which recalled the widely publicized American case of Ahmed Mohamed only months earlier, the fourteen-year-old boy who was arrested by police for making a clock which teachers at his Texas high school believed to be a bomb.[35] Despite their youth (which in the case of white bodies, usu-ally designates "innocence"), the boys' Muslim bodies determined them in advance as "could-be-terrorists." Even on a less controversial note, when I am accosted with a steady stream of *"NiHao!"* while walking around my Parisian neighborhood (an area which also happens to be known for Chinese women's prostitution[36]), my body is imbued with a certain availability and docility, irrespective of the manner of my comportment or presentation. In the existentialist terms employed by Fanon and echoed in Yancy, such encounters cohere with the latter's claim that, "From the perspective of whiteness, I am, contrary to the existentialist credo, an essence ('Blackness') that precedes my existence."[37] Here, inverting the existentialist standard, "existence precedes essence," Yancy points to the fact that as racialized people, the experience is never quite a synchronous coming together of temporal and spatial selves in the synthesis of one's body.

To say that the racialized body appears ahead of itself, however, can under another formulation be to say that one arrives "too late." That is, depending on which perspective we assume when saying, *"she* is determined ahead of *herself,"* the racialized body is *both* too early *and* too late; as pre-determined, she is too early in relation to whom she might reveal herself to be, and at the same time, she is too late in relation to that pre-determination. But as Al-Saji shows us in her article, *"Too Late:* Racialized Time and the Closure of the Past," the language of lateness as employed by Fanon is also useful insofar as it helps us to see how racialized bodies arrive "too late" not only in relation to the identities already carved out for them, but also in relation to the pos-sibilities for action and creativity:

> Though Fanon may sometimes be able to take up the structured possibilities already defined, and follow through their realization according to the routes

deposited by the other (to the degree that this is permitted a black body in a white world), he does not see them as allowing variation, as being able to be worked out *differently*. The structure of possibility allows repetition but not creation or variation; it is a closed map. This seems ultimately to mean that possibilities are not genuinely felt as *mine*, on Fanon's account.[38]

Being "too late" or "behind" oneself is not only a matter of identity and self-presentation—it is also a question of what relation one can take to the world and its others. For example, the language of lateness allows us to consider the distinct role of the past in structuring racism. As Al-Saji argues, for colonized people history is always made present in the form of a caricatured and closed past. This functions doubly to tether down their bodies to stereotypes and paternalistic justifications of colonialism, while also closing off what is for white people an open relation to the past, in which history gets continually taken up, re-animated, re-interpreted, and even re-written. Whereas white subjectivity is open-ended and futural, colonized subjectivity is a closed and past project. According to Al-Saji, an important consequence of this, apart from the obvious problem of agency and authorship, is that despite contemporaneous living, there lacks a shared experience of temporality which may found the basis of a more genuine living- and being-with:

> Indeed, this other is always ahead of Fanon, futurally directed so that s/he cannot be caught up with. This positions Fanon as anachronistic; but more importantly it means that the encounter with the other is a missed encounter, that there is no coexistence in a lived present upon which reciprocity could be built.[39]

The "Non-Event" Nature of Racialization

There is then, in the lived experience of the racialized person, both a spatial and temporal fragmentation at the level of the body schema. That this fragmentation takes place on the level of the body schema is supported by the fact that such ruptures are frequently experienced in the course of *non-events*. (I use the term "non-event" here not in any technical way, but to approximate a sense of "non-occasion" or "non-happening.") In the various examples canvassed above, it is significant to note that many of the racist moments catalyzing bodily and existential stress take place in the midst of mundane goings-about, where race is not otherwise at issue: while riding the train (Fanon), walking along a street (Yancy), weekly grocery shopping (myself), and so forth. (Of course racialization occurs in the course of "events" too: for example, when veiled women enter political debates on the hijab, they are necessarily bound to an identity *as* veiled women, even though the inverse is not true of non-Muslim commentators, who can assume a measure of "impartiality.") Nonetheless, I highlight here the non-event nature of the many other encounters with racism, in order to underscore the way the racializing schema is already present—and indeed *already operative*—on a pre-conscious, pre-reflective level, in situations where race is not already explicitly thematized. As Fanon himself declares, "Below the corporeal schema I had sketched a historico-racial schema."[40] That racism and racialization very often occur in this non-event way means not only that they are enacted on the level of bodily habit and perception as I have argued in chapter 1, but also that they are experienced on the level of the body schema, whereby each unannounced interruption to daily living once again throws into question the otherwise unthematized and uncontested sense of one's own body.

What is the significance of this non-event-ness on the body schema? While I might not experience my body or my self *as* "Asian," or indeed as "anything," when I walk out to buy a baguette in the morning, because of the insidiousness of racialization, I *do* experience my body as susceptible to such racialization at any time; personal and collective experience have prepared me for the possibility that my non-white racial identity can be made into an issue—however big or small—at any unexpected, given moment. Such a possibility permanently marks the body schema of a racialized person in several ways. First, the racialized body schema is such that it lacks a stable formulation, or stable *enough* formulation (for this is not to posit the unchanging body schema as the ideal one). Called into question as it is on a regular basis, even in the course of the most banal activities, the racialized body teeters constantly on the brink of dissolution and undoing. *Wait, is* this *what I am? Is this* all *I am? Even in crossing the road am I first "this" (Asian/ Black/Muslim) before all else?* The racialized body schema is permanently and forcibly held open, in view of the regular but unpredictable moments of racialization. There is no telling, when walking down a street, when someone may yell out "Hey China!," but there is a certainty that this will occur at some point—for one is never *altogether* shocked when it does. When Eritrean British man Mehary Yemane-Tesfagiorgis is escorted off a plane in Rome because a white woman passenger "did not feel safe with [him] on board,"[41] his response to an interviewer's prompt that he "must have been surprised," is telling: "Well to be honest with you—I'm not sure if you've been to Rome, but I was not surprised. As disappointed as I was, and as angered as I felt and still do feel, I was not in the least bit surprised, if I'm going to be brutally honest."[42]

Fanon describes this felt sense of racism's inevitability by highlighting the interplay between certainty and uncertainty:

> The real world challenged all my claims. In the white world the man of color encounters difficulties in the development of his bodily schema. Consciousness of the body is solely a negating activity. It is a third-person consciousness. The body is surrounded by an atmosphere of certain uncertainty.[43]

What is certain in this equation is racism's reality; the way centuries-deep legacies of racism and colonialism continue to shape and structure even our most cosmopolitan living arrangements. The uncertainty then pertains to the when, where, and how—matters of specific occasions—that is, what expression it will take and when. In the face of this, the racialized body schema is one comprising an inherent instability. As one's claims to oneself are constantly challenged, interrogated, or denied, the body schema is plunged into a state of "certain uncertainty."

This brings us back to earlier questions of existential stress and anguish as invoked by Yancy, but also to a kind of perceptual paranoia reflected in Fanon's charting the neuroses of colonized peoples in *Black Skin, White Masks* and *The Wretched of the Earth*. However, this is not to say that all racialized bodies *are* perceptually paranoid or indeed suffer from the neuroses Fanon describes in the extreme cases of war and colonization—we should be careful here to avoid the pathologizing of racialized bodies. My claim, rather, is that the depth and ubiquity of the experience of racism can lead to a kind of existential instability. In experiencing one's body schema as inherently unsettled or at any moment "unsettleable," the racialized body not only becomes accustomed to but indeed *anticipates* these moments of unravelling. When a stranger's eyes widen with curiosity, one might anticipate the opening to "that conversation" (*"Vous venez d'Australie? Mais à l'*origine*?"* or "But where are you *from?*") Or in the case of a Black man, the gentle ruffle of the shoulder bag at the periphery of one's vision might well recall "that movement again." This is to say, racialized bodies, by virtue of the common experience of racism, learn to anticipate and be "on guard" for such occurrences. This tracks our earlier discussion of Yancy's "Elevator Effect," where I argued that to the extent that racialized people "over"-identify[44] incidences of racism, this is politically intelligible and defensible. To this we can now add: such "over"-identifications also make sense insofar as one's experience is knitted together with such encounters. The experience of being constantly marked by others' racialized perceptions and responses becomes incorporated into the body schema such that one comes to anticipate, based on frequent experience, that this identity will once more get called into question. Stripped of a deeper understanding of the experience of racism and racialization, and its influence on the body schema, the so called "over"-identification of racism is often cast as something pathological (*"everything* is always about race for you"), but viewed in light of the workings of racism on the intimate level of the body, we can start to better understand why racialized bodies are not only better placed to identify racism, but also more concerned with calling it out. Moreover, the question of anticipation also draws us back into the discussion of temporality, where in the moment of anticipation and defense, one never quite lives in the present, but always ahead of one's self and situation (in a similar but different way to how disappointment recalls one away from the futuricity of intentional being).

In addition to underlining the racialized body schema of fragmentation and instability, there is also the question of bodily adjustment and comportment. If it is the case as discussed earlier, that racialized bodies bear the burden of adjusting bodily gestures, postures, expressions both to anticipate and to fend off, or even to respond to, racialized projections and racist gestures, then this too takes place on the level of the bodily schema in the form of preparation. Given the often banal nature of racialization, people who frequently experience these kinds of racialized interventions have to learn to become adept at responding to or anticipating and adjusting bodily comportment in the course of non-events. Even in the case where there is no satisfactory response—as in my case of the weekly Parisian market—there is adjustment in the sense that the body must recollect itself and continue in the face of such interruption. Of course, if what we are talking about here is "coping," then this is the human skill *par excellence*, as thinkers such as Dreyfus (influenced by both Heidegger and Merleau-Ponty) have argued.[45] And indeed, in this sense it is not a skill particular to racialized bodies, but open to all body schemata as an inherent mark of our creativity and spontaneity. And yet, there is an important sense in which owing to social and historical practices imposed by oppressive relations (as opposed to the more general human condition of unforeseeability), members of certain groups (such as women, people with visible disabilities) effectively learn to integrate these coping skills into their *modus operandi*.

The kind of body schema fragmentation we have thus far considered, with its spatio-temporal dimensions, as well as its non-event nature, come together to give us a global sense of how deeply the experience of racialization penetrates. In particular, they give weight to Fanon's claims about the primacy of the "historico-racial schema" in relation to the development of the "corporeal schema" (which in this instance refers to the narrower sense of body schema as it bears on motor intentionalities). It is not that racialized persons experience these body schema level deviations from an otherwise "normal" body schema, it is rather that these experiences of fragmentation are woven into the development of the whole (including a motor body schema). The larger point here is that *all* social situatedness not only leaves a mark but also actively shapes the body schema. This is corroborated by Young's analysis of female bodily motility, where again, it is not so much that girls first pass through "normal" body schemas before learning how to move like "women," but rather the *very development* of their body schemas are already shaped by the structuring experience of patriarchal society; the workings of patriarchy help to constitute female body schema. As to the finer question of priority in Fanon's analysis, however, in place of his ordering I would propose a more circular relation, echoing the analysis presented on habitual representation. That is, as much as habitual racialized perceptions are both informed by racist representations while also re-inscribing and thus performing them, so too do the historico-racial schema and the "corporeal schema" (in its narrow sense) have this mutually re-inforcing and re-inscribing relation. As I would argue, neither one is primordial, but they are both co-constitutive.

Resilience, and the Pathologizing of Racialized Bodies

Here I wish to add some remarks on the nature of flexibility and resilience in the face of such bodily fragmentation. One question that may come to mind, given my argument about the body schema level experience of racialization, is: does this mean that racialized people thus experience their bodies in an impoverished or debilitated way? How is the claim of the fragmentation (even dissolution) of the body schema in racialized people's experiences compatible with and justifiable in view of the fact that racialized people *do* live, move, laugh, and love—in other words, do not literally present as fragmented beings in everyday life? Otherwise put, does not the insistence on such fragmentation risk pathologizing racialized people and their bodies? There are several responses one could give to such questions. If we follow the accounts offered by Fanon, Yancy, Sara Ahmed in *Queer Phenomenology*, and others, we see that there is a real sense in which the racialized fragmentation and alienation from one's own body is an experience marked by anxiety, stress, and anguish.[46] Fanon's work, in particular, explores neuroses induced by the racist colonial experience. We could also cite disproportionate rates of incarceration, mental illness, physical health problems, or general unhappiness to support such claims. In other words, there is a real and non-trivial way in which this body schema fragmentation I have been considering embitters and traumatizes the lives of people of color, and it is important not to wash over or diminish this reality.

On the other hand, keeping in mind the dangers of pathologizing such experiences, this is not to say that racialized people do not manage. The claim of body schema fragmentation does not have to mean some kind of utter dissolution of the self. As noted earlier with reference to Dreyfus, the ability to cope in the face of incoherent, unexpected, and even unpleasant experiences is an important quality that gets underplayed in such objections. In particular, if we look at the history of slavery, colonization, and other forms of systematic racist violence, we see that these histories are also often accompanied by stories of resilience, resistance, and creativity. Such stories find their venue in spaces afforded by the arts, political organizing, and so forth. The expectation that body schema fragmentation leads always to visible manifestations such as impoverished movement or social interaction, then, is to reinscribe via alternate means, a pathologizing of racial otherness. What is important, however, is that such measures of coping and resilience do not "gloss over" the nonetheless deep bodily experiences of racism and racialization, or the effort exerted in managing and responding to them. Holding the two thoughts at once, we must do justice to the very real and justified experiences of anxiety, stress, anguish that manifest in racialized bodies in the context of racist societies, while simultaneously giving recognition to the creativity and resilience of those who find themselves in such situations. Indeed to this end, Fanon's *Black Skin, White Masks* is a performative text, both in the way that it lays bare the anxiety he lives through as a Black man in colonial France (and the Francophone world), but also as the text *itself* deploys this narrative to great performative and constructive effect. In it, coupled with his insightful phenomenological and psychoanalytic analyses, we see also how racialized people are, in the face of such challenges, able to work through their experiences in order to make meaning of their lives, to make these lives theirs.

Racialized Bodies in Space and Place

To round out our analysis of the bodily experience of racism and racialization—which has so far taken us through considerations of the bodily work of managing and responding to racism, the experience of existential stress, and the spatio-temporal fragmentation of the body schema—I propose that we turn briefly to the bodily experience in and of one's social space. Although I have thus far been concerned with how the racialized body experiences *itself* as a result of racist and racializing practices (which, of course, is a function of the racialized body's situatedness in a historico-social world), part of this bodily experience is also a question of how one takes up one's body in relation to the world—after all, the account of the body presented by Merleau-Ponty in the *Phenomenology* is always that of the body situated in, and transacting with, its spatial or placial environs. "I am not *in* space and time, nor do I think space and time; rather, I am *of* space and time; my body fits itself to them and embraces them," Merleau-Ponty writes[47] (my emphases). How then does the experience of racism and racialization bear on the way one relates to her surroundings? How does the racialized body experience not just space (in relation to the body schema), but place?[48] In noting above the way in which racism and racialization occur often (but not exclusively) in the course of non-events, it is important to note also that so too they most often occur in the course of movement through public places (streets, airports, train-rides, shops). In Australia, for example, the "Challenging Racism" project coordinated by researchers at the University of Western Sydney claims that some 40% of racist incidents occur in public spaces, most notably on public transport.[49] That this is so, in my opinion, is significant. What is it about the racialized body in movement—occupying and inhabiting shared spaces and places—that so offends and incites racism?[50] And what does this say about underlying claims to ownership of social spaces and places, and the modes of belonging they help to foster?

In the Northern Territory of Australia lies the city of Darwin, a small, tropical city with a long and fraught history of race relations. In part due to its political status as a federal territory (subject thus to federal jurisdiction), First Nations inhabitants of the Northern Territory have historically been subject to many controversial government policies, not to mention the standard problems of over-policing, endemic poverty, and so forth. From this context comes an anecdote by Dawn Adams of her trip to the shops:

> Hi, my name is Dawn Adams, I come from Bagot community and I'm one of the strong leaders in Bagot. I'm originally from Tiwi Islands but I moved in Darwin, I've lived here all- nearly all of my life. And one day, like it was about, 10 o'clock, and my daughter wanted to go to the Nightcliff shopping centre. And me and my cousin—yeah she lives here too—were sitting on chairs at Nightcliff when the other two ladies came and I asked them, come and sit down and have a chat and tell us what's happening at home, y'know. And, all of a sudden these two policemen came and didn't even ask us what was happening, they just said "I think. . . . What are you mob doing? I think you mob better move along." And that wasn't really nice y'know because we weren't doing anything wrong, we were just sitting and gossiping and having a chat about home. I haven't seen my relatives for, that many months and, I was just happy to see them and to ask them how was everything back at home on the Tiwi Islands. But to me it was . . . I find it really . . . offensive, y'know, the way he was saying "lot of you." I don't drink—never drank in my whole life. The way the policeman said—I felt like we were like in South Africa, telling us to move y'know? And all of a sudden I started . . . ended up being angry within myself. . . . You know we had the right to sit there, in a shopping centre—that's what chairs are built for! . . . I don't go out much, I don't like going to the shopping centre, only just go to Woolworths do my shopping and come back home, that's about it. Because I don't like to be told off y'know. And I'm scared of things like that.[51]

Though disturbing, Dawn's account is by no means an exceptional occurrence in Darwin—nor indeed in many other parts of the world. What her encounter offers, however, is a rich snapshot of daily life for Aboriginal or Indigenous peoples in the country's "top end," touching on several themes we have considered so far. In the course of a trip to the local supermarket with her daughter, which turns into an impromptu family catch-up session, Dawn's Aboriginality is made an issue for her as she is evacuated from the pseudo-public space of the shopping center. Not only do we have here the habituated racialized perceptions of the police in question (their seeing Dawn and her family *as* a public nuisance and potentially a threat), but we also see

Dawn seeing herself through their normative white gaze. Her explanation, "I don't drink—never drank in my whole life," tells us that she immediately understands what is really going on, and how she is being perceived; the police need not speak openly or specifically about their habitual perception of Aboriginality and drunkenness when they ask her family to move along. In Dawn's narrative we also get a glimpse into what the affective experience is for her, the sense of frustration, anger, and disappointment it evokes.[52] Finally, recall our analysis of temporal fragmentation: as a Tiwi Islander in Australia's Northern Territory, Dawn is weighed down *in advance* by the tired tropes of Aboriginality and public drunkenness, nuisance, laziness, and her presence, no matter the form, is always "too late" in relation to those tropes. Following our earlier analysis, Dawn is both too early and too late: too early insofar as her pre-determination as "drunk/lazy/troublesome" arrives on the scene always ahead of her, and too late in relation to that pre-determination.

All of these played out in the arena of public space and indeed *shaped by* this "publicness"—the "Aboriginality and drunkenness" trope is only a concern insofar as this takes place in public—translate into her bodily relation to such places. Racialized bodies such as Dawn's do not lay equal claim to the spaces and places that are intended for social gathering. Bodies that are read as "problematic" have more fraught access to and through such places, whether that access is moderated via discriminatory policing, social pressure, or economic means of exclusion (note that Dawn's story happens in a center for commercial trade[53]). That racialized bodies—and Black bodies in particular—have a much more uneasy passage moving through public space is underscored time and time again through stories such as Dawn's and Mehary's (noted earlier). Such bodies are met with obstacle as they attempt to move in and through an anti-Black world; bodies are "stopped" and "slowed down," to evoke Sara Ahmed's terms.[54] Although writing from a different political context, Yancy's words also resonate loudly here: "Black bodies in America continue to be reduced to their surfaces and to stereotypes that are constricting and false, that often force those black bodies to move through social spaces in ways that put white people at ease. We fear that our black bodies incite an accusation."[55]

In addition to this interrupted movement, Dawn's and Mehary's stories bring out for us the way in which experiences of racialization and racism can change one's bodily disposition on the level of *inclination and desire*. In other words, racism can also change what relation one might *want* to take up to one's surrounds, given the experiences one may encounter. As a result of this and most likely numerous other related incidents, Dawn modifies her own behavior: "I don't go out much, I don't like going to the shopping centre, only just go to Woolworths do my shopping and come back home, that's about it." Movement through social spaces has, for Dawn, been reduced to a question of functionality, endured insofar as she needs to meet the basic requirements of living, but not beyond. Since they are not welcoming places for her, she withdraws from them. Brent Staples too, in his "whistling Vivaldi" story, echoes something of this sentiment when he writes: "I began to avoid people. I turned out of my way into side streets to spare them the sense that they were being stalked."[56] Such responses resonate with Yancy's observation that in an anti-Black world, "There are places where you learn that you should not go, spaces that you should not traverse."[57] The space of the shopping center, indeed of most other public places, is not neutral for Dawn, but, rather, a valenced space. It is a space in which her body "sticks out," is more carefully *surveillé*, and consequently, a space in which the spatio-temporal fragmentations of the body are more acutely experienced. Given the affective dimension of such experiences, along with the burden and "work" of bodily adjustment, one can understand why Dawn "chooses" to withdraw, or why Brent "chooses" to take detours on his walks (although I use the term "choose" loosely). However, this is a far cry from Merleau-Ponty's claim that our bodies are not *in* space, but *inhabit it*. Dawn and Brent do not *inhabit* space (and here I include also social space and place) to the extent that they do not take it up as theirs, as a field for being and acting. But insofar as being, and being-with unfolds always in place and among others, this holds broader social, political, and ethical implications. What does this say, for example, about the possibility of genuine social and political participation? How does this translate in political and economic *fora* if racialized bodies do not feel at-ease or at-home in these supposedly shared spaces? These are some of the questions we should keep in mind as we turn now to a consideration of white embodiment.

PART 2—WHITE EMBODIMENT AND ONTOLOGICAL EXPANSIVENESS

Having now considered some of the salient features of racialized embodiment, we might ask in turn: what is the lived experience of whiteness? If as I have argued, the lived experience of racialization is one marked by work, existential stress, and spatio-temporal fragmentation, then how does the bodily experience of whiteness contrast with this foregoing account? Is white embodiment merely the inversion of racialized embodiment, or the model against which racialized embodiment is judged as impoverished? Even in the field of critical race studies, the theme of white embodiment is not one frequently taken up. After all, what is there to say? Against the dramatic narratives presented by the likes of Fanon and Yancy, there appears to be little that is remarkable about the way white bodies move, dwell, and experience their own bodies. But of course this is precisely the point; there is much about the bodily experience of whiteness that is unremarkable because it is not consciously experienced or problematized. And yet, these seldom noticed and remarked-upon bodily movements and sense of lived spatiality speak volumes to the workings of racism and the differential body schemata of racialized and white bodies. In this part of the chapter I take up this question of white embodiment with reference to Shannon Sullivan's work in *Revealing Whiteness: The Unconscious Habits of Racial Privilege*. In particular, I am interested how her description of white embodiment's "ontological expansiveness" presents a striking contrast to our earlier analyses of racialized embodiment. But first, a story:

On a typically hot and sticky New York summer night, a friend and I emerge from an impromptu yoga class in the East Village. The gentle breeze and open air is a welcome relief on our skins as we meander about. Activity is bustling on First Avenue; friendly chatter spills onto the streets, flashing restaurant windows light up the evening with their neon colors, and the odd ambulance whirrs by. We arrive at my friend's bus stop, where I wait with her as we speculate about the kinds of aches we'll surely be waking up to tomorrow. Mid-conversation, we become mildly distracted as a taxi pulls to an unexpected halt in front of us, and the driver rushes around to the passenger's door. Their voices get louder, and the unfolding altercation starts to draw other commuters out of their conversations. The taxi driver—an older South Asian man—holds onto the passenger's handbag, as the passenger—a young white woman—emerges in physical struggle with him, while the two argue. Before any of us can make sense of the dispute we hear a "*whack!*," and the driver falls to the ground. He gathers himself slowly and crouches on the curbside, holding his face and rocking gently. His glasses lay on the ground three meters away. The woman stumbles a little, but remains standing. As if arousing from a moment's stunned pause, people around us spring into action. Some start reproaching the woman. A white man next to me calls the police (after quickly checking with the driver). The woman walks over to the driver again—he has her handbag and holds it tight while on the floor—and starts struggling for it to no avail. A few of us intervene, the woman steps back but keeps yelling, and the man responds. It seems she refused to pay her cab fare, and was trying to leave as the driver came over to stop her. With the driver now slumped on the road, there is a temporary reprieve in the argument, but the woman's spirit is by no means dampened: in her pointy-toed stilettos she loudly threatens to walk over and kick him. She can't of course—there are too many of us who stand ready to stop her—but she is brazen in her posture as she, who I now realize is mildly intoxicated, paces back and forth, demanding her bag. The man on the phone repeats her threat to the police, which she hears and to which replies, "I don't fucking care, *call* the cops. I'll have him [pointing to the driver] fucking deported. He can fucking go back to India." My

friend tells her she is being racist, to which the woman answers, "So what? I
don't care, he can fucking go home, fffucking Indian." With each expletive she
spits out her disdain. The man meanwhile, remains huddled. I bring him some
ice from a nearby bodega, which he places on his cheekbone. He shows me the
light bruising on his face, but tells me that he is alright. He looks visibly shaken
though, and remains on the ground, shoulders hunched and head turned downward, silent. His posture looks to me to express part defeat, part humiliation. He
is quiet. Meters away, the woman continues her barrage of insults and threats,
seemingly unfazed by my friend and the other passers-by who try to silence her.

I walk over to my friend, who is looking fiercely ahead. She is pissed off.
"I'm not leaving," she says. "I'm staying here till the cops come, and until she
gets arrested. She should not get away with this." She continues, "If I spent a
night in jail over a subway ticket, she should go to jail for punching a man.
But she won't, coz she is white, just you see." My friend, incidentally, is not
white. She is a Black woman, who immigrated to the US from Ghana with her
family as a child. Several years earlier, she spent a night in jail for having been
caught jumping a subway turnstile when she forgot her Metcard—not usually
an offence that lands one in jail, but which can if the circumstances are right,
as they were for the many other young Black women in jail that night for similarly trivial offences. On this night, the flashing red and blue lights signal the
arrival of the NYPD—three cars and six policeman in all. They, incidentally,
are all young, male, and white. They start to go about their questioning: a short,
but well-built cop looks to be in charge, and he and his partner walk over to
question the woman. In the course of recalling the incident the woman starts to
cry, insisting that she acted out of fear of the driver: "I'm Italian-American[58],
and I come from a traditional family. Imagine if it was your sister." The police
ignore our loud interjections that it was in fact *she* who was being aggressive
toward *him*. But there is a flicker of recognition across a few of their faces that
this woman has been drinking. They approach the driver, who has now gotten
up, and ask for his license and permit. They ask to see his face too, but seem
unimpressed by the lack of visible marks on his face—at least, not visible in the
evening light. Eventually, some of the police start questioning witnesses: "She
punched him? How hard? And what did he do?." Of the ten or so people who
have lingered, everyone is vocal and offers a more or less a similar version of
events. The police isolate several witnesses to take down official statements,
including the man who had placed the 911 call, who expresses his willingness
to testify in court, if it comes to that. As the police return to confer with one
another, my friend remarks, "She is getting away with it, look. They don't want
to arrest her. They're just gonna let her off with a stupid warning." There is quite
a bit of discussion among the policemen, and with some thirty minutes having
passed since their arrival, it becomes more and more evident that no arrest will
eventuate. In fact, the police seem increasingly annoyed by our ongoing presence, and try to get everyone to move on. A few of the witnesses do. When my
friend and I remain, Number One looks at us with a gaze so steady that its meaning is unmistakable. "Do you have a problem?" he asks. "No," we reply, "we

just want to make sure she gets charged. She punched him, threatened to kick him, and called him all sorts of racist things." His eyes grow rounder and more determined, "We will manage it, ok? So just move along." She is not getting arrested or charged. Soon, the police start returning to their cars. Number One exchanges some words with the woman, then the driver, before getting into his own vehicle. The driver makes his way back to his taxi with an air of resignation. He sits down, adjusts his rear-view mirror, starts the engine, and drives off to resume his night shift. The young woman gathers her things, wipes away the traces of tears from face, and starts walking, her silhouette stumbling slightly as she presses forward, and is swallowed up by the New York City night.

There is much that is both remarkable and unremarkable about this episode. Remarkable, first, because of the very dramatic and public way the events unfolded; in full view of commuters and passersby on a busy East Village night. And particularly remarkable to me was the brazen and confident manner of the young woman, fearing neither the opprobrium of her spectators nor of the police. Her actions, movements, and bodily disposition were all marked with a fluidity and uncaring ease that warrant greater thematization. That she was comfortable being so openly racist in front of a crowd of mostly (though not exclusively) people of color, both struck and enraged me. But the event was also in other ways highly unremarkable. For example, as incongruent as it seemed at the time that the young woman would be let off with merely a "talking-to" by the police, it was not, all things considered, altogether surprising. It is a notoriously known phenomenon that in the United States (and in many other places around the world) whites are under-policed and under-penalized for infractions that would not be tolerated if their perpetrators were Black or Latino/a. The "Criming While White" social media movement that emerged in the aftermath of the decision not to indict the officer who killed Michael Brown, in which whites populated lists of the numerous and often absurd situations where they were afforded leniency by police officers, reads like a modern-day revision of Peggy McIntosh's "invisible knapsack" of white privilege.[59] That the young white woman suffered no legal consequences on this occasion for having publicly punched a man while mildly intoxicated, having fare evaded, and hurled racist insults, is in the age of "Criming While White," unremarkable (and literally so; there exists *no mark* of this incident recorded against her name). Finally, the incident is also unremarkable for the machinations of structural racism at play; that an older, South-Asian migrant man found himself in the relatively disempowered position of cab driver (where the work environment—inherently more volatile, dangerous, and low paying, indeed sometimes non-paying—rendered him more vulnerable to altercations such as these) is again unremarkable, as was the relatively empowered position of the young white American citizen (privileged enough to afford drinking and socializing in Manhattan, nice clothes and shoes, and private transportation). While not the main emphasis of the phenomenological analysis presented in this book, it is of course true that racism is thoroughly embedded in socio-economic and class relations, with the trappings of structural racism already at work in the background of encounters such as these. While there is evidently much in this story to discuss in terms of the different facets of racism, what I am particularly interested in for the purposes of this chapter is the young woman's sense of bodily entitlement. To get this analysis under way, I propose that we turn to Sullivan's concept of "ontological expansiveness."

White Entitlement and Bodily Confidence

Working through the tradition of American pragmatism rather than phe-nomenology, and particularly through the figure of John Dewey, Sullivan is interested in the ways in which our manner of transacting in the world reveal the intimate workings of race and racism. In particular, she is concerned with questions of white embodiment at the level of unconscious habit, arguing that whiteness is most strikingly characterized by what she calls an "ontological expansiveness." The idea, according to Sullivan, is that "[a]s ontologically expansive, white people tend to act and think as if all spaces—whether geo-graphical, psychical, linguistic, economic, spiritual, bodily, or otherwise—are or should be available for them to move in and out of as they wish."[60] She describes in other words, an orientation to the world in which one feels entitled to move fluidly and confidently throughout a variety of spaces and places, uninhibited and unobstructed by one's own body. This entitlement includes the confidence to act in legally (and morally) questionable ways without fear or expectation of adverse consequences; and this is what we observe in the young white woman's bodily comportment in the story above. Having struck the man who as a result falls to the floor, the woman remains upright, pacing back and forth and dishing out further threats and racist abuse. Her body is spatially extended along the vertical and lateral axes; she not only occupies space but she moves through it proprietarily and dynamically, and in doing so, she both claims and re-inscribes the sense of spatial entitlement of the kind Sullivan describes. She enacts her ontological expansiveness. Even her voice (which remains always loud, confident, and clear) occupies aural space in the moments of reprieve and calm that follow the man's initial col-lapse, as well as the later struggle to retrieve her handbag. In these subdued moments her voice interjects and imposes itself in on the impasse, demanding to be heard. The man, on the other hand, remains quiet throughout, and for the most part sits unmoved on the ground; the contrast in bodily comportment and spatial extension between the two could not be more pronounced. It is as if they act out the very difference Sullivan describes:

> Black and white bodily existence differentially licenses people to inhabit space in unequal, non-reciprocal ways. White people may freely transact beyond their immediate inhabited spaces. The whiteness of their space is expansive and enables, rather than inhibits, their transactions.[61]

And this difference is not limited to the two protagonists, either. As the scene unfolds, the responses of myself, my friend, and the other witnesses are telling. Of the fairly mixed group of people who gather, it is interesting that a white man is the first to call the police. Many among us think to do the same of course, but his lightning-fast response suggests not only a measure of faith in the institution to resolve and bring justice to the situation, but also an implicit degree of being-at-ease in dealing with the police, which includes the confidence that his concerns will be answered and his testimony will be received in its "impartiality." I raise this point not to cast a shadow over the man's intentions or actions (which were both necessary and helpful), but rather to show how the racial schema is ever at work, even on the "sidelines" of the action, as it were. Insofar as bodily habits orient our bodies in a futural way, as discussed in the previous chapter, this man's own history and lived experience of whiteness position him to respond swiftly in this way. Compare this with the people of color among the group. Several—myself and my friend included—immediately admonish the young woman for her actions and words, but we take half a step back once the police arrive. In doing so we anticipate (correctly) the frosty police responses to our attempts to remain involved, while giving expression to the often uneasy relations between the NYPD and people of color in the community. This is not to say we give up efforts to hold the police to account in their resolution of the incident, but the relation is marked with a palpable sense of unspoken negotiation, a feeling-out of the boundaries not to cross if we do not wish trouble upon ourselves. Put otherwise, the responses available to my friend as a Black woman with racially tainted experiences with the NYPD are different to those available to me, an Asian woman and international student with my own mixed dealings with the police in other jurisdictions—and both are different again (more dramatically so) from the possibilities available to the white American man who placed the initial call. The ontological expansiveness described by Sullivan is indeed on full display in the white woman's actions toward the cab driver, but so too is a version of it enacted in the white man's response, despite our shared intentions and sense of injustice.

We see here then examples of the different *modes* of ontological expansiveness. While the young woman acts in a way that most white people would not feel comfortable (or indeed inclined) to behave in public, so too is the white man's swiftness to action an expression of this uninhibited being. Ontological expansiveness need not manifest only in extreme cases of racist abuse, but is equally operative in the unobstructed actions and movements of whites in public. As a further example: some 10 years ago, around the time when my hometown of Melbourne (Australia) was undergoing a severe crackdown on fare evasion and "anti-social" behavior on public transport such as "feet on seats" (a period marked by a dramatic increase in the statutory powers of public transport officers), I was struck by the sight of a boisterous group of middle-aged white women on my tram one evening, having a fun and possibly rare night out together. Egging each other on, they performed all sorts of acrobatics on the tram poles and overhanging straps, very loudly enjoying and amusing themselves. Nobody stopped them, or took issue with their lively antics. "Would a group of people of color get away with this same behavior?," I wondered at the time. Would a group of people of color even *attempt* such behavior? The more recent case of 10 Black women who were kicked off the Napa Valley Wine Train in California for being loud and boisterous, with their "offensive" laughter[62]—hence the case being dubbed "laughing while Black"—suggests not, reminding us of the dramatic way in which white and racialized bodies are differentially policed and tolerated in public.

This mode of ontological expansiveness—of moving through the world largely unobstructed—more closely tracks the kind of embodied whiteness Sullivan describes in her book. Drawing on Patricia Williams' examples in *The Alchemy of Race and Rights*, Sullivan considers situations where Black bodies are barred from ostensibly neutral but in reality raced spaces and places. Examples such as Williams' own experience as a Black woman being refused entry into a "closed" clothing shop where white women shoppers were still visibly present, illustrate in a different way the ontological expansiveness of whiteness contra the spatial containment of Black (and otherwise racialized) bodies. In contrast to Williams, the white women in the shop move in and out of places and transact with the world in a way that is unhindered and unobstructed. What this example allows Sullivan to point out more directly is the way in which the ontological expansiveness characteristic of white embodiment often falls under the radar; it is precisely a mode of being that is unthematized and unproblematic—such bodies are *not* experienced "in front of themselves" (to recall an earlier phrase) in the course of their mundane transactions and goings-about. And while the identification of this "unconscious habit of white privilege" once more recalls Peggy McIntosh's work, I argue that there is more at stake here. More than a set of privileges accumulated in some "invisible knapsack," this kind of embodied ontological expansiveness speaks to the very *manner* of one's movement in and through public space and place; it describes the mode of one's embodied being and the expansive constitution of one's world.

It is important to note here that Sullivan extends her account of ontological expansiveness to even more varied situations still. She writes for example: "A white person's choice to change her environment in order to challenge her unconscious habits of white privilege can be just another instance of ontological expansiveness."[63] Thus in her personal example of learning Spanish as a way to foreground her own underlying being-at-ease as a white woman in English-speaking America, Sullivan acknowledges that these exercises in "'world'-travelling" (a term María Lugones uses to describe the work that women of color undertake) can themselves act as another manifestation of the privilege to expand one's lived space, by intentionally *placing oneself* in such positions of dis-ease. We see this frequently in so-called "solidarity movements" when whites don a "hijab for a day" out of solidarity for veiled Muslim women.[64] Despite their "good intentions," among which include the effort to expand one's empathic experience of racism, I argue that what such initiatives fail to recognize is that far from challenging one's white privilege, they may actually *express and extend* it by underscoring the power of whites to *put themselves* in such situations, to move in and out of such worlds or identities at their whim, and to "broaden one's horizons" in such deliberate, calculated, and "safe" ways.[65] As Sullivan writes in a more recent book, *Good White People: The Problem with Middle-Class White Anti-Racism*: "Ontological expansiveness usually disguises itself as a challenge to white privilege, in other words, and as a result it is able to operate relatively undetected (at least by white people) and thus inflict more damage than if it openly declared its aims."[66] In other words, in addition to the questionable effectiveness of putting oneself "in the shoes of" a racialized person in this superficial way, what these exercises unwittingly reproduce is the ontological expansiveness of whites to temporarily inhabit or excursion through such spaces, whether real, virtual, psychical, or otherwise.

That this amounts to an expansiveness—and an expansiveness that whites understand themselves to be entitled to—is made clear when such access is cut short, or challenged. As Sullivan writes in the article "White World-Traveling": "To combat white ontological expansiveness, white people need to accept that there are spaces in which they do not belong. This idea tends to produce a sense of dis-ease for many white people, who are accustomed to being in a position of mastery and control vis-à-vis nonwhite people."[67] Examples of this dis-ease can be found in the indignant responses when whites are called out in their cultural appropriation of the traditions and practices of marginalized peoples, such as the frivolous use of First Nations iconography in sporting paraphernalia or at music festivals, the appropriation and assimilation of Black "ratchet" culture in mainstream music (Miley Cyrus is a notorious offender), or the gentrification of "exotic" cuisines, and so forth. The sense of violation and defensiveness (even claims of "reverse racism") that charges the responses when such protrusions of whiteness are called out, speak loudly to the underlying feeling of entitlement to enter and access to such spaces. Likewise, we see a version of this entitlement expressed when whites are challenged on their authority to define the bounds and limits of racism—when critics such as Yancy, for example, insist on the epistemic privilege of Blacks to name and identify racism. Further still, Sullivan argues that this expansiveness can manifest even the seemingly innocuous example of learning a language, which Sullivan herself grapples with when challenged to reflect upon her decision to learn Spanish:

> This point was brought home to me when a Latina friend and philosopher explained that she did not want white/Anglo people to learn Spanish because their knowledge would intrude on the Spanish/Latina world that she and other Spanish-speaking philosophers are able to create in the midst of white/Anglo-dominated conferences. Opening up her world to white/Anglo philosophers tends to result in the destruction of a valuable point of resistance to white racism.
>
> From the point of view of white ontological expansiveness, the existence of a linguistic space off-limits to white people is an "unjust" violation of the "natural" order of the world that must be rectified. From an antiracist perspective, however, white ontological expansiveness not only presumes a "right" grounded in white supremacy, but also tends to damage and destroy spaces of resistance to white domination. White people's knowledge of the code of African American Language thus can strengthen their sense that it is appropriate for them to inhabit any space they choose to enter.[68]

This, then, is where we are enjoined to wed the structural analysis of power in racism to our phenomenological analyses, since the embodied experience of racialization or whiteness is always one undergirded by their complex relations. That is, the different expressions of racialized or white bodily habits *can never be disassociated from the underlying power relations that structure the meaning of such habits or practices*. In the context of white embodiment, efforts to combat racist habits by, for example, "shaking up" one's milieu or "simulating" an aspect of the racialized experience must be considered through the prism of white ontological expansiveness and the dynamics of power engendered therein. While this can mean that white action or agency often becomes fraught—even when motivated by decidedly anti-racist aims—this is not enough reason, in my opinion, to lay down our critical tools. The task, rather, becomes to think through more carefully the potential trappings of efforts to redress racial harm and inequity, while acknowledging, as Sullivan does, that this sometimes leads to imperfect practices.

By drawing out the highly varied and nuanced expressions of white ontological expansiveness, what we are now in a position to do is think more critically through some of the underlying norms or ideals embedded in phenomenological discourses of the body. That is, returning now to our phe-nomenological register of analysis, we might say that at first blush, one of the key features differentiating racialized and white embodiment is the notion of bodily fluidity and ease of transaction (and the absence of this in the case of racialized embodiment). As Sullivan has identified, phenomenology exhibits a tendency to idealize the smoothness of transactions and the fluidity of bodily movement and motility (evident, for example, in Merleau-Ponty's studies of the "curious deviations" of Patient Schneider in the *Phenomenology*). How-ever, within such a normative framework, this smoothness transforms readily into the ontological expansiveness which Sullivan has described in relation to white embodiment, and this, she argues, translates problematically in the ethical register:

> projective intentionality tends to suggest that it is desirable that all people live in as ontologically an expansive manner as possible. This suggestion is problem-atic from an antiracist and feminist perspective because it licenses white people to live their space in racist ways. It implicitly encourages them not to concern themselves with other people's lived existence, including the ways in which other people's existence is inhibited by white people and institutions. In this way, the non-transactional, unidirectionality of projective intentionality lends itself toward ethical solipsism.[69]

In other words, phenomenology risks idealizing this fluidity of being and transacting in the world even in situations where constraint—or hesitation to invoke Al-Saji's later work—may well be desirable to correct and com-pensate for oppressive asymmetries and inequalities. Thus, while we might agree that all bodies ought to be able to move through spaces and places the way white bodies do in Williams' shopping example (that is to say, in unobstructed and non-discriminated ways), this is not the case with the other examples of white embodiment discussed above. The young woman in my NY cab story, for example, exhibits the modalities of embodied fluidity and being-at-ease, as do the middle-aged white women on the Melbourne tram (all act without concern for others, nor with inhibited intentionality)—and yet this is not to say that they serve as ethical exemplars for how all bodies *ought* to act and move in the world—particularly in the case of the young woman.

This, of course, is because ideal ways of acting and being in the world are highly dependent on situation and context, as well as embedded power relations and asymmetries, as noted earlier. While I do not agree that phe-nomenology necessarily leads us to such ethical positions (Merleau-Ponty's later work in particular answers some of these charges), what is valuable in Sullivan's contribution is her identification of the need to situate implicit normative claims about ideal modes of bodily comportment, in their broader social and political context. Thus as Sullivan writes:

The promotion of a more expansive (though not ethically solipsistic) existence is needed for those, such as black people, who have not been allowed to transact freely. But just the opposite is needed in the case of those, such as white people, who often transact too expansively, aggressively, and solipsistically, living as if they are the only ones who should be allowed to do so.[70]

The sense of transacting "too expansively," I argue, reflects an underlying feeling of "at-home-ness" in the world, a feeling made possible by the fact that the world is organized along racist, white supremacist lines. This is not the case with racialized bodies, and having considered at length here, several salient aspects of racialized embodiment and its experience, I will take up this theme of "home" via an analysis of racialized uncanniness in the following chapter.

NOTES

1. Claude Steele, *Whistling Vivaldi (and Other Clues to How Stereotypes Affect Us)* (New York: W.W. Norton, 2010), 6. I have extracted this quote as it appears in Steele's book, however I note that the passage is presented differently in Brent Staples' own book, *Parallel Time*: Growing Up in Black and White (New York: Harper Perennial, 2000).

2. Ibid., 7.

3. Tressie McMillan Cottom, "Whistling Vivaldi Won't Save You," *Slate*, September 20, 2013.

4. Kamau Bell, "On Being a Black Male, Six Feet Four Inches Tall, in America in 2014," *Vanity Fair*, November 26, 2014.

5. Erving Goffman, *The Presentation of Self in Everyday Life* (New York: Anchor Books, 1959).

6. This work is one-sided since the responsibility falls on the shoulders of racialized people to anticipate, respond to, and counter the racialized anxieties projected onto them. On the other hand, those from whom the anxieties emerge are not called to "work upon" themselves unless and until their behavior is pointed out. Thus it is frequently *from* the labor of racialized people that these habitualized forms of racism get called into question and eventually changed; this point is worth noting.

7. Simone de Beauvoir, *The Second Sex*, trans. Constance Borde and Sheila Malovany-Chevallier (New York: Vintage Books, 2011), 724.

8. This is not to say that one could not also do a phenomenology of women's bodily comportment with a view to considerations such as tone of voice, posture, movement through space—for indeed some of this has been done to great effect by Young. The point rather is that in Beauvoir's account, there is a level of ornamentation that is distinct from the kind of work that I signal here.

9. In another study involving 32,585 participants, questionnaire responses revealed: "Compared to whites, all racial and ethnic minorities experience greater incidence of both emotional and physical stress from perceived racism. Blacks have

the highest rates, with 18.2% experiencing emotional stress symptoms and 9.8% experiencing physical stress symptoms (compared to 3.5% and 1.6% respectively for Whites). Also, racial and ethnic minorities experience significantly more days of poor mental and physical health (except Hispanics for physical health). Blacks and those in the 'other race' category have a notably high number of poor health days compared to whites." Further, Anderson concludes from her data analysis: "Examining the results from the first two binary logic models, we can see that race is related to experiencing emotional and physical stress from racist encounters. First, looking at emotional stress from racism, on which the current literature places more focus, all three race categories when compared to whites have substantial results even when controlling for socioeconomic status, general health status, and mental preoccupation with race. Furthermore, of these three groups, blacks were most likely to experience mental or emotional symptoms from experiences of perceived racism when compared to whites." Kathryn Freeman Anderson, "Diagnosing Discrimination: Stress from Perceived Racism and the Mental and Physical Health Effects," *Sociological Inquiry* 83 (2013): 55–81.

10. Pamela J. Sawyer et al., "Discrimination and the Stress Response: Psychological and Physiological Consequences of Anticipating Prejudice in Interethnic Interactions," *American Journal of Public Health* 102 (2012): 1024.

11. George Yancy, "Walking While Black in the 'White Gaze.'"

12. Frantz Fanon, *Peau Noire, Masques Blancs* (Paris: Éditions Points, 1952), 91–92.

13. I note that Markmann translates *nègre* here alternately as "Negro" and "nigger," although he has in other passages stayed with "Negro" (the famous *"Tiens, un nègre!,"* for example, appears in his rendering as "Look, a Negro!"). The term *nègre* is a difficult one to translate for various reasons, including the fact that in contemporary French usage it is a deeply offensive and profoundly racist term, approximating "nigger"—although possibly even more offensive still, and without the history of reclamation and re-appropriation by African-Americans the word has undergone in the United States. However, around the time Fanon was writing, the term *nègre* had a much broader usage, and while still virulent in many cases of course, it was not used exclusively as a slur (or as an *intended* slur). As I have not been able to discern the different senses in the passage, I have remained with the standard translation of "negro" (a similarly multivalent term), although I accept Markmann's alternation as a viable translation.

14. Markmann translates *tremble* variously throughout the passage (alternating with "shivering" and "quivering") opting not to convey the repetition in Fanon's original. I have retained the repeated citations of "trembling" in my translation, however, both to reflect the original, but also to bring out more strikingly the connection with Yancy's own description. Fanon, *Peau Noire, Masques Blancs*, 92; and trans. Markmann, 114.

15. Merleau-Ponty, *Phenomenology of Perception*, 151. Although it is important to understand that this statement answers directly to the differentiation of body and soul (mapped onto a distinction of object and subject) in Descartes, which Merleau-Ponty there seeks to challenge: "The union of the soul and the body is not established

through an arbitrary decree that unites two mutually exclusive terms, one a subject and the other an object." Ibid., 91.

16. Ibid., 93.

17. Ibid., 92.

18. Ibid., 93.

19. Other iterations of "walking while Black" include the phenomenon of "shopping while Black" (when Black bodies are over-policed or -surveilled, particularly in high-end boutique or department stores), or even the more recent case popularly dubbed "laughing while Black," where 10 Black women from a book club were kicked off the Napa Valley Wine Train for their "offensive" laughter. "Napa wine train controversy: 'I do think it was based on the color of our skin'," *The Guardian*, September 13, 2015.

20. "Men who thought rape would be 'fun' attacked mother and daughter, court told," *The Age*, September 15, 2014; "Rapists jailed for 'vicious, callous and cowardly' attack on mother and daughter," *The Age*, December 19, 2014.

21. Ibid.

22. Ibid.

23. Fanon, *Black Skin, White Masks*, 140.

24. Merleau-Ponty, *Phenomenology of Perception*, 92.

25. Fanon, *Black Skin, White Masks*, 113.

26. Although Fanon sometimes calls it a "triple-consciousness."

27. Fanon, *Black Skin, White Masks*, 109.

28. Consider, for example, Young's discussion of the gendered dimensions of "play" at work in the care/socialization of young children, specifically, the sedentary nature of girls' play as opposed to boys' play.

29. Merleau-Ponty, *Phenomenology of Perception*, 101–102.

30. Ibid., 102.

31. George Yancy, "Trayvon Martin: When Effortless Grace is Sacrificed on the Altar of the Image" in George Yancy and Janine Jones (eds.), *Pursuing Trayvon Martin: Historical Contexts and Contemporary Manifestations of Racial Dynamics* (Lanham: Lexington Books, 2013), 239.

32. Fanon, *Black Skin, White Masks*, 116.

33. Yancy, *Black Bodies, White Gazes*, 15. This sense of fragmentation and hyper-attentiveness to one's bodily movement registered in Yancy's quote is also reflected in Kamau Bell's descriptions of a late night visit to the convenience store: "So, as I walked in the store I had to take some precautionary action. For starters, I took the hood down. I took it down even though my afro had become a flat-fro from being squashed underneath. I didn't touch anything that I wasn't absolutely sure I was going to buy. (Just like my mom had taught me.) I kept my hands out of my pockets with palms clearly visible so the clerk behind the counter could easily see that I wasn't shoving things in—or maybe more importantly about to pull something out of—my pockets. And as soon as I decided on an It's It ice-cream sandwich, I went directly to the counter and *gingerly* placed my selection down, again keeping my palms visible and only making the movements I needed to get the money out of my wallet." While not addressing the question of spatiality directly, Bell's passage evokes powerfully

this sense of bodily and gestural fragmentation. Bell, "On Being a Black Male, Six Feet Four Inches Tall, in America in 2014."

34. "Muslim Boy's 'Terrorist House' Spelling Error Leads to Lancashire Police Investigation," *Huffington Post*, January 20, 2016.

35. "Inventing While Muslim," *The Atlantic*, September 16, 2015.

36. Bordering my Ménilmontant neighborhood is Belleville, an area known for Chinese women's prostitution, and subject to periodic police raids of prostitution rings. In the immediate surrounds of the Belleville *métro* on any given day, there are a considerable number of older Chinese women standing around alone or in pairs, in coded dress, presumably soliciting sex work. This by no means explains the entirety of my encounters with racism and racialization in the area, since women of East Asian appearance are notoriously subject to sexual advances even absent this specific context, but it nonetheless supplies a relevant context and meaning to the frequent callings-out.

37. Yancy, *Black Bodies, White Gazes*, 1.

38. Alia Al-Saji, "Too Late: Racialized Time and the Closure of the Past," *Insights* 6(5) (2013): 1–13, 8.

39. Ibid., 8.

40. Fanon, *Black Skin, White Masks*, 111.

41. "African Man Removed from easyJet flight to Make White Passenger 'Feel Safe'," *TesfaNews*, April 6, 2016. Mehary Yemane-Tesfagiorgis was on board an easyJet flight from Rome back to London (where he is from) when the incident took place. After some delay on the tarmac, Mehary was called up to the front of the plane, where he was met with two security officers and asked to disembark. He was taken aside for extensive questioning, despite there being no substantiated claims of "suspicious activity" being furnished. The airline subsequently apologized for their actions. The case bore remarkable resemblance to two other reported cases of similar incidents only weeks prior. "Third easyJet Passenger Grounded over Security Concerns," *The Guardian*, April 7, 2016.

42. "London Man Escorted Off easyJet Flight by Armed Police because Passenger Felt 'Uncomfortable'," *Evening Standard*, April 7, 2016.

43. Ibid., 110–111.

44. I say here "over"-identify, because that depends on one's perspective; it is not at all over-identification if it is logical and defensible. Also, to say that one over-identifies racism implies that we can arrive at a definitive reading of an encounter. Finally, to say one over-identifies racism is always a relative claim, and risks re-inscribing the white perspective as the norm from which to evaluate incidences of racism (which itself reinscribes racist practices).

45. Dreyfus, *What Computers (Still) Can't Do*.

46. I have not drawn on her work extensively here, but Sara Ahmed's book *Queer Phenomenology* also tracks the phenomenological dimensions of the racialized body, particularly as it is frequently stopped and interrupted. See, for example, her chapter on "The Orient and Other Others" in *Queer Phenomenology: Orientations, Objects, Others* (Durham: Duke University Press), 2006.

47. Merleau-Ponty, *Phenomenology of Perception*, 141.

48. To draw only a very rough distinction between the two, by "space" I refer to the undifferentiated and objectively measurable, whereas by "place" I refer to that which is differentially meaningful. Unlike space, place is embedded with layers of significance—embodied, social, cultural, historical and otherwise—and is experienced in this highly contextualized and situated way. For a richer discussion of the concept of place, see Edward S. Casey, *The Fate of Place: A Philosophical History* (Berkeley: University of California Press), 1997.

49. http://www.uws.edu.au/school-of-social-sciences-and-psychology/ssap/research/challenging_racism, accessed April 26, 2016.

50. Racism almost always happens, or, at least, seems to congeal around the times when racialized bodies *move*—on the streets, in cars, on the train, etc. This is an interesting phenomenon worthy of further thought; it is when racialized bodies are *on the move* that others' racist sensibilities are most offended.

51. "Radio Diary 4: Dawn's trip to the shopping centre," *The Darwin Radio Diaries*, https://open.abc.net.au/explore/32563, accessed December 19, 2012. Transcribed and used with permission from the Larrakia Nation Aboriginal Corporation.

52. Dawn speaks mainly of her anger in this account, but in the audio recording (of which this is a transcript) there are clear notes of disappointment and frustration in her voice, in addition to her brief mention of fear.

53. The point here being that there are significant racial aspects to the distribution of wealth and income too, which in turn affect how racialized bodies engage with different social–commercial spaces. For a compelling analysis of this, see: George Lipsitz, *How Racism Takes Place* (Philadelphia: Temple University Press, 2011).

54. Ahmed, *Queer Phenomenology*, 142.

55. Yancy, "Walking While Black in the 'White Gaze.'"

56. Cited in Steele, *Whistling Vivaldi*, 6.

57. Yancy, *Pursuing Trayvon*, 239.

58. I find interesting the young woman's allusion to her own Italian-American identity in her narrative. For one, it points to some of the complexities of race, highlighting the changing nature, as well as fluid *and* relative boundaries of racism. As scholars such as David Richards have argued, Italian–American identity was formed "under circumstances of injustice based on American racism." However, in the ever-changing racializing schema, the status of Italian-Americans has shifted significantly, not only with the passage of generational time, but also in response to the perceived threat of new foreigners and "more foreign" foreigners. I believe today most would consider Italian-Americans to be white (including Italian-Americans themselves), even if their ethnic identity and sense of cultural heritage remains strong. I note that the experience of Italian Australians has followed a similar, though not identical, trajectory. David A.J. Richards, *Italian American: The Racializing of an Ethnic Identity* (New York: NYU Press, 1999), 181.

59. Peggy McIntosh, "White Privilege: Unpacking the Invisible Knapsack," *Peace and Freedom Magazine*, July/August 1989: 10–12. Examples of stories shared in the #CrimingWhileWhite social media movement can be found at https://mic.com/articles/105694/criming-while-white-brilliantly-destroys-law-enforcement-s-racial-double-standard#.9wQi2HK1a, accessed December 3, 2014.

60. Shannon Sullivan, *Revealing Whiteness: The Unconscious Habits of Racial Privilege* (Bloomington: Indiana University Press, 2006), 10.

61. Ibid., 148.

62. "Napa wine train controversy: 'I do think it was based on the color of our skin,'" *The Guardian*, September 13, 2015.

63. Sullivan, *Revealing Whiteness*, 144.

64. This so-called gesture of "solidarity" has been enacted several times, for example, at *Sciences Po* in Paris in 2016. "French Students Wear Headscarves for 'Hijab Day,'" *The Guardian*, April 21, 2016.

65. I say "safe" because part of the problem with such experiments is that they replicate only a very thin and selective slice of what it is to experience racism, often without the depth of its reality.

66. Shannon Sullivan, *Good White People: The Problem with Middle-Class White Anti-Racism* (Albany: SUNY Press, 2014), 20.

67. Sullivan, "White World-Traveling," *Journal of Speculative Philosophy* 18 (2004): 300–304, 303.

68. Ibid., 302.

69. Sullivan, *Revealing Whiteness*, 163.

70. Ibid., 163–164. I think there is a corollary here with male embodiment in the example of "manspreading" on the subway—it is not that we should all comport our bodies in this expansive way, but that men should actively become more aware of their surroundings and pull back their usurpation of shared public space.

Chapter 3

Die Unheimlichkeit
The Racialized Body Not-at-Home

> Of all our mortal sorrows,
> the worst is
> loss of place.
>
> —Euripides, *Medea*

The experience of racism is an experience in uncanniness. By invoking this term, I draw explicitly on Heidegger's usage in *Being and Time*, where the German *die Unheimlichkeit* gets exploited for its reference to strangeness and alienation, as well as its more literal sense of un-home-liness (*Un-heim-lich-keit*).[1] This basic framework constitutes the main claim of the present chapter; that racialization renders one strange *and* not-at-home. That is, in addition to the bodily fragmentation explored in chapter 2, itself an experience laced with strangeness and disjuncture, it is my contention here that the process of racialization and the experience of one's own body as racialized entails the experience of displacement, and more specifically—and pressingly—of not-being-at-home. But this argument presupposes a basic claim which in turn requires investigation, namely, that the home constitutes an important, positively valenced, or even necessary, place. After all, what is the import of the claim that racialization renders one unhomely if not also for the argument that the home carries with it some ontological, phenomenological, affective, material, or political significance? The two key questions that guide this chapter are: How is racialization a kind of displacement from the home? and, What does it mean to experience one's body or one's surrounds as unhomely? In exploring these two questions, I extend the earlier analysis of the bodily experience of racism and racialization to a more explicitly placial framework in order to illuminate a new dimension to racialized embodiment. Further, by exploring these questions through the schematic of place and home, I advance an account of how both influence and frame our embodied experience.

Despite taking inspiration from Heidegger's meditations on the uncanny and his provocations about being and dwelling in the world, this is not a chapter on Heidegger and racism as such—which, one could imagine, would take on a rather different tone and form, given his own disturbing and controversial political entanglements with national socialism.[2] Instead, this chapter proceeds by borrowing from his philosophical reflections on uncanniness and dwelling, in order to set up an analysis of the experience of racism in placial terms. With this Heideggerian-derived framework established, I then draw in other thinkers of place such as Casey, Bachelard, Young, and Lugones (returning to Heidegger occasionally), in order to explore some different senses of uncanniness and being-at-home, and the insights they yield for our question of racialized embodiment. As such, the structure of this chapter unfolds somewhat differently to earlier chapters, with conceptions of home and dwelling being developed, revised, and fine-tuned as the analysis progresses. In particular, the working account of being-at-home that kick-starts our investigation undergoes significant revision by the end of the chapter, once its shortcomings have been identified and worked through via the thematic of porosity. But to get all of this under way, let us begin by turning to Heidegger's meditation on the uncanny.

PART 1—*DIE UNHEIMLICHKEIT* AND THE RACIALIZED BODY

In *Being and Time*, Heidegger introduces the theme of uncanniness in the course of his consideration of anxiety. After a discussion of how Dasein gets lured into—or lost in—the idle hum of "the They" (*das Man*), he contrasts this kind of Being-in-the-world, a Being in which we are fascinated by the world and absorbed in it, with the experience of prying ourselves away, an experience marked by anxiety. The experience inspires anxiety since the pull away from the unreflective everydayness of *das Man* is at once a confrontation with Dasein itself, with the thrownness and radical singularity of its own being-toward-death. In its absorption in *das Man* and the correlative mode of Being in-the-world, Dasein's involvement, according to Heidegger, amounts to a "fleeing *in the face of itself* and in the face of its authenticity."[3] Thus it is in pulling away from the comfort and everyday familiarity of *das Man* that Dasein experiences anxiety. According to Heidegger, "In anxiety one feels 'uncanny.'"[4] But whereas uncanniness usually refers to a feeling of strangeness, eeriness, or even monstrousness, Heidegger also draws out its literal signification of "'not-being-at-home' [*das Nicht-zuhause-sein*]."[5] In pulling away from the everyday hum of "the They," Dasein experiences itself not only as strange, but also *estranged*: "Everyday familiarity collapses. Dasein has been individualized, but individualized *as* Being-in-the-world. Being-in enters into the existential 'mode' of the 'not-at-home.' Nothing else is meant by our talk about 'uncanniness.'"[6] Dasein's experience of uncanniness, however, is not necessarily or wholly negative, since the uncanniness which characterizes the experience of anxiety represents an authentic mode of Dasein, who is otherwise concealed from itself while still entrapped in the mode of *das Man*. That is, there is a moment of disclosure or unconcealment heralded by this uncanniness. This last point is something that merits further reflection in view of the double consciousness entailed in racialization, and especially in view of Heidegger's later explorations of uncanniness in *Hölderlin's Hymn: Der Ister*. Our starting point here, however, is to take up the descriptive—but not yet normative—claim about how the experience of *die Unheimlichkeit* harbors the twin experiences of strangeness and displacement from the home.

Strangeness and "Not-Being-at-Home"

There are several ways in which Dasein's uncanniness as invoked by Heidegger resonates with the experience of racialization. Of course, many have described the experience of racism precisely in terms of strangeness and alienation—in other words, as uncanny. When Fanon writes for example, "My body was given back to me sprawled out, distorted, recolored,"[7] among other things, we can read this to mean that his body was presented back to him in a way that was strange, unfamiliar, even monstrous—in other words, in line with the ordinary meaning of *unheimlich*. Fanon's body is imbued with meanings that render him a stranger to himself. Indeed, this move is operative more generally in the act of racialized perception: in our earlier analysis we noted how racialized bodies "stick out" visually against a phenomenal field of whiteness and are assigned characteristics of dangerousness, violence, submission, exoticism, and so forth. Such bodies are indeed *rendered* strange, but following our analysis of the always already hermeneutic nature of perception, it is also the case that these bodies stand out against the normatively white visual field *because* the habits of racialized perception operate pre-reflectively. In other words, racialized bodies solicit visual attention and notice by virtue of a discord with pre-perceptual habits of perception; the visual normalization of whiteness renders strange the racialized body in a pre-reflective way. There is thus on this basic level of perceptual racialization already two operations of strangeness at play—both in the visual disjuncture of racialized bodies against a white perceptual field and in their hermeneutic distortion. In addition to these, it is also the case that the experience of racism and racialization is frequently described in terms of an alienation from others.

This may take the form of exclusion from social places and communities (recall Dawn Adams' experience of the shopping center), political membership and discourse (as per the example of veiled Muslim women in France), or even alienation in interpersonal relations (Yancy and Brent Staples). Here we have examples of how the experience of uncanniness in racism gets expressed in the form of alienation—itself a concept that also trades on the twin meanings of strangeness and not-belonging (the Latin *alienus* means "belonging to another").[8]

What Heidegger's conceptualization adds to the mix, however, is how uncanniness entails an experience of strangeness—and "not-being-at-home"—in relation to oneself. In the moment of prying away Dasein is made to feel strange and estranged not only from "the They," but in its anxiety, comes to experience *itself* as uncanny. Likewise, we might say that the racialized body is not only alienated from others, it is alienated from itself; the racialized body is not-at-home in its own body.[9] This we have already seen when considering how the racialized body does not experience itself as the habitual body, but rather as a body that stands in front of and before (or behind) itself. Yancy, for example, put it vividly when he writes:

> The corporeal integrity of my Black body undergoes an onslaught as the white imaginary, which centuries of white hegemony have structured and shaped, ruminates over my dark flesh and vomits me out in a form not in accordance with how I see myself. From the context of my lived experience, I feel "external," as it were, to my body, delivered and sealed in white lies.[10]

Here we get a fuller sense of how the experience of racism lines up with uncanniness in its multivalence: what Yancy gives us is not just an account of his body as strange, but invoking the second Heideggerian sense of the uncanny, his body is made to feel foreign to himself, and he is pushed outside of it. Racism forces upon those whose bodies are racialized, the feeling of being not-at-home in their own bodies, and consequently, not-at-home in their Being-in-the-world.

But what does it mean to be "at-home"? In order to gain a deeper sense of what this "not-being-at-home" means in the context of racialization, I propose that we first explore what it means to be "at-home"—not only in a cultural, emotional, and psychological sense, but also in its ontological and existential registers. This will help us to better contextualize claims about the experience of racism as rendering one unhomely, and to better grasp their significance. In the following section, we therefore proceed with questions such as: What do we mean by the home? What does and doesn't count as a home? and, What does it mean to "not-be-at-home" in one's own body?

Home and House

While we typically begin thinking about the home in terms of its physical cognate—the house—it is not usually the case that we confine the former to the latter. And for good reason, the two are not coextensive. It is often said a home is more than a house: it exceeds the physical structures and materials that come together in the *con*struction of a house, while also outliving its *de*struction. And yet, as Casey points out in *Getting Back into Place*, "in a certain sense a home is also something *less* than a house, since a house has to be constructed while a home need not be built."[11] We can thus invoke tents and caves, which with their varying degrees of construction and materiality qualify for homes though not houses. This aligns with our current investigation into home (and places in which we feel at-home) in the sense that the types of home we have in mind are not limited to materially constructed or even physical places. But what then gives a place the character of a home? Following architectural historian Joseph Rykwert, Casey suggests that another way to think about the home is in relation to its second cognate, the hearth. According to Rykwert in his article "House and Home":

> Home is where one starts from. That much is obvious. . . . Does a home need to be anything built at all, any fabric? I think not. Home could just be a hearth, a fire on the bare ground by any human lair. That may well be the one thing that nobody can quite do without: a fireplace, some focus. After all, if a home had no focus, you could not start from it.[12]

There is in other words an important grounding or orienting function which the home supplies, by virtue of this "focus" (and note that the Latin *focus* designates "hearth"). Rather than in terms of pure enclosure, what Rykwert offers here is the opportunity to think of home as the starting place: "almost always," he writes, "home is at the centrifugal hearth."[13] This offers us our first characterization.

But the home is still more than this. Iris Marion Young, in a similarly titled chapter, "House and Home: Feminist Variations on a Theme," offers a different approach. Recalling psychologist Van Lennep's example of the hotel, she asks: "Why, then, does one not feel at home in a hotel room? Because there is nothing of one's self, one's life habits and history, that one sees displayed around the room. The arrangement is anonymous and neutral, for anyone and . . . no one in particular."[14] The question, for Young, is whether a place *supports and reflects* embodied living: "The home is not simply the things . . . but their arrangement in space in a way that supports the body habits and routines of those who dwell there."[15] In Young's version, home spaces—and this includes places we might not ordinarily think of as "the" home such as stoops, street corners, and coffeehouses, known in urban studies as "third places"[16]—track the goings-about and embodied concerns of its dwellers. In contrast to Rykwert's motif of the centrifugal hearth, here lines of focus and intentionality are circulated throughout the home space and collected through the embodied habits of the subject. Indeed, I would go further to say that not only do homes reflect and support bodily habits, they actively *allow* them. That is, continuing with Young's hotel example, it is not only that they do not display anything of one's self or habits, it is that they are impervious to them; personalized histories and arrangements are wiped clean with each new check-in, with each new morning's housekeeping round. Homes on the other hand not only reflect embodied habits, but actively allow for their cultivation. These functional differences between hotels and homes—which stem from differences in legal tenancy status, duration and purpose of stay, as well as levels of material support and familiarity—come together to create a fundamentally different relation marked by, in the case of homes, the ability to track and foster bodily histories and habits. Homeliness thus is not a separate thing we bring to the house, as Rykwert at times suggests,[17] but rather it is achieved in the very manner of our continued and ongoing interaction with such spaces. This second characterization of home as a place of embodied habit opens up a further connection with our analysis of the uncanniness of racialization insofar as it allows us to explicitly consider whom spaces and places support, or are designed for.[18]

Home and Dwelling

There is, I suggest, one more important way to conceptualize the home, and that is in terms of the activity it most affords—the verb of home as it were, *to dwell*. Though itself an ambiguous concept, dwelling can help us to think further about what marks home *qua* home. In his 1951 lecture, "Building, Dwelling, Thinking," Heidegger distinguishes between simply being housed somewhere [*behausen*] and dwelling there [*wohnen*].

> The truck driver is at home [*zu Hause*] on the highway, but he does not have his lodgings [*seine Unterkunft*] there; the working woman is at home [*zu Hause*] in the spinning mill, but does not have her dwelling place [*ihre Wohnung*] there; the chief engineer is at home [*zu Hause*] in the power station, but he does not dwell there [*er wohnt nicht dort*]. These buildings house [*behausen*] man. He inhabits [*bewohnt*] them and yet does not dwell [*wohnt*] in them.[19]

For Heidegger, there is a critical distinction between being physically housed somewhere and dwelling there, and this distinction trades on the special character of dwelling. In this lecture, given Heidegger is concerned also with the question of building and our technological relation to places, the concept of dwelling gets refracted through the practice of building, and both are found to be fundamentally attuned insofar as they participate in the same endeavor. The clue lies, somewhat predictably for Heidegger, in language: "Now, what does *bauen*, to build, mean? The Old High German word for building, *buan*, means to dwell. This signifies to remain, to stay in a place."[20] We pause here to register a first sense of dwelling that is opened up by its being heard together with building: *staying*. Dwelling and building (insofar as buildings entail a measure of material endurance) both consist in a staying, and this coheres with our earlier attempts to get at a definition of home; the home is where we *stay*, in some significant sense. Indeed, this position echoes Heidegger's earlier remarks in the lecture course, *Hölderlin's Hymn "Der Ister,"* where he claims:

> "Dwelling" is practically and technically regarded as the possession of accommodation and housing. Such things indeed belong to dwelling, yet they do not fulfill or ground its essence. *Dwelling takes on an abode and is an abiding in such an abode*, specifically that of human beings upon this earth. *The abode is a whiling. It needs a while.*[21] (my emphasis)

We should note that this formulation of dwelling as staying or abiding is not unique to Heidegger. For example we hear traces of it in Rykwert's own etymological meditations: "And yet Latin also provides two other words for the house: as a thing built, *aedes, and as a place of rest—which home so emphatically is—mansio, from maneo, I remain or abide*"[22] (my emphases). So too does Young invoke notions of staying and preservation in her description of home-making activity when she writes, "Home is the space where I *keep* and use the material belongings of my life"[23] and, "Traditional female domestic activity, which many women continue today, partly consists in *preserving* the objects and meanings of a home"[24] (my emphases). One curious deviation from this general picture of dwelling as staying, however, appears in Casey's account. For him, dwelling is paradoxically staying *and/or wandering*, and this is curious since he too arrives by way of etymology. Explaining the assertion that his old local mall-arcade afforded a form of dwelling, Casey writes:

> Dwelling as nonresiding? What does that mean? We can find an important clue by tracing the word *dwell* back to two apparently antithetical roots: Old Norse *dvelja,* linger, delay, tarry, and old English *dwalde*, go astray, err, wander. The second root, though rarely invoked, fits my memory of the arcade rather well. There the passerby is encouraged to wander off the street into a world of film and images and fashion. One may *dwalde* in that kind of world, drift with it, follow its lead. . . . Dwelling is accomplished not by residing but by wandering.[25]

Acknowledging the different origins of the word, Casey's exploration of the latter not only allows him to consider much more varied styles and places of dwelling, such as street corners or apartment stoops, but also to announce almost in direct contrast to Heidegger, that, "We may even dwell in automobiles, as commuters do daily."[26] Despite this, Casey admits that some places support more "fully-fledged" modes of dwelling than others, especially those that at a minimum, allow for "repeated return," and possess a certain "felt familiarity."[27]

Dwelling as Resting

Nonetheless, the move to characterize dwelling as staying or abiding is a significant one for our purposes, since it draws us into the orbit of another important term: *resting*. Dwelling as staying and abiding, as heard in Heidegger and echoed in Rykwert and Young, implies restfulness insofar as they release one from the necessity of disorientation and adaptation that accompanies constant change, and the effort these demand. It is likely for this reason that Rykwert links the home with stability and well-being.[28] By resting in the same place, we are *afforded rest*; this bivalence—resting as staying and as repose—is captured well in the English language.[29] Indeed in Heidegger's passage above, it is unsurprising that he follows the discussion on abiding and whiling immediately with the claim, "In such a while, human beings find rest. Rest is a grounded repose in the steadfastness of one's own essence."[30] The home, as a place where we stay—or in Casey's case, the place to which we return—is substantially (though not exclusively[31]) a place of rest. And while Casey's dwelling can be achieved in wandering, it is also the case that, together, Rykwert's home-as-starting-place and Casey's home-as-return bookend the work, exhaustion, even exhilaration, of worldly travel. As Casey writes, "'There is nothing like staying at home' precisely because *at home* we do not usually have to confront such questions as 'Where am I?' 'Where is my next meal coming from?' or 'Do I have any friends in the world?' (original emphasis)."[32]

Of course this characterization of home as a place of rest, which we arrived at through an examination of the activity of dwelling, tugs at a further connection to be considered later in this chapter. Whereas resting harbors both senses of staying and repose, the second sense of resting as repose brings us to the notion of *retreat*, itself a productively bivalent term. In line with the characterization of the home as a place where we are at rest, the term retreat can be employed here to describe the home when it is a place of repose. Retreats are of course places of rest and relaxation, and typically secluded from the hustle and bustle of the world outside. In this sense the nominal use of retreat echoes our earlier acknowledgment of the lack of disorientation and anxiety in home-like places. The home can be a kind of retreat. And yet given the original meaning of retreat as withdrawal, what the term productively highlights is the way in which the home and being-at-home might operate as a kind of disengagement from the world around us, as we will consider later.

Nonetheless, this third characterization of home as where one dwells and rests (in the sense of staying and reposing) folds back into the second question of bodily habit raised by Young. The relationship between habit and rest is, I contend, codependent and cogenerative. For example, on the one hand it is because home supports and reflects our bodily habits that we *do* find ourselves at rest; things are handy to us with a Heideggerian "readiness to hand," and being oriented by such habits, we need not expend additional effort or energy to navigate the home's spatiality. The familiarity of the home puts us at ease, or said differently, our habituation to it opens up the possibility of restfulness. (Such is its restfulness that Gaston Bachelard identifies the house's [his term] single most important quality as the fact that it "shelters daydreaming."[33]) Indeed bodily habits themselves, whether in relation to the home, other places, or situations, allow us to engage in ways that don't call upon or demand our explicit attention, and so afford resting insofar as we are not therefore required to process sensory information anew or navigate bodily spaces and movements with the effort exerted for the unfamiliar. And yet at the same time, it is also the case that we *can* cultivate bodily habits in the home precisely *because* it is a place for rest. As noted above, we accumulate bodily habits in homes and not hotels because we rest (stay) there. In contrast to the hotel where we do not stay, the durational resting at the home allows for ongoing engagement with its space, which is in turn what allows us to make meaning and develop signification. This corner, once empty, now furnished with a desk and a chair, its cupboards repurposed to hold books, and to where I return daily to write, now becomes a study. Spaces get turned into places upon our sustained and meaningful engagement with them, and in doing so they become habitual to us. In the same way that we acquire the "habit" of driving or dancing only once we become at ease with these activities (as discussed in chapter 1), so too do we turn the home space into a habitual place once we are at ease with it. There is in other words, a reciprocity in the way habit and rest unfold in the cultivation of the home.

This meditation on home has brought out three of its key features—the home as it offers a starting place, cogenerates and supports bodily habits, and affords rest or retreat—while also signaling some of the complexities to come. Having laid out these features, which will give depth to our claim about the uncanniness of racialized bodies, I propose that we move now to consider a particular kind of home at stake here—that of the body.

The Body as Home

In what way is the phenomenal body invoked throughout this book *itself* a kind of home, with all that this entails? Of course this body-as-home connection is already present in Merleau-Ponty's treatment of the lived body, a body which is not experienced from some objective or distanced standpoint, but which rather is directly *inhabited*. In the opening line of the essay "Eye and Mind," he declares: "Science manipulates things and gives up living in [*habiter*] them."[34] His own phenomenological project, on the other hand, can be understood as an effort to rescue the inhabited or "lived" body (*le corps veçu*) as a site of philosophical inquiry and insight. But we can be more specific than this. Drawing on the three broadly discerned features of home as proposed above, we find a correlation to each in Merleau-Ponty's account of the body. First, whereas Rykwert identifies the home as our quintessential starting place, so too according to Merleau-Ponty is our body ours. In the *Phenomenology of Perception*, the permanent presence of body—which is a permanence "on my side"—is also that which imposes the first (and lasting) perspective on our access to the world: "for my window to impose on me a perspective on the church, my body must first impose on me a perspective on the world."[35] Our body, in other words, is our starting point for an engagement with the world, meaning that it not only frames this engagement, but makes it possible. The body, too, is where we start. Second, insofar as the home is characterized by its reflection and affordance of bodily habit, Merleau-Ponty writes of the body that it is the "*primordial habit*, the one that conditions all others and by which they can be understood"[36] (my emphasis). The lived body is such that it allows for and is animated through bodily habits. Indeed, as Casey argues in his discussion of memory, habit has a privileged relationship to bodily experience for two reasons: first, insofar it is "the most pervasive and subtle way in which we are in touch with the past that we bear and that bears us", and second, since it is so intimately bound up with the body's expressivity and style.[37] Habits animate bodies as "lived" bodies, and, in turn, the permanence of one's own body is what allows for developments in habit.

Finally, Merleau-Ponty's phenomenal body also converges with our discussion of dwelling and staying. As already noted, we stay in our bodies insofar as they are permanently present to us, and inescapable for us. Such staying interlaces with the development of habit in a way that renders the phenomenal body at ease. In our descriptions of Merleau-Ponty's habitual body, there is a distinct sense in which the habitual body is that which moves without effort or obstruction, rather, it is at ease with itself and its surroundings—indeed this is what our analyses of racialization begin to challenge. In the habitual body, as in the home, we are afforded certain measure of rest. Given such convergences, we can say not only that the body is a kind of home, but that it *is a home* in an original sense, and that we are at-home in it.

Additionally or alternatively, scholars such as Kirsten Jacobson have likewise argued for the parallel understanding of body and home. In her article, "A Developed Nature: a Phenomenological Account of the Experience of Home," Jacobson argues that the notions of home and dwelling, most identifiably associated with Heidegger among the phenomenologists, are in fact equally present in Merleau-Ponty's concepts of "lived body" and "level."[38] Whereas I have proceeded by arguing that the *body* in Merleau-Ponty (and in existential phenomenology more generally) is home-like or indeed *is* a home, Jacobson approaches the question inversely, arguing that the *home is body-like*, or, our "second body."[39] There is then a symmetry to the two analyses; where I noted the body's resemblance to the conception of home as starting place, Jacobson notes the inverse. She writes, for example, "At the most basic level, home is like the body insofar as it is, as we have just been describing, a place of initial stability and a foundation for the self."[40] Further, Jacobson's main contention concerning the developed nature of dwelling and by extension the developed nature of embodied being resonates with our earlier discussion of dwelling as an ongoing enterprise in the cultivation of habit. However, despite our agreement on the convergence of home and body (or what Jacobson sometimes helpfully calls "home-body"), as I will show later, we diverge when it comes to the qualitative characterization of the home. Whereas for Jacobson the home is framed largely in terms of enclosure and refuge (which incidentally, works suitably for the unhyphenated term, "homebody"), I will argue, drawing from the racialized experience, that home—and the body—is more constitutively porous than she allows. This point of departure, as we will see, becomes significant later on in the chapter, as we move to further nuance of the account of the "home-body," in view of concerns around their imagined insularity.

For the moment, however, we can identify in addition to these affinities between home (as characterized so far) and body some more concrete connections. Casey, for example, in *Getting Back into Place* considers the way architectural design often reflects that of body structure, including the "upward action" of buildings as well as their resemblance to the human bodily form. "Built places, then, are extensions of our bodies," Casey writes, "Places built for residing are rather an enlargement of our already existing embodiment into *an entire life-world of dwelling*."[41] Drew Leder in *The Absent Body* agrees: "the very house in which one dwells is both a reconstruction of the surrounding world to fit the body and an enlargement of our own physical structure. Its walls form a second protective skin, windows acting as artificial senses, entire rooms, like the bedroom or kitchen, devoted to a single bodily function."[42] Even when not mimicking or extending bodily anatomy or physiology, buildings are often designed in such a way as to resonate with it; their verticality and groundedness speak to our bodily experience of gravity and uprightness.[43] Buildings—particularly those in which we dwell—are bodily in a multiplicity of ways. Given this, we can understand why Casey concludes that the affinity between houses and bodies is indeed a very thoroughgoing one; the connection is one in which "our very identity is at stake. For we tend to identify ourselves by—and with—the places in which we reside."[44]

Indeed such notes are already present in Heidegger's meditation on dwelling in "Building, Dwelling, Thinking," when he insists that more than a question of emplacement, dwelling becomes a mode of *being itself*:

> What then does *ich bin* mean? The old word *bauen*, to which the *bin* belongs, answers: *ich bin, du bist* mean I dwell, you dwell. The way in which you are and I am, the manner in which we humans *are* on the earth, is *buan*, dwelling. To be a human being means to be on the earth as a mortal. It means to dwell.[45]

In addition to the reflection of bodies in buildings (the noun) and bodies with building (the verb), consider also how the body serves as our first home—not only in Merleau-Ponty's metaphysical sense of our permanent bodily presence, but also in the sense of the mother's body as our *first* dwelling place.[46] The pregnant body is literally our first place of generation, gestation, nourishment, and development[47]—and thus in a non-trivial sense, our first home.[48] Here it is not our own body but that of the *mother's* that offers us a place of rest and a place from which we quite literally "start." While I do not take up fully the complex questions of provenance here, with its distinctive feminist and intersubjective implications as explored by thinkers such as Young and Luce Irigaray among others, I raise the point in order to sound a cautionary note against those eulogies of the home that fail to consider women's roles as first nurturers.[49] Nonetheless, in thinking here through some of the rich and varied affinities between home and body, we see that what is at stake in the coming analysis of racialized uncanniness is how not-being-at-home resonates both at the level of bodily experience and the emplaced experience of one's environs.

Having worked through these affinities in some sustained way, it is important, however, not to overstate the parallels between the home and body; they are alike, but they are not the same.[50] In particular, it is worth remembering that while the body certainly resembles the home, so too does it *relate to* it. That is, as a place, the home is that which the body inhabits, and in which the body moves and unfolds. In this way then the home also serves as something like a world for the body; the home is worldlike. Indeed, for Bachelard the home is "the human being's first world,"[51] it is "our first universe, a real cosmos in every sense of the word."[52] This marks one important point of distinction between the home and body, insofar as the former also provides a milieu for the latter; the relationship between home and body is not only one of resonance, but also one of nesting. Thus despite the many different ways the body seems to mimic the home—such that it might be considered our very own home—we must be careful not to reduce one to the other. The home may be body-like, to recall Jacobson, but that is not to say that it *is* a body, rather, the home subtends the poles of world and body. Keeping this in mind, then, I proceed here on the basis that reflections on the different dimensions of home and being-at-home, while not immediately transferrable to the domain of the bodily, can nonetheless be highly suggestive of the nature of embodied being.

The Racialized Body Not-at-Home, and "World"-Travelling

Having given a conceptual treatment of home, we are now in a position to reconsider the question of racialized bodies, and what it means when we claim that the experience of racialization is an experience of uncanniness, in the sense of feeling not-at-home. We saw earlier that the experience of both racism and racialization is often likened to the experience of estrangement, from oneself and from others, and in both senses of feeling strange and apart from others. This doubling maps onto the cluster of concepts that have been discussed here—uncanniness, alienation, and so forth. Armed with a finer analysis of the home, we can now draw out some of the phenomenological and existential implications of finding oneself not-at-home. In a sense we have already considered how the bodily experience of racialization tracks our first two features of "home." In the discussion of bodily fragmentation and the experience of being in front of and ahead of oneself, there is an originary displacement that stands at odd with our idea of home as the starting place. After all, where is one's starting place if the self is contemporaneously experienced as being located here *and* there? In addition to bodily fragmentation, the analysis of overdetermination and predetermination in chapter 1 also works to render blunt certain notions of genuine "starting" if one is always already "on the scene." Second, in our discussion of bodily habit, we also signaled some of the ways in which the racialized body is experienced as *inhabitual*. Recall Fanon's claim that the development of a corporeal schema is for the Black man, a solely negating activity. In what follows then, I focus on the question of dwelling and rest, which is brought out particularly by the analysis of home. In what way does racialized embodiment run contrary to our third sense of being-at-home, that of being at rest?

In her article, "Playfulness, 'World'-Travelling, and Loving Perception," María Lugones makes the observation that the experience of being an outsider to the mainstream organization of life in the United States—and she has in mind specifically women of color, though the analysis could conceivably extend to others—entails a practice she calls "'world'-travelling." The bivalence of this term is a very productive one, for reasons I will explore. On a first pass, the expression "'world'-travelling" describes the way in which women of color who find themselves on the periphery or outside of mainstream worlds are made to engage in this practice of travelling, in order to negotiate their participation within social and political domains, while retaining a sense of self and identity which is compromised or distorted in those domains. She writes:

> One can "travel" between these "worlds" and one can inhabit more than one of these "worlds" at the very same time. I think that most of us who are outside the mainstream of, for example, the US dominant construction or organization of life are "world travellers" as a matter of necessity and of survival. It seems to me that inhabiting more than one "world" at the same time and "travelling" between "worlds" is part and parcel of our experience and our situation.[53]

The use of "travelling" as a metaphor is a very helpful one, since it allows us to reframe this practice against the terms of being-at-home. In contrast to the experience of being-at-home with oneself and one's world, what Lugones describes here is how women of color experience a constant and unrelenting necessity to travel to and from different "worlds," and to negotiate these worlds in which they are not entirely at-home. Indeed, it is the very experience of feeling not-at-home—or echoing our earlier analysis, not "at ease"—that brings on the necessity of travel. As Mariana Ortega writes in her commentary of Lugones: "Being-at-ease in the 'world,' however, is not a feature of the 'world'-traveller self. It is not the feature of the individual who is considered the 'alien,' the 'stranger,' by the dominant group and who is no longer fully at ease in his or her own culture and is not in the midst of another culture."[54]

This phenomenon of not-being-at-home in the experience of racialization, as discussed earlier in this chapter, and also not-being-at-ease as discussed in the previous, is now supplemented with an account of what one does upon finding oneself so situated. That is, our earlier *descriptions* of the alienating experience of racialization help us to identify and better understand the experience, but here we move to an analysis of how such an experience is to be managed and negotiated. Lugones' concept of travelling is one such strategy for that management. When, for example, Fanon writes that the Black man among his own "will have no occasion, except in minor internal conflicts, to experience his being through others,"[55] he implicitly describes the experience of being through others (and for others) when he is out among the normatively white world. Being as it is, however, that Fanon has to try and live and flourish in a world where he is not among "his own," and indeed in a world which is hostile to him, the task that stands before him in this experience of his world as unhomely is precisely to find ways to *make* himself at-home. We do not only find homes, we have to make them. Being displaced and rendered not-at-home by the experience of racism, Fanon's task becomes to find a home, and to find or make a place which can give him what the home affords. This "finding" is what Lugones might call "travelling."

The *necessity* of such "travelling," however, should not be understated. Where we saw in chapter 2 the way in which racialized people bear the burden of managing racist fears or fetishes projected onto their bodies, of "whistling Vivaldi," there is here a correlate in the burden of managing different and often hostile worlds. Lugones' reference to the necessity of travelling as a matter of survival points to the way in which the burden of negotiation falls largely on the shoulders of those who do not find themselves at-home in such worlds. As in recreational travelling, it is the traveller who displaces herself in order to visit the worlds that stand far enough apart that they require a certain amount of effort, energy, and resources to traverse. The "worlds" do not move, the traveller does. Our earlier discussion of the stress in racialization can thus be taken up and continued under the guise of this mandatory travelling or "forced migration"—a theme we will explore further in relation to the question of power. In addition to the effort exerted in traversing such distances, there is also the work and disorientation involved in making oneself intelligible across these worlds, while holding on to a semblance of a continuous self (even if there are a multiplicity of selves) throughout the process. There is then an important way in which this experience described by Lugones stands in stark contrast to that of the comfort and relief of being-at-home as described by Young, Casey, and others. So too does the earlier discussion of existential stress and the pathologizing of racialized people resonate in our present discussion. If being at home entails a certain measure of stability (physical and emotional) and place for rest and repose, then the experience of having to constantly travel across and between worlds is marked by a distinct lack of those things; it entails constant upheaval. To lack such a home-place can be, as the chorus sings in response to *Medea's* plight, cited in the epigraph to this chapter, a profoundly unsettling and traumatic experience.

But as noted earlier, the metaphor of travelling is one which is productively multivalent. Lugones' description of the activity of negotiation between worlds as "travelling" (as opposed to "managing" or "negotiating"—all of which imply work) is I think, a deliberate effort to encourage us also to think through the valuable, creative, and even joyful moments of such work. After all, travelling can be fun! Or even when it is not, it can be eye-opening. Travelling is a valuable endeavor insofar as it brings us to different places, exposing us to different ways of living and being, and to people and cultures we might not otherwise encounter. Indeed such encounters often hit us with a refreshing new perspective on our own lives and worlds, and can have a transformative effect. Sometimes it is precisely the distance from the home and world in which one is enmeshed that gives us the latitude to try, see, and experience things differently. Or put otherwise, sometimes it is through the eyes (even gazes) of others that we see ourselves afresh. Travelling can then, under certain circumstances, be a valuable endeavor for both those who travel and the worlds they visit. It is in this spirit that for Lugones, travelling can open up new ethical possibilities:

> But there are "worlds" that we can travel to lovingly and travelling to them is part of loving at least some of their inhabitants. The reason why I think that travelling to someone's "world" is a way of identifying with them is because by travelling to their "world" we can understand *what it is to be them and what it is to be ourselves in their eyes.*[56]

Thus, while the home certainly holds important significations in the ways noted above—as a starting place, as a place tracking our bodily habits, as a place of rest—it is also true to say on the other hand that there are certain dangers that come with an over-attachment to or over-identification with it. It is possible, in other words, to become *too much* at-ease or too much at-home with the world, such that one stops encountering others and fails to consider what it is to be herself in the eyes of another. Lugones puts the problem thus: "I take this maximal way of being at ease [in a 'world'] to be somewhat dangerous because it tends to produce people who have no inclination to travel across 'worlds' or have no experience of 'world' travelling."[57] Here we can bring back into the picture the experience of whiteness, which when lived ubiquitously and unreflectively embodies something of this being too much at-home or too much at-ease. As described in the discussion of entitlement and white embodiment in chapter 2, the white body is in the racialized schema, the habitual body, that which is at-home and not presented as a problem for itself. While this certainly brings many advantages and privileges (many of these cumulative and heavily obfuscated), what Lugones's analysis does is to point out the danger and relative impoverishment of such a mode of being. This adds a further dimension—one often underplayed—to those working within critical whiteness movements, where strategies of "race treason," in which one disavows the privileges of whiteness, are deployed in the name of solidarity with people of color. While Emily Lee has called into question the political aims and efficacy of such strategies, arguing that they misplace their efforts,[58] I would add that they also miss the opportunity for genuine solidarity between whites and non-whites in anti-racist struggles. Specifically, what is elided is the way in which white people's *own being* is also at stake, in the system of racist differentiation and subjugation. As Lugones's analysis shows, the kind of being too much at-home that characterizes whiteness comes with its own pitfalls; the lack of a need to "world"-travel or see oneself from the purview from another can lead to a more impoverished mode of ethical being.[59] In the context of anti-racist work, I argue that such multivalenced analyses of home and travel can call forth fuller models of political solidarity, one whose spirit is poignantly captured by Gangulu woman and Australian Aboriginal activist Lilla Watson in her speech to the United Nations in 1985: "If you have come here to help me, you are wasting our time. But if you have come because your liberation is bound up with mine, then let us work together."[60]

Finally, Lugones's analysis should not apply only to those who partake unreflectively in the system of whiteness; it is equally relevant to those who inhabit racialized bodies. That is, while the power dynamics in play are unquestionably and critically different for racialized people, Lugones's caution against the romanticization and reification of the home, taken up more fully by Ortega in the chapter "Hometactics: Self-Mapping, Belonging, and the Home Question," translates politically into a caution against the homogenization of any one kind of being or perspective. In other words, the political response of finding or making oneself a home in a world where racialized bodies experience themselves ill-at-ease ought not to erect new fortresses from which new "others" are kept out. Ortega writes:

> It cannot be denied that even for those who are border crossers and world-travelers, the home question is still a question. Perhaps it is even a more painful question precisely because that home seems harder to find. Yet, despite the determination of this will to belong that may provide a feeling of security and comfort, we cannot avoid recognizing the limits and pitfalls of such security, namely the reification of those who do not fit a version of authentic belonging.[61]

While the possibility of reinscribing oppressive practices leads Ortega to maintain a level of suspicion against what she variously refers to as the "will to belong," as I will argue in part 3 of this chapter, nor is the jettisoning of such an attachment to home necessary or ideal, once we begin to understand the home with greater nuance. That is to say, while the dialectic of home-and-travel presented here opens up important challenges for thinking about the normative analysis of racialized bodies in relation to the experience of home, in my view this is not a problem that can be sufficiently worked through on our current terms. I thus propose in the next part a further consideration of the home and body—this time with explicit reference to its porosity—in order to introduce new terms with which we can consider more satisfactorily the significance of being-at-home for racialized bodies.

PART 2—THE POROSITY OF HOME,
THE POROSITY OF BODIES

Our discussion of the home so far has been limited largely to one characterization, which while rich and itself multifarious also tends to invoke associations of inwardness and enclosure. This has been useful insofar as it has allowed us to underscore the question of identity and the stable sense of self that is afforded in home-places, and as missing when the experience of racialization involves an enduring sense of feeling not-at-home. As noted earlier, the question of home and dwelling is as much a question of being and identity, with the stability and protection of the home affording a certain measure of existential and phenomenological stability and relief. But at the same time, these characterizations of the home also risk imputing a public/private distinction and overstating the home's alignment with the private sphere. Such conceptions are of course rife in philosophy; Hannah Arendt offers one version of this in her conceptual division of the public, private, and social in *The Human Condition*, and more intimately also in the letters exchanged with her husband Heinrich Blücher documented in the aptly named collection, *Within Four Walls*,[62] and even Jacobson is explicit in her treatment of home as such. And yet, it is precisely the characterization of home as private and inwardly oriented that lead Lugones and Ortega to their concerns about the dangers of being too much at-home, and of being too insular in one's political and ethical orientations. We can see this at work in Jacobson's descriptions of the home when she writes:

> I am arguing that home, as a place of and for the self, is a situation of refuge for us, a place or way of being in which 'our own' is privileged and 'the alien' is not manifestly present.
>
> With the exception of our organic bodies, there is virtually no other place in our experience that maintains this kind of inviolable self-enclosure.[63]

For Jacobson, insofar as the home offers enclosure and refuge it also entails a turning away from—or even exclusion of—the other ("the alien"). The home-body is in her words "inviolable." This characterization goes beyond the sense of retreat-as-repose to emphasize retreat-as-*withdrawal*, and echoing Lugones' earlier remarks, I argue that this can be dangerous (especially in the case of white embodiment) insofar as such inwardness may foster a disinclination to "world"-travel. The home, rendered primarily in this inward-facing way, may lead to a kind of ethical insularity that should give us some cause for concern.

But of course, there may be circumstances in which exactly this kind of withdrawal is called for; bell hooks, for example, writes in "Homeplace (A

Site of Resistance)": "Black women resisted [racism] by making homes where black people could strive to be subjects, not objects, where we could be affirmed in our minds and hearts despite poverty, hardship, and deprivation, where we could restore ourselves the dignity denied us on the outside in the public world."[64] Jacobson's characterization of home-as-withdrawal, however, is more general and unlike hooks' it is not specific to a situation where one's sense of being is held under continuous attack and disintegration by the "outside" world, as is the case with Black embodiment. Further, hooks' essay elegantly describes the way in which Black women cultivated "homeplaces" that were not so much a withdrawal from the racist world, but a creative *response to it*; these homeplaces were, she argues, sites of resistance. There is an important way then that the home remains always in dialogue with the "outside" world, and indeed forms part of it. After all, if home is a place (even multiple places) then we ought not to forget that places are themselves relational and embedded in ecosystems of meaning and practices. It is with this in mind that I now turn to a consideration of "porosity" as it pertains to home and body, and which I argue is *constitutive* of them.

The Porosity of the House

In the case of the home, we can trace this porosity in several ways. Given the lingering connection of home with house, we can start with a consideration of the house, whose pores are manifold. As architectural structures, houses are punctuated with doors that afford comings and goings, and windows that let in the world when we don't, won't, or can't cross that portal threshold. Both admit light, weather, and noise from the streets in exchange for that within—carrying forth the smells of a feast in preparation, or the muffled sounds of the evening news on the radio. The house's porosity affords—indeed solicits—an exchange with the world, and this affordance is *constitutive*; a house with no windows and no doors is not a house (much less a home)—it is a dungeon, a prison, or a cellar, structures we deem unfit for human habitation. Solitary confinement in 6 × 8 ft. cells is routinely described by inmates, as documented by Lisa Guenther in her book *Solitary Confinement: Social Death and its Afterlives*, are places for the "living dead."[65] Even at a less extreme end, it is telling that jurisdictions such as New York City legally prohibit the use of non-windowed rooms as bedrooms. Homes, even in their most conventional instantiation of the freestanding, single-family house, are structurally porous.[66]

But we shouldn't take the motif of porosity too literally, if what we are really concerned with is the exchange they afford, for it is not just the "pores" of the house—its doors and windows—that allow it, as if exchange takes place only in the manner of osmosis. Rather, something like the notion of *bearing* could be brought into play: the house as a whole bears the presence of the world, both *carrying it* and *bringing it forth* (to invoke the term's etymology), and in turn bears itself upon the world. Consider the way immediate environs—sunlight, climate, traffic circulation—all bear on the design, composition, and construction of houses. Even laws, population density, conceptions of privacy, economic, technological, and aesthetic practices are embossed into the house, and afford as much exchange as its "pores." And in the same way that porous surfaces allow movement in both directions, inasmuch as houses are constituted by their context and surrounds, so too do they constitute them. Places gain their character as clean, impoverished, uninteresting, rough, and so on through the houses that populate them. In a cursory but nonetheless significant way, then, homes (insofar as they remain connected to houses) exhibit a porosity that is not compatible with the idea of complete withdrawal.

As a cognate and metaphor for the home, the house's porosity is instructive. Despite earlier characterizations of the home as insular and self-enclosed, there in fact remains an important sense in which the home too is constituted by a porosity—and there is no contradiction here. There is nothing, for example, that prescribes that as a starting place (or place of return), the home must be fully enclosed and self-contained. The nature of place, in contradistinction to space, is that it is never definitively demarcated, but rather is marked by boundaries whose precise location remain elusive because they are by their nature unfixed.[67] Second, bodily habits, while highly idiosyncratic expressions of the body and thus in this sense personal, are nonetheless thoroughly mediated by cultural and historical practices, technological affordances, and even interpersonal (and particularly intergenerational[68]) influences. That they are personal and even the fact that they develop behind the "closed door" of the home does not in itself mean that worldly practices are not involved, to the contrary. Finally, though we may ordinarily consider resting to entail retreat in the exclusive sense of removal or withdrawal, this is not strictly true. Looking to Heidegger, for example, we can see how home remains in porous exchange with the world even when dwelling is conceptualized as staying and resting. In his analysis, Heidegger does not speak of a pure staying or preserving *itself*, but, through his concept of the fourfold,[69] a staying *with* things, and *with* place: "To say that mortals *are* is to say that in dwelling they persist through spaces by virtue of their stay among things and *places*" (my modification).[70] Staying, on Heidegger's account, is always staying *with* and *among*. And as Jeff Malpas argues, rendered as such, dwelling can never amount to a full withdrawal:

> Such preserving and sparing is not, however, a matter of our withdrawing from things. This is, indeed, already evident in Heidegger's talk of "letting be"

[*Gelassenheit*] in the 1930 essay "On the Essence of Truth." There Heidegger says that "to let beings be . . . does not refer to neglect and indifference but rather the opposite. To let be is to engage oneself with beings."[71]

Presented in its "middle-voice" between action and inactivity, to dwell *in* place or *among* things means to dwell with an attunement to place as place and things as things. In doing so, dwelling reflects a porosity insofar as it consists of a sensitivity and receptivity to the world as it unfolds to the dweller, and the dweller to it. Even in its stillest moments, dwelling involves a coming and going; dwelling is porous.

The Porosity of the Body, or Intercorporeality

If homes—analyzed above primarily through the structures in which we dwell—are porous, then there is also a strong case to make for the lived body as porous. Indeed, the image of porosity is strikingly evoked by Jean-Luc Nancy in his concept of "ex*peau*sition"[72]—where the body's outer most layer, the skin (*le peau*), marks something of a liminal space between body and world, reminding us of the very literal bodily pores exposing each to the other; we breathe through these pores of the skin. But so too are such philosophical gestures present in our current analyses. In addition to the passage above on dwelling as staying with things and places, Heidegger's *Dasein*—though notoriously lacking a body[73]—is also always already a being-with, or *mit-sein*.[74] More pertinently for our purposes, the distinctively "lived" character of Merleau-Ponty's phenomenal body is already imbued with such porosity to the extent that a "lived" body is one constituted by its responsivity to (and influence by) people, places, practices, situations, and processes. Numerous examples furnished by Merleau-Ponty show this to be the case, including the studies of bodily adjustments to spatial-level inversions,[75] the use and incorporation of bodily prosthetics, and so forth. More than a general demonstration of bodily dynamism and flexibility, these examples serve to demonstrate the body's fluidity and continual experience of change, such that the definite article we use for "the" body misleadingly evokes a constant and identifiably self-same body untouched by time, place, and situation.[76] In other words, the lived body's ever-changing perception of the world (with its endless variety of situations), and its capacity to be affected by and to respond to them, is *constitutive* of its status as a lived body. In our earlier analysis we noted that a house without "pores" no longer serves as a home but rather more aptly as a dungeon, a cellar, or a jail—in a similar sense, a body no longer in porous exchange with its world, no longer affected by and responsive to it, has in some significant sense, become an inanimate body, or a corpse.[77,78] The question of bodily porosity, then, is one of ontological import.

What I have provisionally called "porosity" here, Gail Weiss in her book names "intercorporeality." Drawing on Merleau-Ponty and psychoanalyst Paul Schilder, Weiss argues that our body images are "constructed, reconstructed, and deconstructed through a series of ongoing, intercorporeal exchanges."[79] Such intercorporeality, she argues, is not a deficiency in need of overcoming via the assertion of bodily autonomy—even when expressed in undesirable practices of bodily objectification (racial or gendered)—since it speaks to the fundamental sociality and situatedness of our lived bodies. In her reading of Young's essay, "Throwing Like a Girl"[80] which we considered in chapter 1, Weiss therefore criticizes Young for blaming patriarchy's objectifying gaze (or in Weiss's words, the "socially-referred character of bodily existence"), for inhibiting bodily expression in girls and relegating female bodily experience to the realm of the immanent. While Weiss does not deny that patriarchy has had this effect, her point is that the exclusively negative valuation of this "socially-referred character" of female embodiment remains too tethered to a Cartesian valorization of the transcendental subject. This is because she insists on a relational ontology, one in which we are co-constituted by our relations with others and with the world, even if this sometimes means we are co-constituted through oppressive practices. Given this, she argues that we ought not to be too quick to identify the other's gaze as that which stands to be overcome. For Weiss, such a charge leads us back to the suspect division between transcendence and immanence. She writes: "I would resist viewing the socially-referred character of bodily existence as inherently negative or as leading inevitably to immanence. This is because all of our (men's as well as women's) actions have a socially referred character insofar as they arise in response to a social situation."[81] I take up Weiss's argument more fully in the following chapter on the question of chiasm, but I raise the question here in order to signal that constitutive porosity should not be viewed solely in negative terms since it is precisely what gives both home and body their character. That is, I agree with Weiss that it is precisely by acknowledging the porosity of bodies and homes that we can hold on to their importance, but without falling into the trap of valorizing them as coherent, self-constituting, and self-contained entities. And while there are indeed harmful modes or degrees of this porosity or "social reference" (racial and gendered objectification being but two examples), we should not confuse this with the idea that constitution by the "other" or "outside" is always, and in and of itself, harmful.[82] As Weiss argues, such a stance erases an important aspect of the phenomenologically lived body as constitutively and necessarily intercorporeal. Thus, while the slippage into an existential phenomenology is an easy one (Young and Merleau-Ponty, both make efforts to move beyond this framework, with varying success), it is also something that Weiss (and eventually even Young herself[83]) warns us against.

To return to the question of racialization and "world" travelling then, the argument regarding the constitutive porosity of the body and home helps us now to identify in more nuanced terms the problematic framing of the question as home versus travel. Moreover, it helps us to address some of the concerns raised earlier in relation to the caution of being too much at-home. Specifically, the concern that one is too much "at-home" (whether in the case of whiteness or in the case of clinging to identity markers in response to one's homelessness) risks importing existential frameworks that remain too heavily tethered to their Cartesian commitments. If the home is constitutively porous, this means that even in the stillest moments of rest and withdrawal, dwelling unfolds in and alongside the presence of the world and its others. Being-at-home in a house can never amount to complete isolation or withdrawal, in the same way that being-at-home in one's body never fully dispels the presence or glance (and gaze) of the other.[84] This has implications for our analysis of the racializing gaze, as we will explore in chapter 4. Nonetheless, this constitutive porosity of the home does not displace the value of "world"-travelling as identified by Lugones. This is because to say that the home is porous is not to say that we remain always attentive and attuned to this porosity. Travelling then is one way we are made to thematize this more explicitly. Or put differently, as Weiss argues in relation to the body, there can be situations where it is both productive and valuable to explicitly engage in an intentional objectification of one's body—the micro attention to muscles in elite sports is one such example. But of course the athlete's objectification of their own body (or a coach's objectification of the athlete's body) is distinct from the case of racial or gendered objectification insofar as their endeavors are directed towards the explicit and mutually understood and shared goal of athletic improvement. This meaningful context and shared understanding is of course absent in the case of racial or gendered bodily objectification. What the example invites us to consider then is how relations of power (understood broadly to include political, historical, economic, social, and cultural contexts) remain crucial in our normative valuations of the "ideal" levels of being-at-home.

Power and a Critical Revision of "Travelling"

Indeed I argue that the question of power does more than "factor" into our normative evaluations of intercorporeality and porosity. Remaining within the terms of home-and-travel allows us to see how power injects not just an evaluative metric, but more strikingly, a definitional one. This is because the question of whether an activity can be properly described as "world"-*travelling* as opposed to "forced migration," for example, turns precisely on this question of power. In Lugones' characterization of women of color's travelling to and between worlds, the involuntary *and* necessary nature of this activity calls into question whether it is really "travelling," or whether it is a state of forced nomadism or homelessness. In other words, to what extent does "travelling" presuppose an economy of choice or volition? The term "travel," perhaps especially so in the age of accessible and safe commercial transportation, has come to be associated if not almost exclusively with leisure, then at least minimally with a level of economic, social, and political freedom, as well as worldly curiosity. Can one be said to "world"-*travel* if these minimal conditions (the freedoms) are not met? Those who cross the seas in order to seek political refuge, for example, are not usually considered travellers, although their journeys and subsequent adjustment certainly consist of travelling in its literal and figurative senses. Instead, we understand them more properly as refugees or exiles and not travellers, because the conditions under which they displace themselves—when remaining home is no longer a viable option—do not make room for questions of choice or volition. In what sense, then, are racialized persons *made* to travel by their relatively disempowered social, historical, political, and economic positions? Recall our discussion in chapter 2, of the way racialized people bear the burden of adapting their bodily movements, behavior, and comportment so as to pre-empt or manage racist projections—this is one example of the differential power relations that call into question the term "travel" in such a context. The question of "choice" is not a meaningful one in the face of racist bodily habits which subject the racialized person to anything from disadvantage, discrimination, to bodily danger.[85] Examples abound—the adjustment of African American Vernacular English in order to appear "professional," the adherence to white beauty standards in order to forge careers in news broadcasting, and so forth. While these, as noted earlier, resonate with the work or effort involved in travelling, what I argue here is that they exceed the definition of travelling insofar as they constitute more or less *necessary* activities.

But if the ascription "travelling" is not entirely accurate, then it is at least intelligible insofar as it serves as a way to celebrate the agility, flexibility, and creativity of those who engage in such endeavors. (This is a particularly salient point in view of the tendency to pathologize those whose experiences are framed by their racialization, as discussed in chapter 2.) Lugones is explicit in her wish to pay homage to such work and skill, and as I will argue later, there are certainly productive moments that arise from the often painful experiences of displacement or alienation. In this regard Lugones's concept goes some way to drawing out the multidimensionality of displacement. Further, if the question of power jeopardizes the ascription of "travelling" in the case of racialized bodies (or in the case of "new Mestizas," of whom Lugones writes), this is not to say that the experience of racialization therefore amounts to, at the other extreme, homelessness or refuge. While the unhomely experience of racialization shares aspects in common with these experiences, there are important ways in which they are different. As the experience of homeless people (tellingly called SDFs—*sans domicile fixe*—in French) bears out, the physical dislocation from one shelter to another, or one sleeping area to another, is called homelessness precisely because there is no steady or stable home from which one departs and to which one returns. It is a kind of forced nomadism. But recalling Fanon's suggestion that the Black man *can* feel at-home among "his own," it is not necessarily the case that racialized people lack *any* sense home. Indeed, hooks' earlier description on homeplaces speaks to the richness and importance of home in Black communities, and in addition to this we can look to the success of coalition groups to see how racialized people can and do feel at-home, depending on one's environs and collective projects.

These reflections might also prompt us to think through some of the finer distinctions within the racialized experience of uncanniness. For example, the question of immigration and displacement has loomed large over this discussion, without explicit treatment so far. And yet for many, the experience of racialized uncanniness is also one inextricably bound with the experience of migration (whether that is first- or second-generation), and more often than not, the experience of forced migration. Given the immediate causes of displacement—war, conflict, poverty, persecution, environmental destruction—themselves often flow from the legacies of colonialism and practices of Western economic imperialism, it is people of color who are disproportionately affected and driven into forced migration. Here the experience of uncanniness is doubled and takes on an additional layer, with the status of not-at-home expressing a more literal being-outside of the socio-political membership. Of course these modes of uncanniness remain co-implicated, as evident in the way anti-immigration discourses are invariably laced with racist overtones, and the way they never fail to generate afresh, racist sentiment against people of color irrespective of citizenship status—as evidenced in the immediate aftermath of "Brexit," as well as the presidential election of Donald Trump in the United States. Intertwined as they are, however, what the question of immigration underscores for us is the different and profound experience of uncanniness in another register—that of being forced to leave one's home, and having no home to which one can return—which should in turn caution us against subsuming the experience of migration (particularly forced migration) in our analysis of racialized uncanniness.

Being-at-Ease

Given the complexities entailed in the concept of "world"-travelling, we might turn to Ortega's exploration of the concept being-at-ease, which she traces from Heidegger's existential analytic in *Being and Time*. This, I suggest, might serve to qualify our exploration of *die Unheimlichkeit*, calling for a finer distinction between the uncanny (*unheimlich*), unhomely (*unheimisch*), and the not-being-at-home (*das Nicht-zuhause-sein*). In her chapter on "hometactics" and what she terms our "multiplicitous selves" (a concept loosely equivocating Weiss's "multiple body images," of Merleau-Pontian lineage), Ortega uses this Heideggerian concept of being-at-ease to describe the peripheral marginal experience of lesbian Latina women. Here, it is not so much that these women are homeless, since their multi-dimensionality makes it meaningless to speak of any *single* home. Instead, Ortega argues that it makes more sense to speak of the "multiplicitous selves."[86] Within this schema, we see how despite the change in metric (from homelessness to unhomely or to not-being-at-ease), the power question remains. Ortega writes, for example, that while "there is a sense in which all of us are multiplicitous selves" (a concept here which puts in play our notion of porosity), there is a meaningful distinction between those who find themselves "mostly at ease in the world" and those who do not.[87] For Ortega, this comes down to a question of power and context, and the combination of these can mean that the question of porosity, intercorporeality, or multiplicitous selves only becomes a question for some and not others. She writes, "For example, consider the way in which power relations and other economic, social, and cultural issues related to the north-south border affect the new mestiza self and lead her to feel the contradictory aspects of herself and the sense of being at the limen."[88]

This self- or double-consciousness is thus a phenomenon unevenly experienced, and in the context of the home question, it means that while the home is itself constitutively porous, one's experience of it, given the network of relations in which we are situated, can be more porous—and unwillingly so—than another's. In other words, while the home's porosity guards against the possibility of a romanticized or idealized conception of insularity and self-reference, we should not take this to mean that we all experience this exposure (or ex*peau*sure) to the same extent or in the same way. Or, relating the analysis more directly to the question of porosity and intercorporeality, at what point does our constitutive opening to the world and its others become more like a deluge? Is it still meaningful to speak of a porosity or intercorporeality when one is effectively constituted by the other? Or when one is, to invoke the term once more, "overdetermined" by the other? The experience of oneself as strange for others and strange to oneself (to the extent that one is invited to take a distanced, if not objectifying, stance to the self) are not, in my view, effaced or to be confused with the important fact that all bodily experience is structurally embedded with these possibilities. That is, the fact that we *can* all in one way or another be called to attend explicitly to our bodies, their differences and strangeness, does not diminish the deep anguish when racialized bodies in particular, due to the imposed schema of normative whiteness, are systematically *required* to do so.

PART 3—DO WE NEED THE HOME?

If the previous two sections have been successful in claiming that the experience of racialized embodiment is itself an experience in uncanniness (in the sense of strangeness *and* unhomeliness)—though importantly qualified with the claim that being in general is always marked by a constitutive porosity—then a final analysis is required to give significance to the this claim of racialized uncanniness. That is, if racism and the process of racialization renders one uncanny (in its different valences), we should then inquire after the value or utility of being or feeling canny (in the technical sense of feeling at-home). More bluntly: do we need the home, or do we need to feel at-home, and why? In this final part I explore two contrasting responses to this question through the work of Merleau-Ponty and Heidegger. Looking first to Merleau-Ponty, I examine how his account of the habitual body relies on a sense of being-homely (or being-habitual) in the execution of one's projects. In his account, the home-body is important because it orients us, providing the ground for the bodily sense of "I can." It is from and through the home-body that we can begin to act. Turning then to Heidegger, who of course supplies the initial inspiration for the "homeward" turn in this chapter, our initial response gets fine-tuned. As a pioneering thinker of place and placiality, Heidegger lays great value on the home and, as we have seen, its associated activity of dwelling. And yet, by revisiting his thought we see how his own treatment of *die Unheimlichkeit* passes through different colorations during the course of his thinking. In particular, when we return to a closer reading of Heidegger's lecture course *Hölderlin's Hymn "Der Ister,"* we see how uncanniness (in its full sense of strangeness and not-being-at-home) can also be of existential importance.

Merleau-Ponty and the "I Can" in the Habitual-Homely Body

In a sense the question of the value in being-at-home or being-at-ease has been already intimated in our earlier consideration of the habitual body and its associated modes of motility. Recall our examination of Young's "Throwing Like a Girl," where she tracks the way in which the non-objectified and non-sexualized male body moves with greater fluidity and freedom, generating a greater depth of bodily space for itself and comfortably filling out that space. This body, in contrast to the lived female body in patriarchal society, is not inhibited by a consciousness or double- (or self-) consciousness[89] as a result of its sexualization and objectification, and nor is it a body reined in by the imperatives of tidiness or caution (owing to bodily "fragility"). Lacking these meaningful contexts, the boy's bodily motility is a fitting example of how a sense of being-at-home or at-ease supplies the "I can" of Merleau-Ponty's habitual body. This positively valenced account of the habitual body is also echoed in our earlier account of bodily habit as enabling and forward-looking. Recall that habit as it appears in Merleau-Ponty's rendering accounted not just for a historical sedimentation of acquired movements and bodily dispositions, but also the way in which our bodies become oriented toward certain possibilities. Merleau-Ponty's own example of the organist, along with my example of parkour, illustrated how bodies become oriented through habits, which then open us up to a field of possibility for action and creativity. On a first pass then, to our question, do we need the home?, we are supplied with the answer "yes"; we need the home because it allows us to function, to go about our daily projects unimpeded by an objectifying—and ultimately inhibiting—gaze, and indeed because habits themselves, insofar as they are understood as a bodily habituation or orientation, supply the ground or launching pad for action and creativity.[90]

Note then the resonance with our earlier conceptions of home: the "I can" in the habitual body is in a sense continuous with the characterization of home as starting place. It echoes, for example, Rykwert's notion of home as a launching place, or as the place from which we begin, and Jacobson similarly claims that the familiarity and shelter of home is such that it enables and empowers us to act. Asserting once more the parallel of body and home, Jacobson draws explicitly on Merleau-Ponty's claim that the body is generative of space, in order to make a similar argument about the home:

> It is the body, then, that lets us be spread throughout our world, bring specific things forward from the background of this world, and experience these things as having particular places and positions in the world. Thus, "far from my body's being for me no more than a fragment of space, there would be no space at all for me if I had no body" (Merleau-Ponty, PhP, p. 102). While we do not typically notice this constitutive role of the body, it pervasively shapes every possible activity in which we do take active notice. The body—and, more specifically, the body in its passivity, in its capacity as the receptive, given core in the background of all experience—is fundamentally the base of our action, and this is equally true of our home.[91]

While I have taken issue with Jacobson's characterization of the home as noted earlier, on this point we are in agreement; there is something foundational about the home that is fundamentally productive. Insofar as we all need a "here" from where to begin, the home is not just a place among places but something more; a *particular* place imbued with the exemplary qualities of belonging and orientation, qualities that theorists attribute to place more generally. The home is in a certain sense *a paradigmatic place*.

Despite her reservations, namely, the tendency to romanticize the home and divest it of its intrinsically political character, Young too agrees: "While agreeing with much of this [feminist] critique, I have also argued that home carries a core positive meaning as the material anchor for a sense of agency and a shifting and fluid identity. This concept of home does not oppose the personal and the political, but instead describes conditions that make the political possible."[92] As Young's critical intervention demonstrates, it *is* possible to hold home in a privileged relation to generativity and creativity, while remaining suspicious of the characterization of home primarily in terms of insularity or enclosure. On this view, we can affirm the importance of the home while challenging our traditional conceptions of it. As I have argued, this is precisely the point at which Jacobson's account runs into trouble, but it is a point which I would like to further explore. In order to do so, I propose that we turn to the tension in Heidegger's own thought, working through his account of the home as it emerges in his treatment of the uncanny and dwelling.

Revisiting Heidegger's *die Unheimlichkeit*

Recall that in *Being and Time*, uncanniness appears on the scene concomitantly with Dasein's experience of anxiety. At this point, having pulled itself away from its fallenness into *das Man*, Dasein can now enter into a more "authentic" mode of being. Dasein is thus fundamentally marked by an uncanniness, and it is in its participation in "the They" that this uncanniness is eluded or postponed. Dasein "flees" itself, seeking out refuge in the "tranquilizing familiarity" of *das Man*, a movement from the uncanny to the canny (in the sense of the familiar), from the not-at-home to the home.[93] It bears repeating that this absorption in *das Man* or this "being-at-home" is explicitly characterized by Heidegger as both a *fleeing* and a mark of Dasein's *inauthentic* "potentiality-for-Being-its-Self."[94] Yet this changes in the later Heidegger. Recall the claim in the 1951 "Building, Dwelling, Thinking" that dwelling (the activity most intimately associated with the home) *is* a kind of being. Here, as in other pieces such as "Poetically Man Dwells," home and being-at-home takes on a different valuation, held up even as the exemplary human activity: "The proper dwelling plight lies in this, that mortals ever search anew for the essence of dwelling, that they must *ever learn to dwell*."[95] While it is of course true that the subjects of Heidegger's investigations across these writings are not the same (Dasein is not simply or necessarily "man" or "mortal," though I think one can argue that these terms sufficiently equivocate it), I suggest that we can make better sense of this shift by looking to some of his middle period writing, particularly the 1942 lecture course on *Hölderlin's Hymn "Der Ister,"* where questions of the uncanny figure both prominently and differently.

In *Hölderlin's Hymn* Heidegger's reading and repeated rereading of the opening choral ode in *Antigone* leads him to claim that Sophocles' *deinon*—which he translates as *das Unheimliche* (the uncanny)—captures that which lies at the fundamental core of what it is to be human: "The uncanniest of the uncanny is the human being."[96] In some ways resonant with *Being and Time*, Heidegger claims uncanniness as an ineluctable feature of being human. And yet a significant difference emerges when it comes to the question of how this uncanniness gets taken up; for it is not just that we are ineluctably uncanny, it is also that we *must passage through it* in order to become homely. Heidegger writes, "Coming to be at home is thus a passage through the foreign."[97] This entails two things: first, Heidegger sets up human being as that which always, in spite of itself, veers toward the homely. As fundamentally uncanny creatures, we crave the home. But unlike in *Being and Time*, we do not "fall" or become "absorbed" into it in some idle fashion (as in Dasein's fallenness into *das Man*), rather it is that toward which we explicitly orient ourselves, that toward which we reach out: "In that case, Sophocles' word [*deinon*], which speaks of the human being as the most uncanny being, says that human beings are, in a singular sense, not homely, *and that their care is to become homely*"[98] (my emphasis). Being human—*authentically* human—entails a movement toward the homely, not away from it. And yet, pertinently for our purposes, Heidegger's claim also entails an important second point: that the uncanny constitutes an *essential* encounter in our passage toward the homely. That is to say, becoming homely does not mean overcoming the foreign, sidestepping, or refusing it, but rather, journeying *through* it, and confronting it. As Heidegger writes, "Being unhomely is no mere deviance from the homely, but rather the converse: a seeking and searching out the homely, a seeking that at times does not know itself. This seeking shies at no danger and no risk. Everywhere it ventures and is underway in all directions."[99] Little wonder, then, why Antigone is held up as the "supreme" uncanny. Not only is she uncanny by virtue of her muddied family history, relations to the state, and overall predicament, but she *strives to make sense of these* by pushing ahead (some would say, stubbornly[100]) with Theban burial rites in the face of a situation that is from the outset poisoned. It is her effort at "becoming homely in being unhomely."[101]

This represents a deviation from the earlier accounts of Heideggerian uncanniness and homeliness under consideration, and yet I argue that it does not necessarily amount to a rupture in his thought. Rather, the differential treatment of uncanniness across these works signals the way in which the concept itself provides breadth for—perhaps even solicits—such multi-directional exploitation in drawing out certain emphases. Thus while we see Heidegger embracing the strange and uncanny in *Hölderlin's Hymn* (and more reluctantly so in *Being and Time*), this stands in no contradiction to his insistence on the centrality and importance of home and place throughout his work, and particularly in "Building, Dwelling, Thinking." Instead we see an instructive forking out of the twin senses of uncanniness, of the strange and unhomely, despite the fact that it is he who first alerted us to their entanglement. On the one hand, the affirmation of dwelling in Heidegger's writing reinforces the importance not only of place in general, but also of *home* as a particular and exemplary place of staying, resting, and belonging. However, when we read together his various accounts of uncanniness, it is impressed upon us that this homeliness *cannot and does not* seal us off into a bubble of ownness or familiarity. Since strangeness is experienced and refracted through our encounter with others, milieux, places, or practices, there is a relationality that preserved at the heart of the homely. The interplay between these two analyses is fittingly gathered together in Heidegger's singular imperative, to become "homely in the unhomely." In contrast to Jacobson who insists on the importance of the home and yet goes on to characterize the home in terms of enclosure, in Heidegger we have a way to *simultaneously* think the power of home (or dwelling) while holding onto our fundamental exposure and relationality of the not-at-home.

Racialized Uncanniness, Redux

We have travelled some way from the question of racialized embodiment. But the enquiry undertaken here into the normative value of home lends political and ethical import and urgency to our claim that racialization entails the experience of uncanniness. To begin with, Merleau-Ponty in his account of the habitual body allows us to grasp the necessity of home and a homely orientation as the basis of our participation in the world. Having explored the intimate connection between the habitual and the homely (insinuated as we noted earlier through the pair *wohnen* and *die Gewohnheit*), we saw how the characterization of the racialized body as not-at-home provided an additional dimension to the description of its uncanniness. In particular, our analysis of bodily fragmentation and alienation in chapter 2 is now refracted through an analysis of not-being-at-home. Racialized embodiment entails not only a spatial fragmentation but also a displacement from the home, the consequences of which we see drawn out by thinkers such as Young. Passing this through a Heideggerian analysis, the account yields further nuance. As I have argued, there is room in Heidegger for a deeper and more meaningful encounter with the uncanny, not only as that which inhibits or impedes our embodied being. While it is true that in his broader œuvre, Heidegger gives priority to space and place in the constitution and experience of our being, subordinating (even disregarding) the body and bodily orientation to the power and solicitation of place, and while it is also true that home and dwelling become important cornerstones in his conception of being in both its ontological and poetic figurations, at the same time, he holds onto the uncanny as a quintessentially inexpungible part of what it means to be or become homely. This significantly reframes our current examination of racialized embodiment, in which the experience of uncanniness (as strange and/or unhomely) has almost exclusively been cast in negative or obstructive terms.

For example, I think that Heidegger's multivalenced reading of the concept prevents us from declaring too swiftly that one's racialization is experienced *exclusively* in this impoverished way. By this I refer not only to the deep camaraderie or rich communities that emerge in response to shared experiences of racism, but more pointedly to the way one's direct experience of racialized uncanniness throws a naked light on the mechanisms of power, and the role of history, discourse, and intersubjectivity in the formation of one's sense of self. This is a fact that becomes largely obfuscated (deliberately or not) for those whose whiteness renders their racial identity "invisible." Put differently, for all its fragmentary and interruptive effect—and these are many and real—a racialized double-consciousness is still, quite literally, the acquisition of an *additional* consciousness, a new epistemic standpoint from which to reflect upon one's place in, and relations with, the world. It is no coincidence, for example, that many of those working in critical race philosophy (as well as feminist or queer philosophy) seem to argue for a more relational or historically situated understanding of selfhood. Theoretical work borne of marginal experiences often share this philosophical disposition because of the way the experience of exclusion and marginalization can at the same time, better position one for critique and illumination of the problems with dominant conceptual schemata.[102] But more than intellectual insight and contribution, this speaks to the richness and generativity of such experiences. Couching this in more Heideggarian terms, I think we can maintain, while not wavering in our critique of the disastrousness of racism,[103] that there *can be* something uniquely productive or insightful about the experience of one's own uncanniness (as strangeness *and* unhomeliness), even when this uncanniness is brought upon by the deep wounds of racist habits, actions, and histories.

Of course all this needs to be qualified—heavily and profoundly—with the question of power, and the way it interposes in our analysis of the productive moment of racialized uncanniness. Indeed, as in our analysis of "world"-travelling, the question of power does not so much interject as it frames the analysis, since it more than matters that those who experience themselves as uncanny rarely do so by their own volition. So herein lies a critical point of distinction with Heidegger's more sympathetic reading of *die Unheimlichkeit*: For while he is right to identify an ontological uncanniness that is essential and fundamental to all being, what we have in the case of racialization is an *additional* kind of uncanniness that is *particular* to racialized being. More than the general disorientation and natal condition we all experience having been thrown into the world and charged with the task of making sense of it,[104] racialized uncanniness *arises from a socially and historically constructed system of racist oppression and domination*, a system which imposes upon the racialized body an uncanniness that is not indigenous to it, and moreover, an uncanniness that *benefits* its white oppressors. As we saw in chapter 1, the habitual perception of racialized bodies (e.g., in the case of veiled Muslim women) *serves to reinforce* the normalized invisibility of white bodies, in the same way that our discussion in chapter 2 revealed the ways in which the spatio-temporal fragmentation in racialized bodies (in response to the stresses of navigating a racist world) ensures the smoothness and spatial extension of white embodiment. In other words, whiteness gets installed as the normative center by virtue of this pushing out of racialized bodies to the margins; the canniness of white bodies is predicated on the uncanniness of racialized ones. Our analysis of Heideggerian uncanniness thus needs to be distinguished from racialized uncanniness on that critical score. But what his more subtle reading does contribute to our account of racialized uncanniness, however, is the way in which this uncanniness can be taken up productively and generatively. It gives us a way, for example, to articulate the richness of racialized being, even where that is a richness borne of pain and injustice. At the same time, it also offers us some political insight, with the call to the uncanny prompting us to take up a systematic interrogation of the invisible privilege (and "canniness") of whiteness.

Finally, in my concluding remarks to the chapter, I note that despite the way I have in this last part pitted Heidegger against Merleau-Ponty (concentrating here on the latter's analysis of habitual body), I admit that positioning Merleau-Ponty in this way does not do justice to the full thrust of his work. There is an opening in Merleau-Ponty's thought, if not for the uncanny directly, then at the least for a fundamental encounter with the other and others, that is, a conceptual schema which equally dislodges us from the egoistic center of existential phenomenology. Indeed, we can easily locate points of rejoinder between Merleau-Ponty and Heidegger, moments when Merleau-Ponty's thought echoes centrality of uncanniness in Heidegger's when the latter writes:

All this is true only on the presupposition that initially human beings are not and indeed never "of themselves," or through any self-making, in that which is their own. In that case, however, to dwell in what is one's own is what comes last and is seldom successful and always remains what is most difficult. Yet if the river determines the locality of the homely, then it is of essential assistance in becoming homely in what is one's own.[105]

As I will argue in the following chapter, there is also a pregnant account of this not being "of-oneself" to be found in Merleau-Ponty. But whereas for Heidegger during this period, the source of this "not-ownness" can be found in the uncanny, for Merleau-Ponty this is developed more saliently through his account of the flesh, an account which I argue opens up the space for thinking through our relationality and intertwinement with others, and with the world.

NOTES

1. My occasional literal translation of *unheimlichkeit* (uncanniness) as "unhomeliness" serves to draw out the reference to "home" that Heidegger is so keen to emphasize. In doing so, however, this risks collapsing the term *unheimlich* (uncanny) into *unheimisch* (unhomely), which while very closely related for Heidegger still remains distinct. My invocations of "unhomely" or "unhomeliness," then, are intended only to highlight this important connection, and not to subsume *unheimlich* into *unheimisch* as such. For a discussion on Heidegger's own close pairing of *unheimlich* and *unheimisch* see Richard Capobianco, *Engaging Heidegger* (Toronto: University of Toronto Press, 2010), 58.

2. I admit, however, that these difficult issues ought to be given more consideration than I can give them here. Heidegger's well documented anti-Semitism is cause for concern not just from a biographical point of view, but also from a philosophical one—they prompt us to ask not only whether aspects his thought are infected with racism (a question too bluntly formulated), but also *why* his own deep meditations about the nature of being and Being-in-the-world fail to prevent him from lending support to a party that actively undertakes the extermination of peoples. That is, it raises deeper questions about the nature of philosophical inquiry and its relation to the lived world—and lives in the world. I note that such questions ought to be asked not only of Heidegger, but also equally of other thinkers in the philosophical canon.

3. Martin Heidegger, *Being and Time*, trans. John Macquarie and Edward Robinson (New York: Harper & Row, 1962), 229.

4. Ibid., 233.

5. Ibid.

6. Ibid.

7. Fanon, *Black Skin, White Masks*, 113.

8. This sense of not-belonging is further reflected in the popular racist taunts in Australia: "Go home!" and "We grew here, you flew here." In addition to the xenophobia and historical ignorance they betray (Australia is after all a colonized country), these taunts also speak clearly to how the sense of home and belonging figure strongly in racist conceptions of "us versus them."

9. Recall my earlier remarks in the introduction to the book, regarding my use of the term "body," which I use in its broadest sense to designate something like "self." Thus, this statement is akin to saying that the racialized body is not at home in itself.

10. Yancy, *Black Bodies, White Gazes*, 2.

11. Edward S. Casey, *Getting Back into Place: Toward a Renewed Understanding of the Place-World* (Bloomington: Indiana University Press, 2009 (2nd ed.)), 299.

12. Joseph Rykwert, "House and Home," *Social Research* 58 (1991): 51.

13. Rykwert, "House and Home," 54.

14. Iris Marion Young, "House and Home: Feminist Variations on a Theme" in *On Female Body Experience: 'Throwing Like a Girl' and Other Essays*, 139.

15. Ibid.

16. Both Young and Casey, in particular, do acknowledge that dwelling can take place outside traditional houses: "In many societies 'home' refers to the village or square, together with its houses, and dwelling takes place both in and out of doors. . . . Even in modern capitalist cities some people 'live' more in their neighborhood or on their block than in their houses. They sit in squares, on stoops, in bars and coffeehouses, going to their houses mostly to sleep." (Young, "House and Home," 131–132) and "Parks, which are not 'buildings' in any usual sense, sometimes not offering the barest of shelter or domestic amenities, can be dwelling places. Indeed, the places where people spontaneously congregate such as street corners and stoops of apartment buildings, are genuine dwelling places." (Casey, *Getting Back into Place*, 115). I also thank Brian Irwin for the reference to "third places."

17. Part of Rykwert's goal in this essay is to remind his profession that they are in the business of building *houses*, and not homes. Architects have strayed in their thinking about this, according to him: "Architects tried to fit everything that went on in a 'typical' household into a closely packed shell. It was as if they saw their business not as the provision of houses but the enclosure of Home. . . . They forgot the important moral which Karl Kraus once tried to instil in them, when he said that he expected of the city to provide him with water, gas, electricity, and working roads: *die Gemütlichkeit besorge ich*—I will supply the homeliness, he added." It is perhaps for this reason that the distinction between house and home can seem a little pronounced in his account. Rykwert, "House and Home," 60.

18. One obvious example of this is the issue of urban planning and disability access. The way places (homes or other) are designed can deeply shape the way certain bodies are made to feel at-home or not-at-home, welcome or unwelcome, included or excluded. Questions of body schema and bodily habit thus are intimately connected with the home. In an example more relevant to our investigation, George Lipsitz also looks at some contemporary forms of racial segregation in the context of shared urban space in his book *How Racism Takes Place* (Philadelphia: Temple University Press, 2011).

19. Martin Heidegger, "Building, Dwelling, Thinking" in David Krell (ed.), *Martin Heidegger Basic Writings* (New York: Harper Perennial, 2008), 347–348. I have also inserted the original German terms here in order to more clearly designate the different modes of dwelling and housing named by Heidegger in this passage. Martin Heidegger, "Bauen Wohnen Denken" in Friedrich-Wilhelm von Herrmann (ed.), *Vorträge und Aufsätze* GA 7 (Frankfurt am Main: Klostermann, 2000), 146–164, 147.

20. Ibid., 348.

21. Martin Heidegger, *Hölderlin's Hymn "Der Ister,"* trans. William McNeill and Julia Davis (Bloomington: Indiana University Press, 1996), 20.

22. Rykwert, "House and Home," 52.

23. Young, "House and Home," 139.

24. Ibid., 142. Indeed Young argues that Heidegger does not go far *enough* in exploring preservation as one of the two meanings of building, instead falling into the well-worn trap of privileging its more ostensibly 'active' counterpart—constructing. According to Young, while 'preservation' is one of the two senses of building that Heidegger names, it regrettably ends up being overshadowed by a telling over-emphasis on the second concept, construction. Such a move, she continues, is symptomatic of a broader tendency of the Western philosophical tradition to devalue the importance and creativity of that which outwardly appears as passive, and for that which is typically associated with women's work.

25. Casey, *Getting Back into Place*, 114.

26. Ibid., 115.

27. Ibid., 115–116.

28. Rykwert, "House and Home," 54.

29. In contrast, the French language is one example where a separate verb (*reposer*) is required to designate our second sense of resting, and the verb *rester* refers purely to a physical staying. Interestingly, note that the English bivalence seems to derive from two different etymological sources: rest in the first sense of reposing derives from the Germanic *raston* or *rasten* ("from a root meaning 'league' or 'mile' [referring to a distance after which one rests]"); whereas, rest in the second sense of staying derives from the Latin *restare* which gets taken up as *rester* in Old French.

30. Heidegger, *Hölderlin's Hymn*, 20.

31. An important qualification here: I describe the home as "substantially" but not "exclusively" a place of rest, since there are, of course, many homes in which one does not and cannot rest. Homes in which one finds domestic violence, emotional or sexual abuse, or even homes which are defined by unhappy relationships are all too real examples of where the home is anything but a place of rest (in the sense of repose). Further, we should not romanticize this "restfulness"; what looks from the outside to be restfulness may just as easily be experienced from the inside as boredom or confinement, not to mention the amount of "invisible work" that takes place within a home. I am thinking here of the traditional confinement of women to the home and home-making activity, and the non-recognition (even exploitation) of their labor. In these cases, the kind of home-dwelling afforded is closer to "rest" in the first sense, as a place where one stays, or is made to stay. Such considerations also present a serious

caution against the impulse to eulogize the home, and in the scheme of my exploration, they highlight the need to think home in its three senses (starting place, bodily habit, and rest) concomitantly.

32. Casey, *Getting Back into Place*, 121.

33. Gaston Bachelard, *The Poetics of Space* (Boston: Beacon Press, 1994), 6. Bachelard speaks primarily of "house" (*la maison*) throughout his book, but in a way that leads me to think that he is actually speaking about "home"—noting, of course, that no single term in Bachelard's native French language fully equivocates the English term "home." *La maison* tends to refer to the physical structure (and thus is closer to "house"), whereas *foyer* can mean home, but also designates a hallway or meeting place, much like the English meaning of "foyer." We get closer with the expression *être chez soi* (e.g., "make yourself at home" is *faites comme chez vous*) but this takes us away from the nominal form of "home," and loses the references to building and structures that "home" does carry.

34. Maurice Merleau-Ponty, "Eye and Mind" in Galen A. Johnson (ed.), *The Merleau-Ponty Aesthetics Reader: Philosophy and Painting* (Evanston: Northwestern University Press, 1993), 121. The sentence in the original reads: "*La science manipule les choses et renonce à les habiter.*"

35. Merleau-Ponty, *Phenomenology of Perception*, 93.

36. Ibid.

37. Casey, "Habitual Body and Memory in Merleau-Ponty," 218.

38. Kirsten Jacobson, "A Developed Nature: a Phenomenological Account of the Experience of Home" in *Continental* Philosophy *Review* 42 (2009): 355–373.

39. Ibid., 361. She also writes earlier: "home is phenomenologically akin to our body" at 359.

40. Ibid., 361.

41. Casey, *Getting Back into Place*, 120.

42. Drew Leder, *The Absent Body* (Chicago: University of Chicago, 1990), 34.

43. Brian Irwin, "Architecture and Embodiment: Place and Time in the New York Skyline," *Architext V* (2014): 23–35. I note, however, that this uprightness pertains to the human bodily experience more so than most other modes of non-human embodiment. Moreover, I also note the risk of phallocentrism in overidentifying uprightness in buildings with the human form, over structures that do not emphasize verticality.

44. Casey, *Getting Back into Place*, 120.

45. Heidegger, "Building, Dwelling, Thinking," 349.

46. I acknowledge here Megan Craig's invitation to consider this question in response to a paper I presented based on an earlier version of this chapter. I also use "mother" here in the sense of birth mother, while acknowledging this is not always or necessarily the *only* body that continues to mother or care for the child. (I am thinking here of the scenario of adoption, as well as different possibilities of "mothering" after birth. For a discussion of this, see Sara Ruddick, *Maternal Thinking: Toward a Politics of Peace* (Boston: Beacon Press, 1989).)

47. There is some interesting work around the role of the birth— mother's body and her habits of movement, response, and so forth, in the development of the fetal body schema. Jane Lymer, for example, gives an account of this intimate connection

without resorting to a necessarily biologistic account of bodily movement and mannerism. She writes: "Early foetal movement patterns are therefore maternally structured and regulated and this pattern is observable throughout gestation. Essentially what this means is that foetal movement patterns which form our most primal neurological structures are moulded into existence by the maternal body through what Merleau-Ponty would describe as accouplement—an embodied moving with, or coupling—the functional style of which has implications for how the child develops neurologically." Jane Lymer, "Alterity and the Maternal in Adoptee Phenomenology," *Parrhesia* 24 (2015): 189–216, 196.

48. Although there is, of course, the broader and more complex question of whether a fetus in the womb has a "world."

49. I argue that Bachelard is guilty of this in the *Poetics of Space*, as is Heidegger in "Building, Dwelling, Thinking" (as argued by Young).

50. I thank Alia Al-Saji for prompting me to think about this.

51. Bachelard, p.7

52. Ibid., p.4.

53. María Lugones, "Playfulness, 'World'-Travelling, and Loving Perception," *Hypatia* 2 (1987): 11.

54. Mariana Ortega, "'New Mestizas,' 'World'-Travelers,' and '*Dasein*': Phenomenology and the Multi-Voiced, Multi-Cultural Self," *Hypatia* 16 (2001): 9.

55. Fanon, *Black Skin, White Masks*, 109.

56. Lugones, "Playfulness, 'World'-Travelling, and Loving Perception," 17.

57. Ibid., 12.

58. Lee, "Body Movement and Responsibility for a Situation," 246. Lee's argument is that "race treason" strategies locate the moment of critical intervention in white individuals' divestment from systems of white privilege. She is not only skeptical about the possibility of this (as we noted in chapter 1), but also critical of the way this draws attention away from the overriding social and political structures which continue to shape racism, and which require more than just individuals turning away from their white privilege (which are conferred regardless).

59. Of course, we should also note Shannon Sullivan's critique of "white world-travelling" as an iteration of a white ontological expansiveness, as discussed in chapter 2. Sullivan, "White World-Traveling," *Journal of Speculative Philosophy* 18 (2004): 300–304.

60. Lilla Watson, speech to the *United Nations Decade for Women* Conference in 1985. Note, however, that Watson herself insists that though she is credited for this statement, it emerged collectively from Aboriginal activist groups in Queensland in the 1970s.

61. Ortega, "'New Mestizas,' 'World'-Travelers,' and '*Dasein*,'" 180.

62. I thank Anne O'Bryne for bringing this to my attention.

63. Jacobson, "A Developed Nature," 357.

64. bell hooks, *Yearning: Race, Gender, and Cultural Politics* (Boston: South End Press, 1991), 42.

65. Lisa Guenther, *Solitary Confinement: Social Death and its Afterlives* (Minneapolis: University of Minnesota Press, 2013).

66. I say "conventional" but this of course is qualified the fact that the single-family house (or apartment) is "most conventional" in a certain context—typically in advanced capitalist Western society. It should therefore be acknowledged that my analysis of house and home has been largely grounded in (and limited to) this model, although I make no claims that this represents the most natural or even ideal mode of living. I also note here Shannon Sullivan's discussion of the nomadic lifestyles of the Roma people, and the tendency throughout European history to impose *gaje* (non-Roma) "settled habits" upon them, as one example of divergent modes of dwelling. Sullivan, *Revealing Whiteness*, 151–158.

67. See Casey's discussion of border and boundaries in "Walling Racialized Bodies Out: Border versus Boundary at La Fontera" in Emily Lee (ed.), *Living Alterities*, 191–193.

68. See n.48.

69. This fourfold comprises of the sky, the earth, the divinities, and the mortals.

70. Heidegger, "Building, Dwelling, Thinking," 359. Note that the German reads: *"Die Sterblichen sind, das sagt: wohnend durchstehen sie Räume auf Grund ihres Aufenthaltes bei Dingen und* Orten." The word "Orten," translated as "locales," is I think better rendered as "places."

71. Jeff Malpas, *Heidegger's Topology: Being, Place, World* (Cambridge: MIT Press, 2006), 270.

72. Jean-Luc Nancy, *Corpus* (Paris: Éditions Métailié, 2006), 31.

73. Although for a defense of Heidegger on this point, see, for example, Kevin A. Aho, *Heidegger's Neglect of the Body* (Albany: SUNY Press, 2009).

74. Heidegger, *Being and Time*, 149.

75. Merleau-Ponty, *Phenomenology of Perception*, 259–262.

76. This point is also made by Gail Weiss in her book *Body Images: Embodiment as Intercorporeality* (New York: Routledge, 1999), 1. Iris Marion Young's essay on pregnant embodiment similarly argues that our conception of good health in Western medicine tends to be based on the idea of an unchanging body, when in fact, with the exception of (not yet old) adult male bodies, almost everyone else experiences their own body as a continual process of change—this is true for children, the elderly, menstrual and post-menstrual women. Young, "Pregnant Embodiment: Subjectivity and Alienation" in *Throwing Like a Girl*, 57.

77. It is interesting to note that the skin condition, scleroderma, which involves a hardening of the skin and blockage of its pores—such that the skin no longer "breathes"—can in extreme cases be fatal (as it was for artist Paul Klee: Hans Suter, *Paul Klee and His Illness: Bowed but Not Broken by Suffering and Adversity* (Karger, 2010)). I thank Ed Casey for bringing this to my attention.

78. It should be clear already from the way I have been using "body" throughout this book, but at the risk of misinterpretation: I do not of course mean to say that people whose "physical bodies" do not appear to move or react—such as those with severe physical disabilities or paralysis—are for our purposes "dead." This is because (1) I have been explicit in invoking the Merleau-Pontian sense of body throughout this book, which is to say, using the term to designate (in the case of human bodies) living

persons; and (2) because someone who may not *appear* responsive may nonetheless be responsive, depending on our attentiveness to their modes of bodily expression. This second point is powerfully illustrated in a personal vignette by Eva Kittay, *Love's Labor: Essays on Women, Equality and Dependency* (New York: Routledge, 1999), 147.

79. Weiss, *Body Images*, 165.

80. The turn to feminist philosophy is fitting in this discussion of porosity and intercorporeality, since it was after all, the feminist movement that first insisted that *"the personal is political,"* opening up a whole new domain and mode of political critique and intellectual inquiry.

81. Weiss, *Body Images*, 46. Note that Young addresses these charges and concedes that her account was too pronounced, in a follow up essay, "Throwing Like a Girl: Twenty Years Later" in Welton, *Body and Flesh*, 286–287.

82. Weiss, for example, argues, "In addition, appealing to the particular kind of social reference that contextualizes an individual's movements, comportment, and action in a given situation, also avoids identifying social reference with either immanence or transcendence and encourages a focus on the *type* of social reference operative rather than the *fact* of social reference itself." Weiss, *Body Images*, 47.

83. See, for example, Young, "Pregnant Embodiment."

84. This point also bears implication for how we think about other issues such as privacy in the age of camera surveillance and data collection. It becomes harder, following this analysis, to argue that we hold the "rights" to our images in public, or that we have a right not to be recorded in photos or videos while in public since to be in this space is to give a part of our image (and presence) over to others in the same place.

85. The recent events at Ferguson, Missouri inject a chilling moment of insight into this; the way Black bodies travel (in their mode of self-presentation) in order to avoid most basic harms such as getting shot.

86. I note Ortega's departure from Lugones on this point; the "self" as it is envisaged in Lugones' account is problematic for Ortega. Whereas Lugones deals with the question of the travelling self through the concept of memory and a "multiplicity of selves," Ortega argues that "there has to be a perspective from which I can make a judgment about difference and thus appeals to memory as being that which offers this perspective." She continues: "Given the issues above, we will fare better if we can show that our self is complex, multiplicitous, ambiguous, and sometimes even contradictory, and that even though we are multiplicitous, there is still a togetherness to our multiplicity." Ortega, "'New Mestizas,' 'World-Travelers,' and '*Dasein*,'" 16.

87. Mariana Ortega, "Hometactics: Self-Mapping, Belonging, and the Home Question" in Lee (ed.), *Living Alterities*, 176.

88. Ibid., 176–177.

89. There is a point to make here, however, about how gender norms and expectations can harmfully impact boys as well as girls, insofar as the expectations "not to throw like a girl" place pressure on boys to live up to those (or have their membership into "malehood" questioned). So it is not strictly true to say that boys move without *any* sense of self-consciousness, although I do maintain that it is a different kind of self-consciousness involved (e.g., it is more like a self-consciousness than a

double-consciousness since there is no objectifying gaze, but a self-reflexive one). My thanks to Brian Irwin for prompting me to think further on this point.

90. Recall here Bachelard's claim about the house's quintessential role in making space for "daydreaming."

91. Jacobson, "A Developed Nature," 360.

92. Young, "House and Home," 149.

93. Heidegger, *Being and Time*, 229.

94. To be sure, the kind of being-at-home is different from the kind we have been considering earlier. For example, the canniness of *Dasein*'s absorption in the They is "the 'at-home' of publicness." Ibid., 233, 229.

95. Heidegger, "Building, Dwelling, Thinking," 363.

96. Heidegger, *Hölderlin's Hymn*, 68.

97. Ibid., 49.

98. Ibid., 71.

99. Ibid., 74.

100. Mary C. Rawlinson makes this critique in her chapter "Beyond Antigone: Ismene, Gender, and the Right to Life" in Tina Chanter and Sean Kirkland (eds.), *The Returns of Antigone* (Albany: SUNY Press, 2014), 101–122.

101. "What is worthy of poetizing in this poetic work is nothing other than becoming homely in being unhomely. Antigone herself *is* the poem of becoming homely in being unhomely. Antigone *is* the poem of being unhomely in the proper and supreme sense." Heidegger, *Hölderlin's Hymn*, 121.

102. I qualify this by saying that such "epistemic privilege" is not limited to those subject to racialization (as noted in earlier reference to feminist and queer philosophy), and nor is it an epistemological position that is confined to those with marginal experiences. Echoing Yancy's point on epistemic privilege in chapter 2, it is something that members of dominant groups can of course work on (evidenced, for example, by the many white scholars who offer important contributions to anti-racist philosophy and theory).

103. I have been in this book looking at racism in a fairly limited, though I would argue foundational, way. If we take a broader view of it, however, including the way in which racism has underwritten the colonial project in global history, we can say without exaggeration that racism has been disastrous for humankind.

104. For a discussion of thrownness and natality, see: Anne O'Byrne, *Natality and Finitude* (Bloomington: Indiana University Press, 2010), 23–26.

105. Heidegger, *Hölderlin's Hymn*, 21.

Chapter 4

Racism's Gaze*

Between Sartre's Being-Object and Merleau-Ponty's Intertwining

Déjà les regards blancs, les seuls vrais, me dissèquent. Je suis fixé.
Already the white gazes, the only true gazes, dissect me. I am fixed.

—Fanon, *Black Skin, White Masks* (my translation)

"Look, a Negro!" The disarmingly simple interjection speaks volumes to the workings and lived experience of racism. "Look, a Negro!" In its most basic structure, racism entails a pointing, one which takes place predominantly in the visual register: *Look*.[1] In this final chapter, I turn to what I argue is one of the most salient features of racism and the experience of racialized embodiment, that of being looked at, or better, gazed at. Whatever its form—whether violence, speech, discrimination, or even the more insidious instantiations I have been considering throughout this book (clicking car doors, clutching handbags, etc.)—racism most commonly[2] starts with a kind of looking I call the racializing, racialized, or racist gaze. In this chapter I take up once again questions of this racializing gaze, having briefly encountered them in chapter 2, with a view to fleshing out the ontological bases and presuppositions of the phenomenon and its attendant analyses. As I will argue, much of the discourse around the racializing gaze is grounded in something like a Sartrean account of "The Look," which itself is mapped out across broadly Cartesian divisions of subject and object, looker and looked at. However, following our treatment of porosity and intercorporeality in chapter 3, I argue that such an ontological framework is limited in ways that subsequently confine our analyses of the racializing gaze to the overly dualistic terms of subject or object, immanence or transcendence, self or other. Here I turn to

---

* Based on an essay that originally appeared in *Phenomenology and the Political*, edited by S. West Gurley and Geoff Pfeifer (2016); Rowman and Littlefield International, London

Merleau-Ponty's analysis of the intertwining, and in particular to his account of flesh ontology, to open up a richer and more nuanced way to think about racialized embodiment in its complexity. I argue that such an account can help us to further sharpen our analyses of the racist gaze, and open up further insights into the nature of racialized embodiment and the deep ontological violence of racism.

PART 1—THE BODY FOR-OTHERS, OBJECTHOOD, AND RACISM'S GAZE

Racialized Bodies: From Problem to Object

Australian Aboriginal leader and activist, Michael Dodson, once noted during a speech delivered in his capacity as the Aboriginal and Torres Strait Islander Social Justice Commissioner:

> Since their first intrusive gaze, colonising cultures have had a pre-occupation with observing, analysing, studying, classifying and labelling 'Aborigines' and Aboriginality. Under that gaze Aboriginality changed from being a daily practice to being 'a problem to be solved.'[3]

The racist gaze, both a key instrument and justification of the colonial project, served to transform those who were gazed at, in this case the Aboriginal peoples of Australia, into a "problem." Dodson's speech goes on to give a sample of the long history of the different gazes cast upon Australia's "Aborigines"[4] since first colonial contact, including the juridical, pedagogical, ethnological, religious, and artistic gaze. "Yes," he remarks, "They have had a lot to say about us."[5] Dodson's reflections of course closely recall those of W.E.B. Du Bois who, writing from a different context, drew a very similar connection. Speaking of whites, he wrote that, "They approach me in a half-hesitant sort of way, *eye me curiously or compassionately*" (my emphasis), internally fighting their urge to ask, "How does it feel to be a problem?"[6] The vast differences of time, place, and political history are cut across by the gesture of the same racializing gaze.

We can of course give other examples of this gaze. Edward Said's account of *Orientalism* in his seminal text traces the Occident's fascination with and gaze toward the Orient. Far from benign, such gazes of curiosity and fascination can quickly turn into, as Sara Ahmed argues, a kind of "stranger fetishism."[7] The polite smiles and curious searching looks I encounter at antique markets displaying Buddha-head statues in Paris are no less an expression of the racialized gaze than the obtuse shouts of "Hey China!" hurled at me on the streets of country town Victoria. What these different instantiations of the gaze share in common with the earlier examples, however, is the way in which they entail a process of "thingification" in Aimé Césaire's words, or "objectification" in Fanon's. Recall that for the latter, the experience of being gazed at is that which turns him into an object. Following the fateful interjection opening his chapter on the Lived Experience of the Black,[8] Fanon writes: "I came into the world imbued with the will to find a meaning in things, my spirit filled with the desire to attain to the source of the world, and then I found that I was an object in the midst of other objects."[9] This object-hood is variously described by Fanon as a "nonbeing," or alternately, a being "through others"[10] (specifically, white others). But there is more to this. In earlier passages, Fanon suggests that it is not only the access to or experience of one's Blackness that is filtered through whites, but indeed that Black identity *as such* is created by them. Translated by Markmann as "a white man's artifact," the Black soul as described by Fanon is more than an artefact; it is "a *construction* of the White" (my emphasis) ("*une construction du Blanc*").[11]

In such moments (note also that Said's *Orientalism* is in French subtitled "*L'Orient* créé *par l'Occident*"), we hear the unmistakable resonance of Sartre's famous proclamation in 1946 that "it is the anti-Semite who *makes* the Jew."[12] As we also noted in chapter 2, Fanon's description of Black embodiment as "overdetermined" also borrows directly from Sartre (who himself borrowed the term from Freud). Such references are interesting not only for reasons of philosophical genealogy, but also because they reveal something of the ontological presuppositions to Fanon's work, and to much of critical race and post-colonial scholarship more generally.[13] It is my claim that analyses of the racializing gaze frequently rely on an ontological frame-work whose conceptual pillars are cast in terms of a Sartrean subject–object relation. For this reason, and given the profound contribution these analyses make to fields of critical race and post-colonial studies, in the following section I propose a close and critical examination of Sartre's ontological position with respect to the gaze. In particular, I ask whether there are limits to Sartre's account that in turn delimit our analyses of the racializing gaze. And inversely, are there aspects of the racializing gaze that extend or challenge Sartre's account? Fanon's *Black Skin, White Masks* was, of course, substantially influenced by Sartre's writing on a very proximate subject in *Anti-Semite and Jew*. And while the legacy of that text in Fanon's own writing is something I will consider, in order to excavate the ontological underpinnings of these works, I will first turn to Sartre's work in his seminal text, *Being and Nothingness*.

The Subject–Object Relation in Sartre's Gaze

In this text, Sartre outlines the three ontological dimensions of the body. The first is the body *for-itself*—the first-person, perspectival body of phenomenology that grounds or supplies our opening to the world, while itself receding into the background (or in Sartre's terms, surpassing itself to that world). This is not the body as made conspicuous to me, but rather, the body intuited, experienced, or felt from "within"[14]; the body that I simply "exist."[15] For the second ontological dimension, however, the body does appear in a thematized way. Here we have the body *for-others*, that is, my body as it appears for the Other, and equally (according to Sartre[16]), the Other's body as it appears for me. It is this dimension that is most relevant to our present inquiry, since it describes the relation between the Other's appearing for me and their object status. In a section entitled *"Le Regard"*—often translated into English as "The Look" but which in the context of his analysis, I argue, is more appropriately rendered "The Gaze"[17]—Sartre opens by drawing a clear correlation between the gaze and one's object status:

> This woman whom I see coming toward me, this man who is passing by in the street, this beggar whom I hear calling before my window, all are for me *objects*—of that there is no doubt. Thus it is true that at least one of the modalities of the Other's presence to me is *object-ness*.[18]

Just as the Other appears for-me as an object in this second ontological dimension the body, so too can I appear for it in the manner of being-object. As Martin C. Dillon surmises in his chapter, "Sartre on the Phenomenal Body and Merleau-Ponty's Critique": "When—through the phenomenon of 'the look'—I become aware of my body as the object of another's consciousness, when I feel his objectifying gaze upon my body, my experience is one of being objectified."[19] These first two modes or "ontological dimensions" of the body, *being-for-itself* and *being-for-others*, map roughly onto the Cartesian dualism of subject and object, and as Dillon has argued, do so by importing a version of the Cartesian distinction between immanence and transcendence, despite Sartre's own stated efforts to overcome this. The look (or the gaze), then, plays a defining role in the determination of one's experience either as subject-self or object-Other, and this we see reflected in Fanon's own analyses of the Black body as the object gazed at or pointed to.

That the gaze turns the approaching woman or the street beggar into objects is in part, according to Sartre, a function of the spatial dimension of vision. For Sartre the spatial relation of distances undergoes transformation through the gaze. In his words, the Other's gaze *"holds me at a distance,"*[20] or conversely, my gaze holds the Other-as-object at a distance. Note here the resonance with Yancy's analysis of the locking car door, a gesture which seals in the white body, securing it from the passing Black (male) body-object, a body which is now held at a safe felt or *lived* distance—even as the physical, measurable, distances remain unchanged. And as the object held "out there," such distances foreclose possibilities of near-dwelling; the object is she who dwells (stays) far from us, with whom there is minimal chance of porous exchange. This removal is significant for Sartre, given that he earlier describes subjectivity precisely in such spatial terms; to be a subject is to have space organized and oriented around oneself, it is to have distances run—or in Sartre's word, "unfold"—from you. (This echoes both early Heideggerian and Merleau-Pontian treatments of spatial experience.) But as Sartre elaborates, to be object is thus to be stripped of such spatial privilege, it is to be spatially emptied:

> In particular the Other's look, which is a look-looking and not a look-looked-at, denies my distances from objects and unfolds its own distances. This look of the Other is given immediately as that by which distance comes to the world at the heart of a presence without distance. I withdraw; I am stripped of my distanceless presence to my world, and I am provided with a distance from the Other.[21]

The situation becomes more complicated, granted, as Sartre goes on to consider how the Other can appear for us differently and distinct from other objects, since she too has a gravitas that can pull the world to her distances: "Thus suddenly an object has appeared which has stolen the world from me. Everything is in place; everything still exists for me; but everything is traversed by an invisible flight and fixed in the direction of a new object."[22] This is the beginning of the slippage between the Other's status (for-me) as object and subject, through the phenomenon of reversibility. And while, as we will see later, it is possible in Sartre's ontological schema to switch between these two modes of subject and object, we cannot experience them concurrently. Thus Sartre returns frequently to the phrase, as if in refrain, "But the *Other* is still an object *for me*. He belongs to *my distances*."[23] Distances may start to emerge in relation to the Other, but ultimately the space of the Other is still, and according to Sartre "made *with my space*."[24]

A second important operation in the gaze's transformation of the Other-into-object, intimately tied up with the function of distance, is the synthesizing concept of power. In holding out the Other at a distance, the gaze effects an objectification by way of an asymmetrical power relation. The seer *imposes* her distances, her spatial orientation, onto the Other-as-object, or subsumes the Other into them. The distancing entailed in vision becomes a matter of force and imposition; one is pulled into the seer's spatial field.

Moreover, in Sartre's analysis of shame there is a distinct sense in which the gaze leaves the Other-as-object both revealed and exposed. In his example of the person who peers through a keyhole but then is caught (*seen*) doing this, the moment incites a feeling of shame because the *voyeur/voyeuse* is revealed in their naked being; she in turn becomes exposed and seen in her seeing. Sartre writes of shame, that "it is the *recognition* of the fact that I *am* indeed that object which the Other is looking at and judging. I can be ashamed only as my freedom escapes me in order to become a *given* object." (original emphasis)[25] This "vision-power-object" triad is perhaps most compellingly treated by Michel Foucault in *Discipline and Punish*. (And it is interesting to note that in the original French title, what gets translated into English as "Discipline" is the verb "*Surveiller*," a term that already invokes the visual register.) In an incisive chapter on panopticism, Foucault demonstrates how the economics of visibility can be leveraged to effect and sustain disciplinary power, a mode of power which trades on the in principle omnivisibility of prison inmates within the structure of the panopticon, set against the centralized watchtower whose guards remain, for the inmates, invisible. This unidirectional system of optics leads inmates to internalize their own policing, such that it becomes "at once too much and too little that the prisoner should be constantly observed by an inspector: too little for what matters is that he knows himself to be observed; too much because he has no need in fact of being so."[26] As Foucault's analysis shows, extending what is intimated in Sartre's account, questions of power[27] are deeply implicated in the relations of visibility.

Racism's Gaze and the Racialized Object

There are then some undoubtedly powerful resonances between Sartre's ontology of the gaze (and Foucault's extension of it), with the experience of racialized embodiment. Indeed, the precipitous cry, "Look, a Negro!" in many ways exemplifies the Sartrean gaze. Fanon is spotted in and as his Black body, and in the moment of the look ("Look!") his being is crystallized into a *being-for-others*; he has become the white boy's object to call out, point out, and fear. From the mode of *being-for-itself* while travelling along uneventfully in the train, merely "existing his body" to borrow Sartre's locution, he has in the instant of the gaze been swept up and transformed into the object of the Other's gaze. And insofar as the Sartrean gaze entails a distancing, so too can we easily identify moments of distancing in the case of the racializing gaze. The intransigence of Western representations of veiled Muslim women can be put down to not only the habitualized modes of perception as discussed in chapter 1, but also to the way these women are held at a distance. As Al-Saji has argued in a later piece: "Living with Muslim women who wear the hijab, and forming attachments with them" offers possibilities for redrawing our "affective maps" in ways that arguments and cognitive shifts cannot.[28] In other words, the intimacy of "living with" and among veiled Muslim women (and this can take the form of dwelling, socializing, organizing, or working with) renders difficult the objectification of them, as these distances become harder to sustain. Moreover, as we saw in our investigations of the home in chapter 3, racialized embodiment can be characterized as a kind of not-at-home, which among other things entails a displacement from centers of being, dwelling, and subjectivity. To feel not-at-home is precisely to be pushed out, to be at a distance from wherever one feels to be at "home," and to be pushed out of what Heidegger calls "Being-in," or *In-sein*.[29] This recurrent sense of being-at-a-distance is thus concordant with the sense of objecthood experienced by the racialized body.

Finally, the Sartrean description of the gaze and its ontological framework dovetails with our account insofar as power constitutes an essential element of the racializing gaze. That power is thoroughly implicated in the dynamics of looking/being-looked-at are borne out compellingly in a story recounted by Lewis Gordon in his book, *Bad Faith and Antiblack Racism*, which, it should be noted, is set explicitly within a Sartrean framework:

> The white body is expected not to be looked at by black bodies. This is because the black body's situation of being-without-a-perspective cannot be maintained if blacks are able to unleash the Look.
>
> There was a period in the American South when, for blacks, looking a white in the eye carried the risk of being lynched. Calvin Hernton reports, for example, an infamous case of rape by "reckless eyeballing" that occurred in Mississippi in the 1950s: "The Negro was on one side of the street and the [white] woman was on the other side. She screamed. What happened? 'That 'nigger' tried to attack me.' 'But he's way over there across the street going in the opposite direction!' 'Why he *looked* at me as if he were going to attack me.' The Negro was arrested, tried, and sentenced!" As absurd as this case may be, the white woman in the example exemplifies a point: The Look is sadistic. Thus the Negro had, indeed, attacked her, apparently, simply by looking at her.[30]

While I do not agree with Gordon that the look is necessarily sadistic, I do agree that power is always a constitutive dimension of the racializing gaze. The fetishizing gaze of Orientalism is one example of a non-sadistic and yet still colonizing gaze, as explicated by Egyptian sociologist Anwar Abdel Malek in a passage cited in Said's *Orientalism*:

> the Orient and Orientals [are considered by Orientalism] as an "object" of study, stamped with an otherness ... a constitutive otherness, of an essential character. ... This "object" of study will be, as is customary, passive,

non-participating, endowed with a "historical" subjectivity, above all, non-active, non-autonomous, non-sovereign with regard to itself[31]

The racializing gaze expresses an underlying sense of epistemic and perspectival entitlement, and so in the case relayed by Gordon, we see why the Black man's so-called attempt to assert or exercise that power proves so offensive and violent to the white woman. Moreover, we see iterations of this story in contemporary society when white people respond to reversals of the racialized gaze—whether through film, blogs, comedy, or even academic work—with anger, contempt, and even in more extreme cases, threats of personal violence. That such work is sometimes met with death threats speaks to the ferocity and intensity of feeling evoked when the white gaze is unwillingly reversed. (And there exists an important parallel with feminist critiques of male dominated fields such as online gaming, as the "gamergate" controversy in 2014 demonstrated.) This is despite the fact that such generalizations and caricatures of non-white people saturate the everyday cultural imaginary. As Sullivan notes in her article "White World-Traveling," citing bell hooks: "Given the history of white control of the Black gaze, white people generally do not think of themselves as the object of Black vision and judgment. White people tend to 'think they are seen by black folks only as they want to appear' (hooks, 1992)."[32] Insofar as the dynamics of the gaze in Sartre's account bear direct relation to the poles of power, we can see why the gaze's reversal can solicit such strong responses. Recalling that in his analysis of shame, to find oneself suddenly looked-at, when voyeuristically bent over a keyhole, is to find oneself naked and exposed. The moment of vulnerability is thus experienced as a disempowerment, or in Sartre's term, a deflowering: "What is seen is possessed, to see is to *deflower*."[33] The visibility of racialized bodies within the topography of the gaze is, then, as Said and Fanon have variously argued, deeply structured by such relations of power.

PART 2—COMPLICATING THE GAZE-OBJECT ONTOLOGY: MODES OF LOOKING, SEEING ONESELF BEING SEEN, AND BODILY AMBIGUITY

Having given a broad, schematic overview of Sartre's account of the gaze and how it gets mobilized in analyses of racism and the white gaze, I now propose a more detailed look into aspects of this conceptual framework, as relevant to our enquiry. For example, while what we have seen so far of Sartre's account appears to resonate with the machinations of the racializing gaze, isn't there also a more nuanced account of the bodily experience of racism and racialization that remains to be articulated? The objectification of one's body via the gaze constitutes an enduring part of the experience of racism to be sure, but it seems too much to claim that the subjective experience is in this moment entirely eclipsed. After all, the racialized body is seen, but *also sees itself being seen.* This is where we will turn to Sartre's third ontological dimension of the body and ask whether his account sufficiently anticipates and addresses this concern. Relatedly, we also take up the question of ambiguity in racialized bodies, and drawing on Gail Weiss's account of intercorporeality and critical reading of Sartre's *Anti-Semite and Jew*, a reading that further nuances our account of the racializing gaze. But before turning to these questions, it is worth pausing for a moment to ask whether what we have been referring to as "the gaze" throughout this analysis, taking our cue both from Sartre and postcolonial thinkers such as Fanon, has indeed been appropriately thematized as such, or whether it would benefit from further conceptual precision.

Modes of Looking: the Gaze, the Glance, and the Stare

Through the course of his phenomenological investigations into the nature of looking, Edward Casey in *The World at a Glance* carefully delineates different modes of looking, noting that the glance and the gaze "represent the two ends of an entire axis that extends from steady, continuous looking to darting and discontinuous seeing."[34] Whereas the gaze is most often associated with the characteristics of slow, patient, and contemplative looking, "plumbing the depths" of its visual object (think of lovers gazing into each other's eyes), Casey argues that the glance represents a flightier mode, prone to distraction and "alighting on surfaces." He writes: "The glance is a literally superficial activity, and that is its very strength."[35] He points, for example, to the way one can take in the tenor and gravity of a situation—such as the scene of a domestic dispute—through the fleeting glance. And yet, these taxonomies do not quite square with our own descriptions of the racializing gaze. While it may be true that the racializing gaze, in line with Casey's description, "lingers" on the racialized body—the white boy's gaze, when calling out Fanon, is not easily drawn away, despite his mother's increasing embarrassment—is it not also the case that this gaze transacts primarily with surfaces? After all, it is the *surface* of Fanon's skin that draws the boy's gaze, a gaze that never attempts to plumb deeply enough to discover Fanon's "refined manners, knowledge of literature, or understanding of the quantum theory."[36] What Casey's analysis prompts us to consider then, beyond Sartre's topography of the gaze-relation, is the *quality* of looking. For example, in what way does the racializing gaze entail a *non-seeing*? Such a characterization would help to explain the phenomenon of racialized *invisibility*, described powerfully by African American author Ralph Ellison: "I am invisible, understand, simply because people refuse to see me."[37] Likewise, the legal doctrine of *terra nullius*, activated by the British to justify colonization in Australia (and legally overturned only in 1992), entailed a comparable *non-seeing* of Aboriginal peoples, with their highly developed cultural and social practices. Such examples, which may intuitively appear to run counter to our analyses of the racializing gaze, in fact are continuous with it insofar as we understand the latter as a distorted kind of gazing. As Yancy writes of Ellison, "To be 'seen' in this way is not to be seen at all."[38]

Likewise, we may want to delineate the kind of looking entailed in the racializing gaze from that of the *stare*; a kind of looking which has been the subject of much analysis in fields such as critical disability studies.[39] Rosemarie Garland-Thomson in her book, *Staring: How We Look*, outlines some variations of staring, including what she terms "dominance staring," that which is operative in the case of looking at women's bodies and racialized bodies. (Indeed, her analysis of dynamics of power entailed in this mode of staring echoes much of what we outlined earlier in relation to the racializing gaze.) In contrast to dominance staring, however, Garland-Thomson also outlines a mode she calls "baroque staring," a "gaping-mouthed, unapologetic staring"[40] experienced most keenly by those whose bodies bear visibly pronounced marks of physical disability or divergence. While this too is enmeshed in relations of power and normalizing vision, what distinguishes baroque staring from other modes is that, driven by curiosity and fascination with the "freakish," starers become unable to pry themselves away in accordance with the usual rules of social decorum. This is illustrated in the case of conjoined twins, Reba and Lori Schapell, of whom Garland-Thomson writes:

> Emerging from twenty-four years of institutionalization into a world of people shaped quite differently from them, Lori and Reba draw baroque stares wherever they go.
>
> Their myriads of first-time viewers, however, are awestruck, stopped in their tracks with mouths agape and eyes out of control. The twins . . . anticipate and maneuver staring encounters, often instructing starers how to handle themselves appropriately. . . . With some indulgence and often strained patience, the twins let us know that they understand their starers' loss of composure and social grace as simply ignorance about the intricacies of human variation and of alternative ways of being in the world.[41]

While the starers in this case cannot bring themselves to look away absent the explicit intervention of the twins, a different yet related phenomenon is that of "ocular evasion." Garland-Thomson refers here to the testimony of anthropologist Robert Murphy, whose book *The Body Silent* chronicles some of his experiences as a later-life quadriplegic: "People refuse to look at Murphy . . . partly because they know that they are not supposed to stare at him and have no easy way to relate to him. . . . The new quadriplegic Murphy found that acquaintances 'did not look [his] way' and that he was 'virtually ignored in crowds for long periods, broken by short bursts of patronization.'"[42] Interestingly, as Robert Bernasconi reports, Sartre makes a similar observation in relation to the white aversion of Black gazes during his first visit to the United States in 1945 (after the publication of *Being and Nothingness*), writing in a Parisian newspaper: "You can pass these untouchables on the street at any time of day, but you will not meet their gaze."[43] As Bernasconi goes on to elaborate,

> Sartre had discovered an imperative of White American society: Blacks are not your business, nor are you theirs. Their business is with the elevator, your luggage, or your shoes. 'They perform their tasks like machines and you ought not take any more notice of them than if they were machines.'[44]

Despite their superficial differences, then, both "baroque staring" and "ocular evasion" articulate an attempt to navigate encounters with non-normative bodies, and more pointedly, in ways that demean the personhood of those bodies. In the same way that Ellison's racialized *invisibility* is a variation rather than a negation of racialized visibility, so too does this looking-away operate along similar axes to that of staring. As Garland-Thomson argues,

> looking away from people who make us uncomfortable differs from granting them visual anonymity. Looking away is an active denial of acknowledgment rather than the tacit tipping of one's hat to ordinary fellow citizens expressed in simply not noticing one another. Looking away is for Murphy a deliberate obliteration of his personhood.[45]

As this analysis shows, by delving deeper into the varied modes of looking or non-looking, we uncover nuances that are not available to us in Sartre's account of the (objectifying) gaze. Following this, we might ask if there exist other modes of seeing that are foreclosed by this Sartrean account, and which may be pertinent for our purposes. For example, in the analysis so far, I note that the visibility of the body is cast almost exclusively in negative terms. But aren't there other kinds of looking—even at racialized bodies—that are not framed in this way? The "Black is Beautiful" movement of the 1960s, with its reclaiming of the Black body as a site of beauty and pride, is one such example disrupting existing taxonomies of the gaze and instituting new ways of seeing. Sartre's viewer–viewed (subject–object) ontology under consideration here, however, insofar as it remains tethered to the idea of visibility as disempowerment or vulnerable exposure does not appear to accommodate such shifts. As commentators such as Glen A. Mazis have argued, this represents a failure on the part of Sartre to seriously consider other kinds of gazes (or in Mazis' term, regards[46]). Whereas Sartre's gaze "turned to the power of vision to deflower, to strip away, to violate, and to possess"[47], Mazis argues that a vision more attuned to the sense of touch (and in particular to the caress) may open up different possibilities of seeing:

> In the loving regard, one is seen within the web of one's actions and possibilities. Therefore, one can be comfortable or even pleased by this nudity, because it does not strip away one's identity and reduce one to pure object. Sight borrows a lesson from tactile experience as here one uses vision not to register the other at a distance or deflower or violate or even unmask the other, but rather one *touches* the other with the regard of one's glance, and allows the other's visual appearance to *touch* one with the atmosphere of their entire being.[48]

The criticism, which might at first appear merely to exhort Sartre to broaden his range of seeing in the treatment of the gaze, in fact holds a deeper criticism insofar as it throws into question the alignment of seer–subject and seen–object. Specifically, it challenges the characterization of seen always *as object*, given there are ways in which, as Mazis points out above, visual appearances can also speak out to or "touch" us. This is the case not only for art–objects such as the dancer (in Mazis' example), but also in everyday situations when we are, as the phrase goes, "struck by the sight of something." Agreeing with Mazis, I contend that Sartre's treatment gives too much power to the objectifying gaze, allowing its taxonomy to dominate, perhaps even direct, his ontological imagination. For his part, Mazis is interested in how the structure of touch—and specifically a Merleau-Pontian account, which we will explore later in the chapter—offers possibilities for a more sophisticated and nuanced ontology. And while Mazis is not alone in calling for a more central treatment of touch in our thinking—Elizabeth Grosz makes a similar call in *Volatile Bodies*—it should be noted that the power of visual-thinking is not easily shaken off. It is interesting to note, for example, that whereas Mazis relies on Merleau-Ponty in order to usher in a new ontology grounded in touch, for Grosz (following Irigaray) Merleau-Ponty does not sufficiently disentangle the touch from vision. In fact whereas Mazis turns to Merleau-Ponty over Sartre for a more haptically grounded ontology, Grosz argues that Merleau-Ponty remains nonetheless too beholden to visual analyses in his consideration of the tangible; that he does not shake off the visual register *enough*.[49] While Grosz goes on to consider some of the important feminist implications from this failure,[50] I mention this here to signal some of the difficulties encountered in attempts to move away from sedimented conceptual schemas. And while we defer our consideration of Merleau-Ponty's account of touch for the next section, it is worth registering here that some of the criticisms raised by Mazis in relation to Sartre were already anticipated in our discussion of visibility and the racialized body in chapter 2.

The Racialized Body Seeing Itself Being Seen, Reversibility, and Sartre's Third Ontological Dimension of the Body

Taking up the suggestion that the seer–subject and seen–object division warrants further interrogation, we return here to the question of racialized embodiment, which if considered from the vantage point of its lived experience, we see is already laced with such moments of ambiguity. For example, we noted in chapter 2 that the visibility (even hyper-visibility) of the racialized body extends beyond being seen, to also *seeing oneself being seen*. Fanon captures this powerfully in the retelling of his experience, that is, in the performativity of his own writing. The young boy's increasingly desperate cries at "the Negro" are interspersed with Fanon's own internal reflections and responses to his being so publicly singled out and gazed at. That he documents the inner turmoil, exasperation, amusement, and angst he experiences by being called out demonstrates to us a seemingly benign yet highly significant point: *he sees himself being seen*. Du Bois makes a similar point when he says, "It is a peculiar sensation, this double-consciousness, this sense of always *looking at one's self through the eyes of others*, of measuring one's soul by the tape of a world that looks on in amused contempt and pity"[51] (my emphasis). And even Brent Staples's description of "whistling Vivaldi" among other strategies discussed in chapter 2 chronicles not only the extent to which the racializing gaze is itself seen and seen-*through*, but also the way in which this gaze is anticipated, negotiated, diffused, and deflected. Of course this "looking at one's self through the eyes of others" also has a correlate in gendered analyses of body-objectification, and in the case of women of color, this very often entails a *doubling* of that double-consciousness (where the experience of double-consciousness arising from one's racialization is itself doubled or compounded through the sexual objectification of women's bodies in patriarchal society—and in the case of women of color, sexually objectified in racially coded ways). What this points to, then, is the way in which racialized embodiment entails a richness, complexity, and ambiguity that seems to resist the clean compartmentalization into being-subject or -object. This in turn, prompts us to ask whether a more fluid and nuanced ontological account of the body is available, one in which we can more seamlessly slide between, or perhaps even concurrently exist, these different ontological dimensions.

The Reversibility of the Gaze, and Sartre's Third Ontological
Dimension of the Body

Our treatment of Sartre, however, is not yet complete. For while it is true that
Sartre presents the two distinct modes or ontological dimensions of being-for-
itself and being-for-others, there is also a third (and according to commentators such as Dermot Moran, more "complicated and difficult to grasp"[52])
ontological dimension of the body that is especially relevant for our analysis.
For this dimension Sartre offers no name, but Dillon has proposed the term
"the Body-for-Itself-for-Others."[53] Sartre describes it thus:

> But in so far as I am for others, the Other is revealed to me as the subject *for*
> *whom I am an object.* Even there the question, as we have seen, is of my fun-
> damental relation with the Other. *I exist therefore for myself as known by the*
> *Other.* . . . This is the third ontological dimension of my body. (my emphases)[54]

In other words, while it is the case for Sartre that we apprehend the Other-
as-object, it is also true that in the relation of the gaze, we can be *looked at*,
that is, we can be objects *for* the Other. There is a reversibility of the gaze in
Sartre's account, where it becomes possible for the Other and I to trade places
in the gaze-relation, thereby marking the possibility of one's moving between
the poles of subject and object. Indeed, this reversibility is not just a *possibil-*
ity for Sartre; it also represents the *means* by which I come to apprehend the
Other—not the Other as-object, but *as-subject.* In his earlier analysis of 'The
Look' Sartre writes:

> my fundamental connection with the Other-as-subject must be able to be
> referred back to my permanent possibility of *being seen* by the Other. It is in and
> through the revelation of my being-as-object for the Other that I must be able to
> apprehend the presence of his being-as-subject.[55]

But what we have in the "Body-for-Itself-for-Others" is more than a mere
reversal of the gaze (and the subject–object positions entailed therein), and
which after all Sartre grants later in Black Orpheus when he writes, "Today
these black men are looking at us, and our gaze comes back to our own
eyes."[56] Moreover, as we will see later in the chapter, the phenomenon of
reversibility by itself is not enough to account for the experience of racialized
embodiment since, as thinkers such as Fanon argue, the white gaze is securely
embedded in our imaginary owing to its hegemonic power. ("For not only
must the black man be black; he must be black in relation to the white man.
Some critics will take it on themselves to remind us that this proposition has a
converse. I say that this is false. The black man has no ontological resistance
in the eyes of the white man."[57]) What the third ontological dimension of the

body potentially contributes, then, is a way to think about how we become aware of, and indeed *exist*, our own being-object, our "me-as-object."[58]

It is with this in mind that commentators such as Moran have defended Sartre for giving a more sophisticated account of the body than he is often given credit for. For example, Moran points to the way in which Sartre's account installs relationality as a fundamental feature of the body: "[Sartre] claims that my experiencing my body in the gaze of the other does not make my body a simple object to me, rather I experience the 'flight of the body which I exist.' In other words, the other both presents me as I really am and also takes control of my body-image away from me."[59] The question of the Other's access to "who I really am" aside, what Moran picks up on here is the way in which relationality necessitates a holding open and maybe even a making vulnerable of our bodily being to and for the Other. This point I return to later. Moran's broader point, however, is that this intersubjective intercorporeality, so often credited to thinkers such as Merleau-Ponty (and to a lesser extent, Husserl), is often overlooked in Sartre. For him, there is already a Sartrean account of how the being-object (or *for-others*) of the body gets folded back into the experience of oneself through the phenomenon of the reversibility of the gaze, as described in the third ontological dimension of the body.

Returning then to the question of racialized embodiment, at first glance it seems that this development in Sartre's account speaks directly to the problem we identified earlier: the idea that the object-status of the racialized body is reflected back to that body, the racialized body as it apprehends and lives its objectification. However, this is worthy of some closer examination. For example, while the third ontological dimension appears to reconcile the first two dimensions of being from-within and from-without, this reconciliation is a qualified one. This is because according to Sartre my apprehension of my body's being-object for the Other is only an apprehension of "certain of its formal structures," not the actual "me-as-object" itself, which for him remains an "unknowable being," an objectified *alienation*.[60] In other words, while I can become aware of myself as object-for-the-Other, this does not make me privy to *how* I appear to them, or to the substance or meaning of my "objecthood." There remains for Sartre a gap between the "incommunicable levels"[61] of being-subject and being-object of the body that can never close over, even in this third ontological dimension:

> We can not, I said then, perceive and imagine simultaneously; it must be either one or the other. I should willingly say here: we can not perceive the world and at the same time apprehend a look fastened upon us; it must be either one or the other. This is because to perceive is to *look at*, and to apprehend a look is not to apprehend a look-as-object in the world (unless the look is not directed upon us); it is to be conscious of *being looked at*.[62]

To be aware of one's being looked-at, according to Sartre, is to be aware only of the contours of being looked-at, but not necessarily its content.

However, this is not the case with the racializing gaze. As we saw at the end of chapter 2 with Dawn Adams' encounter while shopping in Darwin, the particulars of a gaze need not be spelled out in order for her to grasp their meaning. The weight of the racist gaze communicates not only the fact of being looked at, but also its meaning. Consider Fanon's experience of being gazed at, about which he writes:

> In the train it was no longer a question of being aware of my body in the third person but in a triple person. . . . I was responsible at the same time for my body, for my race, for my ancestors. I subjected myself to an objective examination, I discovered my blackness, my ethnic characteristics; and I was battered down by tom-toms, cannibalism, intellectual deficiency, fetishism, racial defects, slave-ships, and above all else, above all: "Sho' good eatin."[63]

It seems that what Fanon apprehends here is *precisely* the contents of this looking, over and above a consciousness of being looked at. Moreover, this folding in of the gaze functions not only on the reflective level of "objective examination," but also I would argue pre-reflectively; think for example the ways in which racialized beauty standards (which implicate a certain kind of gaze) can weave their way into pre-reflective modes of self-perception.[64] Racist histories, political discourses, and social practices come together in supplying the horizon from which the meaning of a gaze (and one's being gazed at) becomes eminently graspable.

Additionally, while it is possible in Sartre's account to be aware of one's being-object for the Other, to *be* that object for oneself is to exist in bad faith. This is why Dillon has called this mode "the Body-for-Itself-for-Others." Far from offering a mediating position between the first and second ontological dimensions of the body, this third dimension, as Dillon has argued, actually serves to remind us of the "impossibility of any rapprochement" between the first two modes of being-for-itself and being-for-Others.[65] That is, we are on Sartre's account, either being for-ourselves or for-others, but never both. This in turn tugs at a deeper underlying problem of his position. Recalling our analysis of being-at-home in chapter 3, and in particular the discussion of porosity in relation to the home, we note how modes of being are very often doubled up; in the case of dwelling, it is not just that we can shift *between* different modes of being-at-home and not-being-at-home, but rather, how each is already permeated by the experience of the other. We can find ourselves *simultaneously* at-home *and* not-at-home. Of course it is true that one mode might strike us as more salient than others at any given time, but it is structurally the case that we can experience both concurrently; this is what the double-consciousness of racialized experience expresses. However, this is what Sartre's account expressly forbids. In the earlier analysis of the gaze's reversibility, we did not yet mark the fact that while reversibility allows the possibility of the Other's movement beyond their object-status (for me), it comes at the price of my assuming that object position (for her). And accordingly, to find myself at the end of the Other's gaze is to concurrently find myself divested of my subjectivity. In the relation of self and Other, one of us must always remain the object. As Moran writes:

> Sartre clearly distinguishes between my body as experienced (ambiguously and non-objectively) by me in the first person, and the body as it is perceived or known by me occupying the perspective of another person. These points of view are irreconcilable and indicate an ontological gulf that separates the two dimensions. These different "bodies" underpin different and *irreconcilable* ontologies. Sartre's analysis of the well-known phenomenon of the double sensation aims to reinforce this irreconcilability between these opposing "ontological" dimensions.[66]

We see here how this aspect of Sartre's ontology remains firmly rooted in the Cartesian terms of subject–object, immanence and transcendence, and being such, his framework does not permit the kind of double lining which marks the experience of racialized embodiment. As Dillon has argued, this position carries over to Sartre's analysis on touch. In response to what classical psychology terms "double sensation"—the notion of simultaneously touching and being touched, therefore a suitable correlate of this visual reversibility—Dillon argues that Sartre's rejection of it stems from his Cartesian positioning of subject and object: "The body is either subject (being-for-itself) who is touching or object (being-for-others) that is touched; to be both at once is impossible: there can be no such thing as a double sensation."[67]

As Dillon goes on to argue, however, not only is clear separation of the two "incommunicable levels" of being-subject and being-object rendered suspect on the basis of the lived experience of ambiguity (to be discussed later), but it also reveals an internal inconsistency within Sartre's own schema. This is because in his discussion of shame, Dillon argues that this affective response makes sense only if the object-seen holds at the time of their being seen, an expectation of subjecthood. That is, the affective response of shame arises only because one has certain expectations of subjectivity and invisibility. As Dillon explains in this passage, employing here the term "alienation" in lieu of shame:

> "Alienation" connotes more than mere difference, mere otherness. It conveys the idea of estrangement and exclusion, and has overtones of *disappointed expectations*. To be different is not necessarily to be alien. Alienation arises

when hopes and anticipations of inclusion and familiarity are thwarted and frustrated by exclusion and estrangement. . . . In the present context, then, to find a difference between the body one lives (and experiences nonthetically) and the body one knows (by thematic reflection) is to experience alienation *only if that otherness appears where one had anticipated solidarity.*[68] (my emphasis)

This analysis, though proceeding in terms of shame and affectivity, calls to mind Heidegger's later treatment of uncanniness, which as we saw in chapter 3, called for the move to *become homely in the unhomely*. Recall that, for him, Antigone stood out as the supreme figure of uncanniness precisely because she held fast to her alien (and tragic) fate, demanding its recognition within the homely realm of the city. We can also certainly relate Dillon's analysis to the case of the racializing gaze; in an earlier quote we noted how Fanon himself was explicit about his coming into the world with hopes and desires, only to have the racializing, Medusa-like gaze freeze him in place as object. What these reflections push us to question then is the desirability of such clean subject–object distinctions, which seem to wash over the moments of ambiguity and bivalence in the gaze relation as it pertains to the racialized body.

Ambiguity, "Overdetermination," and Intercorporeality

In this final section we turn to Gail Weiss, who takes up precisely the question of ambiguity in relation to Sartre (and Fanon) in her essay, "Pride and Prejudice: Ambiguous Racial, Religious, and Ethnic Identities of Jewish Bodies." Importantly for our purposes, her critique addresses Sartre's work with explicit regard to questions of race, and is built around the very closely related question of Jewish identity. In this piece Weiss challenges what she claims to be the overly simplistic picture of Jewish identity presented in Sartre and inadequately remedied by Fanon. In particular, she is concerned that Sartre overstates the account of objectification and the constitution by the other. The analysis is twofold: first, Weiss argues that the term "overdetermination" as employed by Sartre (and Fanon, following him) is a misappropriation of Freud's term, leading to too-hasty a conclusion on the nature of bodily identity. That is, in famously claiming that "it is the anti-Semite who *creates* the Jew" in *Anti-Semite and Jew*, Sartre moves Freud's term from its original domain of experiences and objects, to people. That *people* (such as Jews) and not experiences (such as Dora's dream) are described as "overdetermined" gives too much power, she argues, to the Other in the constitution of one's self-identity, indeed in the objectification of one's self—something Freud himself never claimed, and something which fails to fully account for the role of Jews in the experience of their own bodily identities.

This criticism warrants a closer look. As we have seen in chapter 2 and again in this chapter, the influence of *Anti-Semite and Jew* on Fanon's *Black Skin, White Masks* is evident. And yet it is also true that Fanon draws some important distinctions between the situation of the Jew and the situation of the Black: "The Jew is disliked from the moment he is tracked down. But in my case everything takes on a new guise. I am given no chance. I am over-determined from without. I am a slave not of the 'idea' that others have of me but of my own appearance."[69] Thus while Fanon does appropriate Sartre's version of "overdetermination" in looking at the constitution of the Black body by the Other, his distinction is such that it reintroduces some ambiguity (though for Weiss, ultimately not enough) into the case of Jewish identity.[70] In this passage Fanon reserves this experience of visual overdetermination for Blacks (though perhaps not exclusively), implying that Jewish identity is not as visually fixed or given, since it is possible for the Jew to "pass." The identification of a Jew then takes place not in the seamless perception of their skin color or morphological features, the argument would go, but through other physical features such as religious garments, hair, or even the yellow star. However, despite this reintroduction of ambiguity in the case of Jewish identity, Weiss contests the implication that because Jewishness is not inscribed (exclusively[71]) in skin color, that, it is any less embedded visually and bodily. She thus challenges the too-hasty ascription of "voluntary" versus "involuntary" bodily appearance that Fanon's distinction seems to invite, arguing that it is both dangerous and divisive to fall into the trap of comparing prejudices.[72]

For Weiss, then, although Fanon adds nuance to Sartre's use of the term "overdetermination," he does not do this in ways she finds productive. In part we might say this is because Fanon is too narrowly focused on a certain economy of visibility, privileging the visibility of the epidermal layer as prior and more significant than other visible aspects of the body. Such a line would place us back in the earlier criticism pertaining to rigid modes of seeing. And yet, recall that Weiss's criticism is not directed exclusively at Fanon, but rather primarily Sartre (who after all, initiates the appropriation). Weiss's primary criticism is that *both* Sartre and Fanon, in describing the Jewish and Black experiences respectively in the language of overdetermination, misapply Freud's original concept. But moving to the second part of Weiss's critique, more than a textual misstep, she argues that the characterization of these identities as overdetermined fundamentally misunderstands the intercorporeal nature of bodily identity. She writes: "Crediting the other with the ability to define one's identity . . . not only eviscerates the agency of those who are oppressed by the other's essentializing descriptions, but also forecloses some of the inherent ambiguity that, I am claiming, always attends each of these identities."[73] In other words, Weiss argues that in their misappropriation of the concept, Sartre and Fanon do a disservice to Jewish and Black identities by washing over the critical space of ambiguity and indeterminacy. Recast in the language of the gazed-at-object, Weiss' argument is that it is too much to say that the object of the gaze becomes, merely and wholly, an object.

It is not the case, however, that Weiss grounds the argument of ambiguity solely in the nature of Jewish identity and its complexity. While it is true that Jewish identity comes together through a complex mosaic of race, ethnicity, religiosity, culture, history, and nationality, this is something that Sartre does, to some extent, acknowledge. He asks, for example, "Failing to determine the Jew by his race, shall we define him by his religion or by the existence of a strictly Israelite national community?"[74] Indeed Sartre's thesis that the Jew *is his or her situation* speaks to the idea that there is nothing else which intrinsically defines the Jew as Jew. But this is where, for Weiss, Sartre goes wrong. For in saying that the Jew *is* their situation, Sartre denies the way in which the Jew's corporeality plays a significant role in their identity, indeed, in the formation of their situation. As Moran notes, "Sartre maintains that one must start from the recognition that, first and foremost, our experience is not of *the body* as such (or indeed of our own consciousness as such), but rather, of the *world*, or the *situation*."[75] However, for Weiss, the Jew is *not only* his or her situation insofar as this suggests one's situation can be exclusively external (remember that for Sartre it is the anti-Semite who *creates* the Jew). Instead, she argues that one's situation derives equally from the one's corporeal engagement with the world and with others. To cast it in Fanonian terms, the racialized body does have *some* "ontological resistance." But even to speak in terms of resistance may be to suggest too heavily that we are in a zero-sum relation of subject and object. As in her argument on intercorporeality as explored in chapter 3, it is Weiss's contention, following Merleau-Ponty, that one's identity is arrived at *through* the embodied navigation of situations, that is, one is *constituted* through the intercorporeal transactions with institutions, practices, and other bodies. For as Weiss argues, *no* body is overdetermined, at least, never *wholly* constituted by the other—even those embedded in oppressive relations with the other, such as racialized bodies. She argues, in other words, for an account of racialized embodiment that adequately takes into account the constitutive intercorporeality of bodies, which does not dissipate in the face of oppressive racist relations.

We encounter yet again, this time through Weiss's argument, a critique of the sharp dualism grounding Sartre's analysis—a theme that has emerged consistently throughout our consideration of the limits of his ontological position. Given this recurrent theme, and its potential to recast or further nuance our account of racialized embodiment, let us now turn now to a direct engagement with Merleau-Ponty's account of the chiasm.

PART 3—MERLEAU-PONTY'S INTERTWINING
AND THE SUBJECT–OBJECT DISSOLUTION
IN RACIALIZED EMBODIMENT

Merleau-Ponty's final but incomplete work, *The Visible and Invisible*, cut short by his untimely death, sketches out the beginnings of a phenomenology which seeks to shed its existentialist hangover along with the Cartesian dualism that it imports. In particular, it is his reflections on the intertwining or chiasm, sometimes also known as his "flesh ontology," that marks a key turn away from the ontological commitments of existentialism as we have seen in Sartre (with its attachment to Western philosophy's deeply rooted subject–object distinction), to one where subject and object and/or world are more fully and fluidly integrated. In this following section, I examine how this turn in Merleau-Ponty's thought can be productively leveraged for the analysis of racialized embodiment, in ways that offer insight into the nature of the racializing gaze in lived experience.

The Chiasm

Touch and Vision: A Doubling

In a widely celebrated chapter of *The Visible and Invisible* called "The Intertwining—The Chiasm," Merleau-Ponty develops what later becomes known as his "flesh ontology." Two leitmotifs invoked in his account help us to set the analysis in motion: first, that of the two hands touching (famously considered by Husserl, and which we will recognize as "double sensation" from our earlier mention of classical psychology), and second, the seeing eye which is itself visible. Together, they help him to develop an account of the intertwining.

What is central to both cases, according to Merleau-Ponty, is the essential doubling and folding back of each upon the other. In the first case of the two hands—my right hand touching my left—if we are attentive to this phenomenon we realize that it is difficult to truly distinguish the touching from the touched. In a very real sense, each hand is *touching* the other, while at the same time being *touched by* the other. Moreover, we see that the status of touching and touched designate positions that are easily unsettled: "when my right hand touches my left hand while it is palpating the things, where the 'touching subject' passes over to the rank of the touched, descends into the things, such that the touch is formed in the midst of the world and as it were in the things."[76] It is better to say that both hands participate in the touch, and that this participation is not one of fixed positionality, but of fluidity and interchangeability. In a later passage, Merleau-Ponty gives in passing a different but related example of the handshake saying that "[it] too is reversible; I can feel myself touched as well and at the same time as touching."[77] It seems that there are two things to be noted here. First, that of reversibility in the sense of *interchangeability*. What happens when the handshake lingers on for too long; when my hand is not released from the shake despite my readiness to be done with it? Or if my hand gets caught in too vigorous an encounter, finding itself squeezed to the bones and shaken all about? Such fumbling may cause my hand—once an active participant in the handshake, as both touching and touched—to "pass over to the rank of the touched." And now what if perhaps expended from the vigor of the handshake, the other hand turns limp? Then my hand, left prolonging the doomed shake, returns to the rank of touching. My participation in the transaction is thus a dynamic one, susceptible to reversal and permutation, and my hand cycles between the modes of touching and being touched. But in addition to this interchangeability, what we have in the handshake—even more so than in the right hand touching the left hand touching the things—is a *doubling* of touching and being touched. In the handshake we have not only the possibility of passing over into the rank of the touched, but also the possibility of experiencing this touching and being touched synchronously, although granted, this takes place in the context of a self-other transaction. While not developed further in his (unfinished) manuscript, the example of the handshake is a highly suggestive example of how we might begin to think the reversibility of touch in terms of its simultaneity—the right and left hands touching each other perhaps (and not touching the things), or the hand touching itself. Taken together, these explorations in *The Visible and the Invisible* point to the variability and ambiguity of touch and the flesh.

A similar analysis can be unfurled in the visual register, and, indeed, for Merleau-Ponty (contra Husserl), the tangible and visible ought to be treated continuously, since each is "promised" to the other.[78] It is not only touch that is doubled for Merleau-Ponty, then, but also vision. For him, vision unfolds within the visible, and each seeing is itself capable of and vulnerable to being seen; a point well understood by those who are trained to attend to their seeing, such as the painter who is said to "feel myself looked at by the things."[79] This "narcissism" of the seer consists not only in her seeing the outside world according to and from the contours of her own body (the perspective imposed by one's body as discussed in chapter 2), but it also includes the experience that her body too is seen from this world. This is more than the Sartrean moment of recognition that one can exist "for-others," however. In Merleau-Ponty's account, one's being-seen "by the outside" (in a way that extends beyond the superficial seeing of one's body-contours) is equally something we participate in. To be seen in such a way, he continues, is to "exist within it, to emigrate into it . . . so that the seer and the visible reciprocate one another and we no longer know which sees and which is seen."[80] In contrast to Sartre, then, we find here notes of activity within the passivity of being-seen, traces of agency or maneuver within the possession of the look.

It is true that this represents a departure from Merleau-Ponty's earlier account in *Phenomenology of Perception*, where, for example, his exploration of perception was considered most saliently from the vantage point of one's own body (*le corps propre*), identified there as our frame and anchor in perceptual experience. And as Al-Saji has argued in her article, "Bodies and Sensings: On the Uses of Husserlian Phenomenology for Feminist Theory," where Merleau-Ponty does address the question of touch in *Phenomenology*, he often casts the experience of touching and touched in mutually exclusive terms, along the lines of the for-itself and in-itself, activity and passivity, and in doing so losing the moment of doubling that Husserl is able to advance.[81] On the other hand, commentators such as Dillon—in comparing Merleau-Ponty to Sartre—have pointed to former's references to the body as a "subject–object" in *Phenomenology*, and "its unequivocal status as touching and touched,"[82] to show how the traces of the intertwining are anticipated in this earlier work. But granting that the *Phenomenology* is indeed deeply wedded to the body's perspectival starting point—or by Al-Saji's analysis, still too tethered to subject/object dichotomies—the shift in Merleau-Ponty's *The Visible and Invisible* is not entirely discontinuous with his earlier work. For example, in the later work, it is not so much that this egoistic phenomenological starting point is repudiated (*my* vision starts still and always from the perspective imposed upon me by my body), it is rather that there is a paradigmatic shift, since now my vision *is not all that exists*, nor all that matters; there exist many other visions emanating from many other vantage points, and indeed, I find myself at the end of some of those. Thus it is not merely a case of bifurcating vision, but rather, situating one's vision in the broader network of vision and visibility in their generality and anonymity. In this schema, it becomes less important *who* sees, as we shift emphasis away from the subject and its perceptual horizon, to the phenomenon of vision itself: "There is here no problem of the *alter ego* because it is not *I* who sees, not *he* who sees, because an anonymous visibility inhabits both of us, a vision in general."[83]

Reversibility and Flesh Ontology

The insights drawn from the reversibility of touch and vision allow Merleau-Ponty to develop what is often referred to as his "flesh ontology." For him, the fact that the eye, as the seeing organ, has itself a visible existence is no mere factical truth, it also bears ontological significance. The same can be said of touch; the sensitive and receptive nature of the body's skin—the outermost layer of the flesh—points us to something about the structure of embodied being. Taking up these cues, Merleau-Ponty claims that in the case of vision, in order to see one must already be installed in the world as a participant, and installed in the schema and economy of visibility itself. In fact, this is the very *condition* of seeing. Weiss, speaking here in the register of touch, puts it this way: "It is because I touch that I can be touched, and if I am not touched, then I will not be able to touch; neither experience is reducible to the other, and yet each makes the other possible."[84] Of course such a position pits Merleau-Ponty in stark contrast to Sartre, for whom the ability to be seen by the other served only as a possibility or (in relation to the double sensation in touch) a *contingency*.[85] For Merleau-Ponty, however, this reversibility is a *condition* of our seeing; we are receptive to and of the world only insofar as we are already embedded in it, or in his words, only if *we are of it* ("*s'il en est*"). Elizabeth Grosz describes this as a "belongingness."[86] And yet, in being so installed, we too are rendered visible; we participate not just as seers but also as entities seen. The two sides, according to Merleau-Ponty, come together thus:

> It suffices for us for the moment to note that he who sees cannot possess the visible unless he is possessed by it, unless he *is of it*, unless . . . he is one of the visibles, capable, by a singular reversal, of seeing them—he who is one of them.[87]

And as commentators such as Grosz have argued, this ontological claim pertaining to the reversibility of the flesh is not one that always bears out factically, since the claim is "not an actual but only an in-principle reversibility of seer and seen or toucher and touched."[88]

The difference between Merleau-Ponty and Sartre on the question of reversibility is a significant one. As we have already intimated, whereas the reversibility of the look is possible for Sartre, in Merleau-Ponty's account we have something more than mere possibility, but closer to an interdependence; we can see *only because* we participate in the visible, and this participation mandates that we are, in principle, ourselves visible. In Merleau-Ponty, as in Husserl before him, it is not just a case of reversi*bility*, then, which in its suffix misleadingly intones ability or possibility; there is something more. Recall that for him, what is in question is the reversibility of the *flesh*. But what does the flesh designate? On one level, the flesh is simply the "in-between," the space mediating the distances of seer and seen. It is thus often described variously as a thickness, a lining, or a tissue, one that "for its part is not a thing, but a possibility, a latency."[89] Such descriptions borrow from our *actual flesh*, the skin which lines the outer epidermal boundaries of our body and interfaces with the world and its objects, serving thus as a *limnus* between the body and world. In Grosz's reading, Merleau-Ponty's "flesh" at times sounds like a precursor to Irigaray's concept of the "interval," although, of course, significant differences separate the two thinkers. Whereas the interval in Irigaray serves as the space of sexuate difference, or the space between the (at least) two originary beings, Merleau-Ponty does not ground his analysis in any real distinction between differently embodied beings (which opens him to criticism), and nor indeed is it the case that his concept of the flesh functions only as an in-between.

In Merleau-Ponty's case, it is more helpful to think of the flesh through the motif of "folding back" or what he sometimes also calls "invagination," although his use of this term can also be problematic from a feminist perspective.[90] We can think of the flesh as this folding back on itself, in the way that the seer's vision folds back on itself by being herself visible. As in biological and morphogenetic invagination, such folding renders ambiguous the outer and inner boundaries of its organs or organisms, and as Derrida's later deployment of the concept shows, in doing so the stability of these identities become compromised; we can speak of an "inner" or "outer" only insofar as we understand them to represent transient modes or moments of being, and not fixed entities. Indeed, on this reading, the flesh is neither simply inner nor outer, but both. This being-both-at-once, which we saw earlier in the case of touch and the simultaneous possibility of both touching and being touched, is alternately invoked by Merleau-Ponty in the following description:

> If one wants metaphors, it would be better to say that the body sensed and the body sentient are as the obverse and the reverse, or again, as two segments of one sole circular course which goes above from the left to right and below from right to left, but which is but *one sole movement in its two phases*. (my emphasis)[91]

This image helps us to understand and better situate his references to the doubling of vision and touch. Contrary to Sartre's presentation of the being-for-itself and being-for-others as oppositional and mutually exclusive modes, according to Merleau-Ponty when my body passes through the different modes of "seeing" and "being seen" it expresses the same movement, that of my body's participation in the visible.

Finally, we should note that for the late Merleau-Ponty, the ambiguity of this reversibility, of the flesh proper, is not presented as an impediment to sense making, but is rather *generative* of it. As various commentators have pointed out, his distinct affirmation of ambiguity sets him apart from his peers—even Husserl, from whom he borrows the notion of obscurity (as Weiss has argued, in Husserl's work such obscurity is framed in the negative terms of obstruction[92]). Merleau-Ponty, on the other hand, insists on the ambiguity of the flesh as ultimately productive: "It is that the thickness of the flesh between the seer and the thing is constitutive for the thing of its visibility as for the seer of his corporeity; it is not an obstacle between them, it is their means of communication."[93] In other words, it is the ambiguity of being able to pass through subject- and object-modes of being, *as well as* the bivalence of experiencing both modes concurrently, which gives meaning to our encounters.

Merleau-Ponty's Chiasm and Racialized Embodiment

How does this account, in which we have noted significant departures from Sartre, challenge or extend our existing account of racialized embodiment, the racializing gaze, and the lived experience of being-object or objectified? In what follows, I argue that there are three main ways our account becomes further nuanced by a Merleau-Pontian flesh ontology.

Seeing Oneself Being Seen, and the Subject-Object Dissolution

The first point is relatively straightforward. Earlier we encountered some of the limitations of the Sartrean model insofar as it struggled to account for the more complex dimensions of racialized embodiment. As I have argued, the lived experience of racism and racialization entails not just being seen, but also seeing oneself being seen; it entails an objectification of the body but also *living* that objectification, which is to say, making sense of and navigating it. In fact, to borrow Yancy's words, it becomes a matter of "political and existential survival" to learn how one's body appears within the racialized schema, in order to navigate one's way through social, political, cultural, and even professional worlds. As one example, we can point to the way white standards of beauty can have a crushing effect on the way young women of color see and relate to their own bodies, with many documented stories of girls and women engaging in skin bleaching or even cosmetic procedures to emulate certain prized white features. So hegemonic is the white gaze that racialized bodies can quickly learn to see themselves according to it, that is, to see oneself according to another's gaze. But whereas Sartre's dualism prevented us from moving beyond the mutually exclusive terms of subject and object, in Merleau-Ponty's later schema we find a way to articulate the complexity of racialized embodiment in relation to the gaze. In particular, his account of the reversibility of the flesh and the intertwining of the traditional poles of being allows us to see how we are, in Shannon Sullivan's words, "ambiguously subject and object at the same time, reversing [our] positions as subject-touching and object-touched."[94] Racialized embodiment, I argue, *is this intertwining*; as much as we are gazed at, stereotyped, discriminated against, abused, refused, imitated, alienated, and so forth, we respond. We anticipate, we "world"-travel. The *lived* experience of racialization is one of multiple-consciousness and of perennial negotiation. Racialized embodiment is, as Lugones and others have argued, to be constantly embroiled in a sophisticated existential gymnastics. We move between the modes of being-subject and being-object, and very often, we are synchronously being-subject-*and*-object—that is to say, the distinction between subject and object ceases to be meaningful in our navigating what Cornel West calls, "the *funk* of life."[95] While this is to some extent true for all human beings, I argue that racialized embodiment in the context of a racist world engenders a certain kind of "schizophrenic" being[96]; neither for-oneself nor fully for-others, neither at-home nor fully homeless—in short, neither subject nor object, but always both and somewhere in-between.

The Hegemony of the Racializing Gaze and the Impossibility of Reversal

And yet, this is not to obscure or wash over the very real ways in which racialized bodies get "trapped in" the mode of being-object or being-for-others. Nor is it to trivialize the weight of that defining and traumatic experience. As we noted earlier the Sartrean paradigm of the gazing-subject/gazed-at-object resonates powerfully with critical race scholars precisely because it describes an enduring dimension of what it means to be racialized and to live one's body in and through a racist world. Recall that Fanon experiences himself as "object in the midst of other objects." Others too have deployed this paradigm to explain the deep disempowerment of those bodies who are routinely subject to racist acts, comments, gestures, and the like. It is my view, however, that these express only one aspect—though surely a salient and profoundly important one—of the lived experience of racialized embodiment. More importantly, I think they serve to show us how the hegemonic gaze in oppressive systems can get us "stuck" in a certain mode being-object, foreclosing the breadth of chiasmic being, the implications of which I explore more fully in the concluding remarks of this book. Though in principle reversible, the hegemony of the white gaze is not easily shrugged off by a reversibility of the visibles. Thus while Bernasconi is right to credit Sartre for holding up a mirror to whites in his controversially received "Black Orpheus,"[97] disrupting their millennia-long "privilege of seeing without being seen," it is not the case that this returned gaze stands in symmetrical relation to the white gaze of Black (or otherwise racialized) bodies. Indeed, the "shock of being seen" that Sartre hoped to effect through his support of the *Négritude* movement ("Black Orpheus" first appeared as a preface to Senghor's seminal *Anthologie*) was a "shock" only to the extent that it rallied against the deep entrenchment and steadfast hold of the white gaze—a gaze which remains very much in place today. The point about reversibility, then, ought not distract us from the way we can become ensnared in paradigms that foist upon us certain modes of being, and in the case of racialized bodies, the mode of being-object. But having worked through an analysis of the intertwining, what we can now say is that in the racializing gaze, it is as if the hegemonic directional force from white subject to racialized object is itself a crystallization of that which *ought to* remain ambiguous and fluid. Through the racializing gaze we become stuck in a model of subject and object, missing out on the productive ambiguity and ambi-valence of the in-between.

Interestingly, we seem to find conceptual space for this question of the hegemonic gaze in Merleau-Ponty's qualifying comments on reversibility in *The Visible and Invisible*. Despite his highly integrated and intertwined account of flesh ontology, at a certain point in the manuscript Merleau-Ponty declares convergence to be never fully realized nor realizable. Rather, it is a reversibility that is only ever *almost* attained, eluding us always in the final moment. I quote at length:

> To begin with, we spoke summarily of a reversibility of the seeing and the visible, of the touching and the touched. It is time to emphasize that it is a reversibility always imminent and never realized in fact. My left hand is always on the verge of touching my right hand touching the things, but I never reach coincidence; the coincidence eclipses at the moment of realization, and one of two things always occurs: either my right hand really passes over to the rank of the touched, but then its hold on the world is interrupted; or it retains its hold on the world, but then I do not really touch *it*—my right hand touching, I palpate with my left hand only its outer covering. Likewise, I do not hear myself as I hear others, the sonorous existence of my voice is for me as it were poorly exhibited; I have rather an echo of its articulated existence, it vibrates through my head rather than outside. I am always on the same side of my body; it presents itself to me in one invariable perspective.[98]

In other words, it is never the case that we *fully* reach both modes of touching and touched in the same moment, although we may come very close. This, I think, leaves an important space in which we can insist on the centrality of one's historical and political milieux, and the way that certain norms or racialized paradigms have a gravitas that are not easily transcended. That is, it is important that the notion of reversibility does not downplay the power of habituated modes of perception or comportment that derive from these norms. When Weiss writes that, "just as in the famous duck/rabbit Gestalt, we cannot experience both at once,"[99] we are reminded of how certain habits of seeing can "stick"; thwarting attempts to move fluidly between different paradigms, or better, to move *from* dominant ones.

Racialized "Passing," and the Persistence of the Visual Register

Finally, much has been made of the move from an ontology informed by the taxonomy of vision to one informed by the touch. As already noted, for Mazis this is what makes Merleau-Ponty's ontology more viable than Sartre's[100], whereas for Grosz, Merleau-Ponty still does not make enough of a transition from the visual to the haptic. Despite their different readings, what is shared across both commentators is the affirmation of touch as a productive paradigm through which to develop a more nuanced ontology. (And on this count, the work of thinkers such as Derrida and Jean-Luc Nancy speak powerfully to this potential.[101]) I contend that this shift can also be an instructive one for us, insofar as our own analyses of racism and racialization have predominantly unfolded within the visual register (unsurprisingly, given the stated focus of this chapter on the gaze). In a way, the push from the visual to the haptic register in Merleau-Ponty prompts us to question whether we too have overstated or over-relied on the visual register in our own analyses of race, succumbing to Western philosophy's "ocularcentrism," to use Linda Alcoff's term. Surely there exist a multitude of registers through which racism and racialization operate. Does this emphasis on the visual serve to obfuscate certain other aspects of the lived experience of racism and racialization? To answer this, I turn briefly to a consideration of the phenomenon of "passing."

In fact we have already encountered this phenomenon in our earlier engagement with Weiss' writing on the ambiguity of Jewish identity. While her argument extended the notion of ambiguity to the category of racialized bodies more generally, the *visual* ambiguity of the Jew in particular (especially in the twenty-first century[102]) calls to mind the question of passing. Sartre raises the point in *Anti-Semite and Jew*, when recounting the story of a Jewish friend who according to him was easily recognizable among the French, but not (since he was "blond, lean, and phlegmatic") among the Germans. Sartre recalls of this friend: "He occasionally amused himself by going out with SS men, who did not suspect his race. One of them said to him one day: 'I can tell a Jew a hundred yards off.'"[103] While this example, along with others (including Alcoff's own reflections on her experiences as compared with her more phenotypically Latina sister's[104]) document some of the advantages of "passing" within a racist world, there exist also narratives that explore its more painful side. For example, Allyson Hobbs explores some of the personal struggles of those who "pass" in her recent book, *A Chosen Exile: A History of Racial Passing in American Life*, and it is striking the way her reflections recall some of our earlier discussion on homelessness:

> This book is about loss. Racial passing is an exile, sometimes chosen, sometimes not. . . . Between the late eighteenth and the mid-twentieth centuries,

countless African Americans passed as white, leaving behind families, friends, and communities without any available avenue for return.[105]

While eliding the visual experience of the racializing gaze, those who pass may nonetheless share in the lived experiences of bodily fragmentation or uncanniness in ways that directly reference and flow from the racialized schema. The emphasis on the metric of visibility thus may blind us, as it were, to other equally harmful lived experiences of racism.

And yet, this need not undermine the centrality of the visual register in our analysis of racism; rather, it serves to draw attention to the *racialized schema's own reliance on the visual field*, such that "passing" becomes the anomaly it is. An example may help to illustrate. In what has since come to be known as the Stolen Generations affair, thousands of Aboriginal Australian children—especially those with lighter or "fairer" skin and features—were systematically and in many cases forcibly removed from their families and communities throughout the twentieth century by government agencies. This was a practice that spanned decades and its policy justifications were many and various, including the idea that these children would fare better in life in "mainstream Australia" (in many cases "passing" as whites), and for some, the hope that this would conveniently resolve Australia's "Aboriginal problem."[106] The harrow and distress of this affair have been well documented; families and communities were not only torn apart, but longstanding cultural and linguistic practices also dissipated along with them. Stories recount the atmosphere of fear and terror that engulfed the lives of such children and their families:

> Every morning our people would crush charcoal and mix that with animal fat and smother that all over us, so that when the police came they could only see black children in the distance. We were told always to be on the alert and, if white people came, to run into the bush or run and stand behind the trees as stiff as a poker, or else hide behind logs or run into culverts and hide.
>
> There was a disruption of our cycle of life because we were continually scared to be ourselves. During the raids on the camps it was not unusual for people to be shot—shot in the arm or the leg. You can understand the terror that we lived in, the fright—not knowing when someone will come unawares and do whatever they were doing—either disrupting our family life, camp life, or shooting at us.[107]

In many ways this example appears to run contrary to dominant analyses of race and visibility, since it documents an example of racist harm *reserved specifically* for those whose bodies could "pass" for normatively ideal white bodies.[108] In other words, it was the ambiguity of these children's bodies that rendered them more vulnerable. And yet as I would argue, far from bypassing it, this harm was effected *through* the visual register (e.g., bodies blackened so as not to solicit attention), in the context of a broader racist schema that deemed the bodies of Aboriginal peoples unworthy of family, culture, community, and the basic right to steer one's life path.

The visual register then remains a powerful—though not exclusive—site for the machinations of racism and racialization. This is a position shared by leading race scholars such as Alcoff and Al-Saji, and clearly implicit in the writings of Fanon and Yancy. Moreover, I would argue that to the extent that other bodily and sensory registers are also sites of racism, they often take their cue from the visual register. It once took several friendly encounters before an artist neighbor in Brooklyn—and fellow Australian—realized that I too shared his Antipodean roots. Puzzled by his attempts, in the course of a discussion of his painting, to explain to me Tasmania's location ("a little island off mainland Australia"), I mention that I grew up close by in Melbourne. He was flabbergasted. "But, your accent—*ohhhh, I hear it now.*" Somehow in all our conversations prior, my Australian accent—his self-same—did not register for his ear; the very same accent which at the time amused my two American housemates and gave much trouble to my third Korean-becoming-American housemate. The visual presentation of my Asian body served to structure and ultimately muffle his hearing, to pass over the cues of my broad vowels and tonal shifts, in short, to pass over the mimicry of our speech in a place where ours were the ones that stood out. In a contrasting example, it was not an uncommon occurrence for my white partner to be mistaken for German while living in Berlin, despite his Australian accented speech and beginner level German language—a problem I never seemed to have despite my more advanced German. The visual encounter of a body can, I argue, serve to frame our perceptions across other sensory registers of the body. No real need then, for the Martinican man in Fanon's story, to have worked so diligently on rolling his French *R*s ("*Garrrçon!*"[109]); his body remained Black, his voice heard as Black, despite the effort. While Fanon is of course right that language and speech serve as important gateways for the colonial subject, they by no means dislodge vision as the structuring force of our bodily encounters.

As I have argued here, there is something about the racialized schema that compels us to the visual register, and its persistence is tracked in the discussions above. However, this is not to say that the visual register is without its own complexity, as I have tried to argue in the case of "passing." Thus following our earlier analysis on the different ways of looking, and Merleau-Ponty's own dynamic presentation of the doubling of vision, I suggest that we can be more attentive to the nuances of the racializing gaze.

Coda—The Ontological Violence of Racism

In moving between Sartre's and Merleau-Ponty's different accounts of vision and visibility and their pertinence for our analyses of the racializing gaze, we have in turn moved through different ontological frameworks and the alternate accounts of racialized embodiment they make possible. Having done so, it is a timely moment for us to take a step back and ask: What in fact is the ontological violence of racism?

In the earlier parts of this chapter we considered how the experience of racialized embodiment is most saliently described as a kind of being-object. Certainly as we have seen in Fanon, it is an enduring aspect in the lived experience of his Black body in world organized according to the white imaginary. But insofar as racism is understood primarily as an objectification of racialized bodies from subjects into objects, we will tend to conceptualize the ontological violence of racism as violence against one's subjectivity. This, I think, is certainly intelligible in the political domain—insofar as racism disempowers certain peoples, renders them alien from their own bodies, identities, and communities, it is politically defensible that efforts are directed toward the reclamation of these bodies and identities for themselves. The language of self-determination and autonomous organizing in the context of decolonial movements, for example, speaks to the critical importance of this work. However, in a philosophical register, I think there is something more we can say. Thinking as we have, through the prism of the relational, phenomenal body, a body which is not static, pre-given, or self-contained, but rather one that is situated, animated, and co-constituted by its world, and which in turn *co-constitutes* its world, what we have available to us now are the tools for a more complex articulation of racialized embodiment, as well as that which is violated by the practices, or habits, of racism. The ontological violence of racism is not a violence against our subjectivity, as traditional accounts of racism would have it, but rather—and more urgently—a violence against our *intersubjectivity*. It is a violence against our embodied *being-with*. If, as we move closer to a Merleau-Pontian account of flesh ontology, the meaning of one's being is not given nor willed, but rather *forged* through the embodied interaction with others, places, situations, and practices, then what is cut short by the overhanging and overpowering force of racism is the possibility to do precisely that—to make meaning of one's world through embodied engagement with it. Moreover, racism pushes us into a model of subject–object ontology, despite the necessarily messy and ambiguous nature of our being-subject-*and*-object, and attempts to devise a world split into (white) subjects and their (racialized) objects. In doing so it threatens to efface the fluidity and ambiguity of embodied being, creating instead a world of dualisms, a world of literal and figurative Blacks and whites.

Philosophers of color have often described the experience of racialized embodiment in terms of a forestalled motility—a freezing of one's bodily and ontological registers of being. George Yancy, for example, has on various occasions described racism not only as that which "ontologically truncates," but also as that which ontologically *paralyzes*.[110] Fanon, in the epigraph to this chapter, writes: *Je suis fixé*, "I am fixed." We can take this to mean both that he is substantively predetermined in the content of his being, but also that he is *frozen* in the movement of his being; cornered and left no room to move or expand. Set against the thrownness that Heidegger famously attributes to reflective being, to *Dasein*, the paralyzed or frozen being cannot take up the dynamic temporality proper to it. And as we noted in chapter 2, racism leaves its racialized subjects no shared present, to borrow Al-Saji's point, in which to live with others. The removal of the possibility for meaningful encounters with others in the world, as philosophers such as Guenther has argued, amounts to an ontological violence. While Guenther's work considers how the extreme cases of prisoner isolation in solitary confinement violates the "structure of open relationality" that lies at the foundation of our being,[111] we can draw parallels with the theme of isolation (even if only figuratively) or alienation in the case of racialized bodies. This denial of the fundamental being-with (whether *Mitsein* in Heidegger, intercorporeality in Merleau-Ponty, or *être avec* in Nancy), and the motility to actively participate in the world while navigating one's way through the weight of its historicity, is what I identify as the ontological violence of racism.

NOTES

1. Note that the original is *"Tiens, un nègre!"* The verb *tenir* literally means "to hold." And yet, in its imperative form, *tiens!* does translate well to "look!" It can also mean variously: "wait!" "hold on!" "here (you go)." The temporal dimension of the verb *tenir* indicates the sense of pause or waiting, and thus it functions to inject a moment of interruption, soliciting one's (often visual) attention. For this reason, its translation as "look!" is appropriate; however, it is important not to lose its other senses of holding, waiting, even hesitating (to invoke Al-Saji's work on racialized habits and hesitation).

2. I say "commonly" and not "exclusively" because I think there are expressions of racism which do not directly or explicitly invoke the racist gaze. One example is that of white entitlement, as explored in chapter 2; this does not function on the basis on a gaze of the other—in fact it functions via a non-gaze of the self.

3. Michael Dodson, "The End in the Beginning: Re(de)finding Aboriginality," delivered as the Wentworth Lecture to the Australian Institute of Aboriginal and Torres Strait Islander Studies, 1994. Transcript available here: https://www.humanrights.gov.

au/news/speeches/end-beginning-redefinding-aboriginality-dodson-1994 (accessed January 11, 2015).

4. I put quotation marks around this word, following Dodson, to mark its pejorative tone. Though grammatically correct in its nominal form, in the contemporary Australian context the term is avoided at most levels of society—in government, the community sector, news broadcasting—precisely because of its connotations of a specimen under investigation. The preferred terms are "Aboriginal Australians" or "Indigenous Australians" though there remain some controversy over these.

5. Dodson, "The End in the Beginning: Re(de)finding Aboriginality."

6. W.E.B. DuBois, *Strivings of the Negro People*, 194

7. I also argue that the different examples of the gaze can bring out more clearly the distinction between "racism" and "racialization" as I have been employing the terms throughout the book. In particular, the fetishizing gaze serves as an example of what we can readily count as racialization, though not so readily as racism (even though I maintain that it is still *racist*).

8. This chapter entitled *l'Experience vécue du Noir* has been poorly translated as "The Fact of Blackness" in Markmann's translation.

9. Fanon, *Black Skin, White Masks*, 109.

10. Ibid. This is likely a deliberate variation of Sartre's "being-for-others."

11. Fanon, *Peau Noire, Masques Blancs*, 11; *Black Skin, White Masks*, 14.

12. Sartre, *Anti-Semite and Jew*, 69.

13. I focus primarily on Fanon in this section, given his importance in the field of critical race scholarship, but also because of the relative convenience of being able to draw a clear lineage from Sartre to him. There are many other important critical race and post-colonial scholars however (such as W.E.B. DuBois, Edward Said, bell hooks, Sara Ahmed), for whom Sartre is not an influence (he comes chronologically after in some cases), but for whom I argue Sartre's account might still provide a compatible theoretical foundation. My specific treatment of Fanon and Sartre then functions also metonymically, to invoke other common discourses of racism which proceed around the touchstones of racism—gaze—object.

14. This is Moran's term, see: Dermot Moran, "Sartre's Treatment of the Body in *Being and Nothingness*" in Jean-Pierre Boulé and Benedict O'Donohoe (eds.), *Jean-Paul Sartre: Mind and Body, Word and Deed* (Newcastle: Cambridge Scholars Publishing, 2011), 15.

15. Jean-Paul Sartre, *Being and Nothingness*, trans. Hazel E, Barnes (New York: Washington Square Press, 1992), 460.

16. Sartre writes that they amount to the same thing (Ibid., 445); however, Martin C. Dillon disagrees, arguing that Sartre wrongly understands the two (the Other's being-for-me and my being-for-Other) as reciprocal when in fact they are not. Martin C. Dillon, "Sartre on the Phenomenal Body and Merleau-Ponty's Critique" in Jon Stewart (ed.), *The Debate between Sartre and Merleau-Ponty* (Evanston: Northwestern University Press, 1998), 127.

17. I think "the gaze" works as a translation for *le regard* here, since it soon becomes clear that the kind of look Sartre has in mind most closely equivocates the gaze in English; however, this is not to say that his treatment is *always* one of "the

gaze" over the "look." Indeed one of the advantages of the French term is that it allows greater movement or slippage between the two senses of "gaze" and "look." It is also relevant to note in this context that Lacan's and Foucault's separate works on *le regard* are often translated as "the gaze" (although a fuller examination of their respective treatments of *le regard* would be required before making the case for the translation of "the gaze" on this basis alone).

18. Jean-Paul Sartre, *Being and Nothingness*, trans. Hazel E, Barnes (New York: Washington Square Press, 1992), 340.

19. Ibid., 129.

20. Sartre, *Being and Nothingness*, 347.

21. Ibid., 360.

22. Ibid., 343.

23. Ibid.

24. Ibid.

25. Ibid., 350.

26. Michel Foucault, *Discipline and Punish: The Birth of the Prison* (New York: Vintage, 1976), 201.

27. It is important to note that Foucault's analysis in *Discipline and Punish* speaks of *institutional power* insofar as his analyses pertain to institutional contexts such as prison, schools (and in other works, the medical and scientific contexts). However, I speak here of power in its generality, since I believe that his account of institutional power and its entanglement with the visual register is also generalizable to power in non-institutional contexts.

28. Although note that this is not some naive claim that all racism would dissipate if we all just live together. Rather the argument is that forms of racist perception are thoroughly embedded in our "affective maps," not always accessible or changeable by our cognitive efforts. Al-Saji, "A Phenomenology of Hesitation," 160. Note also that Lewis Gordon agrees on the point of affectivity: "It is difficult to imagine a racist who is without some form of emotional or affective response in the presence of the people whom he regards as his racial inferiors." Lewis R. Gordon, *Bad Faith and Antiblack Racism* (Amherst, NY: Humanity Books, 1999), 78.

29. Heidegger, *Being and Time*, 79.

30. Gordon, *Bad Faith and Antiblack Racism*, 103.

31. Edward W. Said, *Orientalism* 25th Anniversary Edition (New York: Vintage Books, 2003), 97.

32. Shannon Sullivan, "White World-Traveling," 303.

33. Sartre, *Being and Nothingness*, 738.

34. Casey, *World at a Glance*, 132.

35. Ibid., 140.

36. Fanon, *Black Skin, White Masks,* 117.

37. Ralph Ellison, *Invisible Man* (New York: Vintage, 1980), 1.

38. Yancy, *Black Bodies, White Gazes*, 76.

39. I thank Eva Kittay for prompting this line of inquiry.

40. Rosemarie Garland-Thomson, *Staring: How We Look* (New York: Oxford University Press, 2009), 50.

41. Ibid., 112–113.

42. Ibid., 83.

43. Cited in Robert Bernasconi, "Sartre's Gaze Returned: The Transformation of the Phenomenology of Racism," *Graduate Faculty Philosophy Journal* 18(2) (1995): 201–221, 201.

44. Ibid.

45. Garland-Thomson, *Staring*, 83.

46. Mazis opts for the language of "the regard" even though this transliteration of *le regard* does not work well in contemporary English. But we can understand his decision insofar as it does allow him to refrain from committing to either look or gaze (see note 17 for a discussion of the translation of *le regard* as "the look" or "the gaze"). Glen A. Mazis, "Touch and Vision: Rethinking with Merleau-Ponty Sartre on the Caress" in Stewart (ed.), *The Debate between Sartre and Merleau-Ponty*, 144.

47. Ibid., 150.

48. Ibid., 151.

49. Elizabeth Grosz, *Volatile Bodies: Toward a Corporeal Feminism* (Bloomington: Indiana University Press, 1994), 105–106.

50. Grosz (following Irigaray) argues, for example, that the visual register as the register in which phallocentric "lack" can be most effectively thematized: "... the visual is the domain in which lack is to be located; it is the order of plenitude, gestalt, and absence: the order which designates female genitals as missing, an order which is incompatible with the plenitude, enfolding and infinite complexity of the tactile and the tangible." Ibid., 106. I disagree, however, that the visual register is bound to an economy of "lack"; in the case of racialized bodies, it is not "lack" that is thematized, but "excess." The racialized body is that which has an excess, of pigmentation, of meaning. Notably here, the white body is not conceived as a "lack," but as the neutral, or a non-lacking nothing.

51. W.E.B. Du Bois, *The Souls of Black Folk* (Chicago: Dover, 1994), 2.

52. Dermot Moran, "Revisiting Sartre's Ontology of Embodiment in *Being and Nothingness*" in Vesselin Petrov (ed.), *Ontological Landscapes: Recent Thought on Conceptual Interfaces between Science and Philosophy* (Frankfurt: Ontos-Verlag, 2011), 273.

53. Dillon, "Sartre on the Phenomenal Body and Merleau-Ponty's Critique," 126.

54. Sartre, *Being and Nothingness*, 460.

55. Ibid., 344–345.

56. Jean-Paul Sartre, "Black Orpheus," *The Massachusetts Review* 6(1) (1964): 13–52, 13.

57. Fanon, *Black Skin, White Masks*, 110.

58. Sarte, *Being and Nothingness*, 461.

59. Moran, "Revisiting Sartre's Ontology of Embodiment in *Being and Nothingness*," 274.

60. Sartre, *Being and Nothingness*, 461 and 463.

61. Ibid., 404.

62. Ibid., 347.

63. Fanon, *Black Skin, White Masks*, 112.

64. I raise this point since Sartre makes a distinction between the pre-reflective and reflective levels, writing for example: "The object-state of my body for the Other is not an object for me and can not constitute my body which I exist. . . . It is therefore on the level of the reflective consciousness that the Other's knowledge can be brought into play." Sartre, *Being and Nothingness*, 464. My claim, however, is that this apprehension of oneself as-object can occur across reflective and pre-reflective registers.

65. Ibid., 133.

66. Dermot Moran, "Sartre's Treatment of the Body in *Being and Nothingness*: The 'Double Sensation' in Jean-Pierre Boulé and Benedict O'Donohoe (eds.), *Jean-Paul Sartre: Mind and Body, Word and Deed* (Newcastle: Cambridge Scholars Publishing, 2001), 9–26, 20.

67. Ibid., 134.

68. Ibid., 137–138. I think Dillon's term "disappointed expectations" resonates powerfully with my own earlier reflections in chapter 2 of "doing the markets" in Paris, where the racially objectifying interjection registered in me as an overriding feeling of disappointment (in addition to anger and humiliation). Dillon's analysis here gives a rich analysis of why that was the case, noting the underlying expectations of selfhood and solidarity which get thwarted.

69. Fanon, *Black Skin, White Masks*, 115–116.

70. Weiss also notes that another key difference is that Sartre speaks of overdetermination from within, whereas for Fanon it is primarily overdetermination from without. Gail Weiss, "Pride and Prejudice: Ambiguous Racial, Religious, and Ethnic Identities of Jewish Bodies" in Lee (ed.), *Living Alterities*, 221.

71. Of course, as Weiss notes there are Black Jews and other Jews of color. Ibid., 220.

72. That is, Weiss argues that Fanon's sharp distinction between the Jew and the Black seems to suggest that Jewishness is visible on the visual register primarily through "voluntary" modes of presentation (clothing, hair, style). While I think she is right to demand a more nuanced treatment of the relation of racial identity to the epidermal layer (especially viz., the phenomenon of racial "passing"), I wonder if she is perhaps too critical of Fanon here. For one, he does acknowledge the way in which bodily physiognomy is one salient aspect "exposing" Jews to a level of visibility. But second, I think his claim concerns the immediacy of the flesh, and the way in which racist structures of perception *do* home in on certain aspects of bodily presentation before others as a primary indicator of race (which is different from saying that they ought to). Ibid., 227.

73. Ibid., 216.

74. Sartre, *Anti-Semite & Jew*, 64.

75. Moran, "Sartre's Treatment of the Body in *Being and Nothingness*," 18.

76. Maurice Merleau-Ponty, *The Visible and Invisible*, trans. Alphonso Lingis (Evanston: Northwestern University Press, 1969), 133–134.

77. Ibid., 142.

78. Ibid., 134.

79. Ibid., 139.

80. Ibid.

81. Alia Al-Saji, "Bodies and Sensings: On the Uses of Husserlian Phenomenology for Feminist Theory," *Continental Philosophy Review* 43 (2010): 13–37, 20–22.

82. Dillon, "Sartre on the Phenomenal Body and Merleau-Ponty's Critique," 134.

83. Merleau-Ponty, *The Visible and Invisible*, 142.

84. Gail Weiss, "Ambiguity, Absurdity, and Reversibility: Indeterminacy in de Beauvoir, Camus, and Merleau-Ponty," *Journal of French and Francophone Philosophy*, 5 (2010): 81.

85. And as Moran notes, this bodily contingency for Sartre is the origin of our nausea.

86. Perception "entails a reversibility based on the belongingness of the material subject to its material world" Grosz, *Volatile Bodies*, 102. This is a nice way of putting it, since it also evokes our earlier discussion of home and belongingness.

87. Merleau-Ponty, *The Visible and Invisible*, 134–135.

88. Grosz, *Volatile Bodies*, 101. Although it is perhaps misleading to describe it as *only* in-principle since this in-principle-ness means that reversibility is always *accorded in advance*, even it does not factually eventuate.

89. Merleau-Ponty, *The Visible and Invisible*, 132.

90. In an article on Irigaray's critique of Merleau-Ponty, Grosz opens by asking: "Is Merleau-Ponty's notion of the flesh—'fold back, invagination, or padding' simply another masculine appropriation of the metaphors of femininity to ground an ontology, epistemology or theoretical system? Is it simply another way of asserting the sexual neutrality (i.e., the implicit masculinity) or theoretical paradigms and systems which, as Irigaray so astutely observes, has characterized Western philosophy since its inception? . . . Is he participating in that centuries-old practice of recuperation and unacknowledged reliance on femininity and its conceptual and linguistic representations which is the defining characteristic of phallocentric thought?" Elizabeth Grosz, "Merleau-Ponty and Irigaray in the Flesh," *Thesis Eleven* 36 (1993): 37.

91. Merleau-Ponty, *The Visible and Invisible*, 138.

92. Weiss, "Ambiguity, Absurdity, and Reversibility," 72–74.

93. Merleau-Ponty, *The Visible and Invisible*, 135.

94. Sullivan, *Living Across and Through Skins: Transactional Bodies, Pragmatism, and Feminism* (Bloomington: Indiana University Press, 2001), 83.

95. Cornel West, "Afterword: Philosophy and the Funk of Life" in George Yancy (ed.), *Cornel West: A Critical Reader* (Malden: Wiley Blackwell, 2001), 346. West's discussion of the mess or "funk" of life calls to mind Merleau-Ponty's own emphasis on the meaningfulness of the everyday aspects of one's life, no matter how banal. "So that's what he does with his time? So that's the ugly house he lives in? And these are his friends, the woman with whom he shares his life. These, his mediocre concerns? ... One admires as one should only after having understood that there are not any supermen, that there is no one who does not have a human's life to live, and that the secret of the woman loved, of the writer, or of the painter, does not lie in some realm beyond his empirical life, but is so mixed in with his mediocre experiences, so modestly confused with his perception of the world, that there can be no question of meeting it separately, face to face." Maurice Merleau-Ponty, "Indirect Language and the Voices of Silence" in Johnson (ed.), *The Merleau-Ponty Aesthetics Reader*, 95.

The shared resonance is I think not coincidental insofar as West's pragmatism and Merleau-Ponty's interest in embodiment bring them both to engage with the materiality of life.

96. I use this term loosely in order to track the neuroses of Black embodiment explored by Fanon, and those who follow him, for example: William Miles, "Schizophrenic Island, fifty years after Fanon: Martinique, the pent-up 'paradise,'" *International Journal of Francophone Studies* 15 (2012). But while Fanon's own work crosses into the psychoanalytic register, my own reference to "schizophrenic" being seeks to reference the more general and chronic disorientation, displacement, and fragmentation explored throughout this book, and not psychical or clinical senses of the term.

97. Bernasconi writes: "[Sartre's] hope was that White readers of the anthology would experience, as he had, 'the shock of being seen.' Whites, having been what in *Being and Nothingness* he had called the we-subjects of Blacks, now found that 'our gaze comes back to our own eyes.' In Sartrean terms, so long a Europeans and European-Americans failed to pass through that totally disarming reversal of the gaze, their sense of their own superiority would remain untouched." Bernasconi, "Sartre's Gaze Returned," 207.

98. Merleau-Ponty, *The Visible and Invisible*, 147–148.

99. Weiss, "Ambiguity, Absurdity, and Reversibility," 81.

100. As Mazis argues, even though Sartre does consider the touch imposes this structure of the gaze in his analysis of touching, and in particular, the caress. In doing so, Mazis argues that Sartre not only fundamentally mischaracterizes touching, overlooking its distinctive features, but in doing so, he thereby misses the opportunity to think different possible modes of interaction or being-with. What Sartre misses, according to Mazis, is how "In touch, the distinction between touching subject and touched object blurs: in other words, the distinction between activity and passivity dissolves. Rather than a confrontation and appropriation, there is a permeability of boundaries and an opening up of interpenetration, of communion." Mazis, "Touch and Vision," 148.

101. See, for example: Nancy, *Corpus* and Derrida, *On Touching*.

102. That is to say, many Jews who would not have "passed" as easily in the last century, especially around the period of WWII, might well "pass" quite easily today. This demonstrates how "passing" (and indeed the visual identification of "obviously racialized bodies") is thoroughly embedded its social, cultural, and historical contexts.

103. Sartre, *Anti-Semite & Jew*, 61–62.

104. Alcoff, *Visible Identities*, 266.

105. Allyson Hobbs, *A Chosen Exile: A History of Racial Passing in American Life* (Cambridge: Harvard University Press, 2014), 4.

106. *Bringing Them Home: Report of the National Inquiry into the Separation of Aboriginal and Torres Strait Islander Children from Their Families* (Sydney: Human Rights and Equal Opportunity Commission, 1997).

107. Ibid., 21.

108. In other words, it is not a case of mere reversal where whites are targeted in a majority Black society.

109. Fanon, *Peau Noire, Masques Blancs*, 16.

110. George Yancy, "Forms of Spatial and Textual Alienation: The Lived Experience of Philosophy as Occlusion," *Graduate Faculty Philosophy Journal* 35 (2014): 2.

111. Guenther, *Solitary Confinement*, 156.

Conclusion

During a 2014 panel discussion on the narratives of hope, progress, and despair in the context of the race discourse in America, guest panelist and Latino studies/political theory scholar Cristina Beltrán commented: "what a lot of African-American intellectuals and race scholars in general ask people to do is to *sit with the tragedy* of white racism, or to sit with the tragedy of racial violence, and *really sit with it*, and think about it and engage it, and not always shift to the happy ending, to the language of innocence."[1] Beltrán identifies here a tension frequently encountered in critical race work, especially when undertaken by people of color; namely, how to present analyses and critiques of longstanding and far-reaching systems of white oppression without having these all washed over by claims of "progress" in racial justice, even where that progress may be real and measurable. Or conversely, how to, when charting the markers of this progress, *hold open* the space for the brutality, pain, and violence of racism to be aired, and equally, to be heard.

In a book on her experience of a traumatic rape and its aftermath, Susan Brison explores the importance of two activities for survivors of rape and trauma: remembering and listening. And yet in spite of their importance, she argues that our culture fails chronically on both counts. Of the former, she writes:

> As a society, we live with the unbearable by pressuring those who have been traumatized to forget, and by rejecting the testimonies of those who are forced by fate to remember. As individuals and as cultures, we impose arbitrary term limits on memory and on recovery from trauma: a century, say, for slavery, fifty years, perhaps, for the Holocaust, a decade or two for Vietnam, several months for mass rape or serial murder. Even a public memorialization can be a forgetting, a way of saying to survivors what someone said after I published my first article on sexual violence: "Now you can put this behind you."[2]

Brison goes on to explore the importance of "empathic listening" in the recovery of survivors of rape and trauma; a listening that does not seek to close over the depth of the traumatic experience nor rush to move on from it. According to Brison, such modes of "bearing witness" are essential to the "remaking of the self" after trauma.[3] While different in several important respects to the case of racism and even racial trauma, Brison's reflections help underscore the ethical importance of attending to the experiences of those who suffer.

But there is something more to this "sitting with" that Beltrán speaks of, than the acts of remembering and listening, though these are surely important. In the case of racism, given that the system of white power and privilege is founded upon—and actively sustained by—the suffering of racialized bodies, it seems that this "sitting with" should involve something more. In George Yancy's words, it should involve the need for whites to engage in a "tarrying." Recounting an experience with audience members after having delivered a guest talk, Yancy describes an exchange with an older white male professor who remarks irritably, "You leave us with *no* hope."[4] This comment, which we are told is not an uncommon response to his talks on the phenomenological experience of being an "essence" *vis-à-vis* the white gaze, reveals something else about the status and expectations of critical race scholarship. As Yancy argues:

> [The criticism on the absence of hope] functioned to elide the gravitas of the immediacy of black pain and suffering and the virulent ways in which white racism continues to function with such frequency in our contemporary moment. In my analysis, both men failed to *tarry* with the reality of racism and the profound ways in which people of color must endure it.[5]

This failure to "tarry" (to delay, to linger), and its correlated groping for glimmers of hope and progress, recalls Beltrán's comments about the impatience to "shift to the happy ending," a move which spares whites and those unaffected by the harms of racism, the discomfort and dis-ease of confronting its reality and their entanglement in it. Yancy writes, "The unfinished present is where I want whites to tarry (though not permanently remain), to listen, to recognize the complexity and weight of the current existence of white racism, to attempt to understand the ways in which they perpetuate racism, and to begin to think about the incredible difficulty involved in undoing it."[6]

This book has been an effort to "sit with" the tragedy of racism, and to give air to the many and varied experiences of it—to the breadth of its reach, and to the depth of its weight. In this project I have been concerned with mapping the different expressions and dimensions of racism, from the banal annoyances to the profound ruptures, and to register its bodily and lived experience.

This has taken us through an exploration of the subtle yet habitual modes of racist perception and bodily orientation, the fragmentation of the racialized body schema, the affective work and stress entailed in the experience of living with racism, and the chronic disorientation of finding oneself not-at-home in one's own body and lived environment. Along the way, we have also tracked some of the correlating experiences of whiteness as being-at-home, being-at-ease, and being invisible in order to draw contrast with our explorations of racialized embodiment, and in some cases, to show how these aspects of white embodiment rely on the dispossession of racialized bodies.

In doing so, however, I have also sought throughout the book to draw important philosophical insight from the lived experiences of racism. I have argued, for example, that traditional conceptions of the lived body in phenomenology and the subject in existentialist philosophy fail to adequately account for the experience of racialized embodiment, highlighting the way in which their frameworks proceed on the basis of fluidity and cohesion of experience that is strained in the case of racialized bodies. I have also considered how the complexity of this experience pushes us toward more relational philosophical models that dispose with neat subject–object (viewer–viewed) distinctions, even where their deployment may be tempting and useful for race theorists in describing the sense of objectification and dispossession. Merleau-Ponty's thought has served as an anchor throughout much of this work, even as my own position in relation to the different dimensions of his thought have at times been constructive, and at other times critical. In engaging with his thought, along with that of Heidegger, Fanon, Sartre, and many other contemporary thinkers, I hope to have carved out a space at the intersection of phenomenology and critical philosophy of race—a space in which we can engage with the important and urgent questions of racism and embodiment, and invite others to sit and tarry with them.

NOTES

1. This discussion was instigated by the public debate between race commentators Jonathan Chait and Ta-Nehisi Coates in 2014 across *The Atlantic* and *The New York Times*. MSNBC's *Melissa Harris-Perry* hosted a panel of guests to discuss aspects of this debate on April 6, 2014. http://www.msnbc.com/melissa-harris-perry/watch/breaking-down-narratives-of-racial-discourse-218234435944, accessed April 8, 2014.

2. Brison, *Aftermath*, 57–58.

3. Ibid., 59.

4. George Yancy, *Look, A White! Philosophical Essays on Whiteness* (Philadelphia: Temple University Press, 2012), 154.

5. Ibid.

6. Ibid., 158.

Bibliography

Ahmed, Sara, *Queer Phenomenology: Orientations, Objects, Others* (Durham: Duke University Press, 2006).

Aho, Kevin A, *Heidegger's Neglect of the Body* (Albany: SUNY Press, 2009).

Alcoff, Linda Martín, *Visible Identities: Race, Gender, and the Self* (New York: Oxford University Press, 2006).

Al-Saji, Alia, "A Phenomenology of Hesitation: Interrupting Racializing Habits of Seeing." In *Living Alterities: Phenomenology, Embodiment, and Race,* edited by Emily S. Lee, 133–172 (Albany: SUNY Press, 2014).

———. "Too Late: Racialized Time and the Closure of the Past." *Insights* 6(5) (2013): 1–13.

———. "The Racialization of Muslim Veils: A Philosophical Analysis." *Philosophy and Social Criticism* 36(8) (2010): 875–902.

———. "White Normality, or Racism against the Abnormal: Comments on Ladelle McWhorter's Racism and Sexual Oppression in Anglo-America." *Symposia on Gender, Race and Philosophy* 6 (2010).

———. "Bodies and Sensings: On the Uses of Husserlian Phenomenology for Feminist Theory." *Continental Philosophy Review* 43 (2010): 13–37.

———. "A Phenomenology of Critical-Ethical Vision: Merleau-Ponty, Bergson, and the Question of Seeing Differently." *Chiasmi International* 11 (2009): 375–398.

Anderson, Kathryn Freeman, "Diagnosing Discrimination: Stress from Perceived Racism and the Mental and Physical Health Effects." *Sociological Inquiry* 83 (2013): 55–81.

Bachelard, Gaston, *The Poetics of Space* (Boston: Beacon Press, 1994).

Beauvoir, Simone de, *The Second Sex*, trans. Constance Borde and Sheila Malovany-Chevallier (New York: Vintage Books, 2011).

Bernasconi, Robert, "Sartre's Gaze Returned: The Transformation of the Phenomenology of Racism." *Graduate Faculty Philosophy Journal* 18(2) (1995): 201–221.

Bourdieu, Pierre, *Outline of a Theory of Practice* (Cambridge: Cambridge University Press, 1977).

Brison, Susan J. H., *Aftermath: Violence and the Remaking of a Self* (Princeton: Princeton University Press, 2002).

Butler, Judith, "Endangered/Endangering: Schematic Racism and White Paranoia." In *Reading Rodney King/Reading Urban Uprising*, edited by Robert Gooding-Williams, 15–22 (New York: Routledge, 1993).

Casey, Edward S., "Walling Racialized Bodies Out: Border versus Boundary at La Fontera." In *Living Alterities*, edited by Emily Lee, 189–212.

———. "Habitual Body and Memory in Merleau-Ponty." In *A History of Habit: From Aristotle to Bourdieu*, edited by Tom Sparrow and Adam Hutchinson, 209–226 (Lanham: Lexington Books, 2013).

———. *Getting Back into Place: Toward a Renewed Understanding of the Place-World* (2nd ed.) (Bloomington: Indiana University Press, 2009).

———. *The World at a Glance* (Bloomington: Indiana University Press, 2007).

Crossley, Nick, "Habit and Habitus." *Body & Society* 19 (2013): 136–161.

———. "The Phenomenological Habitus and its Construction." *Theory and Society* 30 (2001): 81–120.

Dillon, Martin C., "Sartre on the Phenomenal Body and Merleau-Ponty's Critique." In *The Debate between Sartre and Merleau-Ponty,* edited by Jon Stewart, 121–143 (Evanston: Northwestern University Press, 1998).

Dreyfus, Hubert, *What Computers (Still) Can't Do: A Critique of Artificial Reason* (Cambridge: MIT Press, 1993).

Du Bois, W. E. B., *The Souls of Black Folk* (Chicago: Dover, 1994).

Ellison, Ralph, *Invisible Man* (New York: Vintage, 1980).

Fanon, Frantz, *Black Skin, White Masks*, trans. Charles L. Markmann (New York: Grove Press, 1967).

———. *Peau Noire, Masques Blancs* (Paris: Éditions Points, 1952).

Foucault, Michel, *Discipline and Punish: The Birth of the Prison* (New York: Vintage, 1976).

Gallagher, Shaun and Dan Zahavi, *The Phenomenological Mind: An Introduction to Philosophy of Mind and Cognitive Science* (New York: Routledge, 2008).

Gallagher, Shaun and Jonathan Cole, "Body Image and Body Schema in a Deafferented Subject." In *Body and Flesh: A Philosophical Reader,* edited by Donn Welton, 131–148 (Oxford: Blackwell Publishers, 1998).

Garland-Thomson, Rosemarie, *Staring: How We Look* (New York: Oxford University Press, 2009).

Goffman, Erving, *The Presentation of Self in Everyday Life* (New York: Anchor Books, 1959).

Gordon, Lewis R., *Bad Faith and Antiblack Racism* (Amherst, NY: Humanity Books, 1999).

Grosz, Elizabeth, *Volatile Bodies: Toward a Corporeal Feminism* (Bloomington: Indiana University Press, 1994).

———. "Merleau-Ponty and Irigaray in the Flesh." *Thesis Eleven* 36 (1993): 37–59.

Guenther, Lisa, *Solitary Confinement: Social Death and its Afterlives* (Minneapolis: University of Minnesota Press, 2013).

Hawley, John C., *Encyclopaedia of Postcolonial Studies* (Westport: Greenwood, 2001).

Heidegger, Martin, *Being and Time*, trans. John Macquarie and Edward Robinson (New York: Harper & Row, 1962).

———. *Hölderlin's Hymn "Der Ister,"* trans. William McNeill and Julia Davis (Bloomington: Indiana University Press, 1996).

———. "Building, Dwelling, Thinking." In *Martin Heidegger Basic Writings,* edited by David Krell, 343–364 (New York: Harper Perennial, 2008).

Hobbs, Allyson, *A Chosen Exile: A History of Racial Passing in American Life* (Cambridge: Harvard University Press, 2014).

hooks, bell, *Yearning: Race, Gender, and Cultural Politics* (Boston: South End Press, 1991).

Human Rights and Equal Opportunity Commission, *Bringing Them Home: Report of the National Inquiry into the Separation of Aboriginal and Torres Strait Islander Children from Their Families* (Sydney: HREOC, 1997).

Irwin, Brian, "Architecture and Embodiment: Place and Time in the New York Skyline." *Architext V* (2014): 23–35.

Jacobson, Kirsten, "A Developed Nature: A Phenomenological Account of the Experience of Home." *Continental Philosophy Review* 42 (2009): 355–373.

Kittay, Eva, *Love's Labor: Essays on Women, Equality and Dependency* (New York: Routledge, 1999).

Leder, Drew, *The Absent Body* (Chicago: University of Chicago, 1990).

Lee, Emily S., "Body Movement and Responsibility for a Situation." In *Living Alterities*, edited by Emily Lee, 233–254.

Lipsitz, George, *How Racism Takes Place* (Philadelphia: Temple University Press, 2011).

Lugones, María, "Playfulness, 'World'-Travelling, and Loving Perception." *Hypatia* 2 (1987).

Lymer, Jane, "Alterity and the Maternal in Adoptee Phenomenology." *Parrhesia* 24 (2015): 189–216

Malpas, Jeff, *Heidegger's Topology: Being, Place, World* (Cambridge: MIT Press, 2006).

Mazis, Glen A., "Touch and Vision: Rethinking with Merleau-Ponty Sartre on the Caress." In *The Debate between Sartre and Merleau-Ponty*, edited by Jon Bartley Stewart, 144–153.

McMillan Cottom, Tressie, "Jonathan Ferrell Is Dead. Whistling Vivaldi Wouldn't Have Saved Him." *Slate Magazine*, September 20, 2013.

McWhorter, Ladelle, *Racism and Sexual Oppression in Anglo-America: A Genealogy* (Bloomington: Indiana University Press, 2009).

Mendieta, Eduardo, "The Somatology of Xenophobia: Towards a Biopolitical Analysis of Disgust and Hate" (publication forthcoming).

———. "The Sound of Race: The Prosody of Affect." *Radical Philosophy Review* 17(1) (2014): 109–131.

Merleau-Ponty, Maurice, *Phenomenology of Perception*, trans. Donald A. Landes (New York: Routledge, 2012).

———. *Phénoménologie de la Perception* (Paris: Gallimard, 1945).

————. "Eye and Mind." In *The Merleau-Ponty Aesthetics Reader: Philosophy and Painting,* edited by Galen A. Johnson, 121–150 (Evanston: Northwestern University Press, 1993).

————. "Indirect Language and the Voices of Silence." In *The Merleau-Ponty Aesthetics Reader,* edited by Johnson, 76–120.

————. *The Visible and Invisible,* trans. Alphonso Lingis (Evanston: Northwestern University Press, 1969), 133–134.

Miles, William, "Schizophrenic Island, fifty years after Fanon: Martinique, the pent-up 'paradise.'" *International Journal of Francophone Studies* 15 (2012): 9–33.

Moran, Dermot, "Revisiting Sartre's Ontology of Embodiment in *Being and Nothingness.*" In *Ontological Landscapes: Recent Thought on Conceptual Interfaces Between Science and Philosophy,* edited by Vesselin Petrov (Frankfurt: Ontos-Verlag, 2011).

————. "Sartre's Treatment of the Body in *Being and Nothingness*: The 'Double Sensation.'" In *Jean-Paul Sartre: Mind and Body, Word and Deed,* edited by Jean-Pierre Boulé and Benedict O'Donohoe, 9–26 (Newcastle: Cambridge Scholars Publishing, 2001).

Nancy, Jean-Luc, *Corpus* (Paris: Éditions Métailié, 2006).

O'Byrne, Anne, *Natality and Finitude* (Bloomington: Indiana University Press, 2010).

Ortega, Mariana, "'New Mestizas,' 'World-Travelers,' and *Dasein*: Phenomenology and the Multi-Voiced, Multi-Cultural Self." *Hypatia* 16 (2001): 1–29.

————. "Hometactics: Self-Mapping, Belonging, and the Home Question." In *Living Alterities,* edited by Emily Lee, 173–188 (Albany: SUNY Press, 2014).

Rawlinson, Mary C., "Beyond Antigone: Ismene, Gender, and the Right to Life." In *The Returns of Antigone,* edited by Tina Chanter and Sean Kirkland, 101–122 (Albany: SUNY Press, 2014).

Reynolds, Joel Michael, "Merleau-Ponty's Aveugle and the Phenomenology of Non-Normate Embodiment," *Chiasmi International* 18 (2017).

Richards, David A. J., *Italian American: The Racializing of an Ethnic Identity* (New York: NYU Press, 1999).

Ruddick, Sara, *Maternal Thinking: Toward a Politics of Peace* (Boston: Beacon Press, 1989).

Rykwert, Joseph, "'House and Home." *Social Research* 58 (1991): 51–62.

Said, Edward, *Orientalism* (New York: Pantheon Books, 1978).

Sartre, Jean-Paul, *Being and Nothingness,* trans. Hazel E. Barnes (New York: Washington Square Press, 1992).

————. "Black Orpheus." *The Massachusetts Review* 6(1) (1964): 13–52.

————. *Anti-Semite and Jew: An Exploration of the Etiology of Hate,* trans. George J. Becker (New York: Schocken Books, 1948).

Sawyer, Pamela J. et al., "Discrimination and the Stress Response: Psychological and Physiological Consequences of Anticipating Prejudice in Interethnic Interactions." *American Journal of Public Health* 102 (2012): 1020–1026.

Steele, Claude, *Whistling Vivaldi (and Other Clues to How Stereotypes Affect Us)* (New York: W.W. Norton, 2010).

Sullivan, Shannon and Nancy Tuana, *Race and Epistemologies of Ignorance* (Albany: SUNY Press, 2007).

Sullivan, Shannon, *Revealing Whiteness: The Unconscious Habits of Racial Privilege* (Bloomington: Indiana University Press, 2006).

———. "White World-Traveling." *Journal of Speculative Philosophy* 18 (2004): 300–304.

———. *Living Across and Through Skins: Transactional Bodies, Pragmatism, and Feminism* (Bloomington: Indiana University Press, 2001), 83.

———. *Good White People: The Problem with Middle-Class White Anti-Racism* (Albany: SUNY Press, 2014),

Waldenfels, Bernhard, *The Question of the Other* (Albany: SUNY Press, 2007).

Weiss, Gail, *Body Images: Embodiment as Intercorporeality* (New York: Routledge, 1999).

———. "Pride and Prejudice: Ambiguous Racial, Religious, and Ethnic Identities of Jewish Bodies." In *Living Alterities*, edited by Emily Lee, 213–232.

———. "Ambiguity, Absurdity, and Reversibility: Indeterminacy in de Beauvoir, Camus, and Merleau-Ponty." *Journal of French and Francophone Philosophy* 5 (2010): 71–83.

West, Cornel, "Afterword: Philosophy and the Funk of Life." In *Cornel West: A Critical Reader,* edited by George Yancy, 346–362 (Malden: Wiley Blackwell, 2001).

Yancy, George, *Black Bodies, White Gazes: The Continuing Significance of Race* (Lanham: Rowman & Littlefield, 2008).

———. "Forms of Spatial and Textual Alienation: The Lived Experience of Philosophy as Occlusion." *Graduate Faculty Philosophy Journal* 35 (2014): 1–16.

———. "Walking While Black in the 'White Gaze.'" *The New York Times*, September 1, 2013.

———. "Trayvon Martin: When Effortless Grace is Sacrificed on the Altar of the Image." In *Pursuing Trayvon Martin: Historical Contexts and Contemporary Manifestations of Racial Dynamics,* edited by George Yancy and Janine Jones, 237–250 (Lanham: Lexington Books, 2013).

Young, Iris Marion, *On Female Body Experience: 'Throwing Like a Girl' and Other Essays* (New York: Oxford University Press, 2005).

———. "Throwing Like a Girl: Twenty Years Later." In *Body and Flesh*, edited by Welton, 286–290.

Index

About the Author

Helen Ngo is lecturer in philosophy at Deakin University, Australia. She completed her PhD in Philosophy at Stony Brook University (USA), and works in the areas of phenomenology, critical philosophy of race, and feminist philosophy.

Printed in Great Britain
by Amazon

22231321R00119